Staying Connected
Managing contact arrangements in adoption

British Association for Adoption & Fostering
(BAAF)
Skyline House
200 Union Street
London SE1 0LX
www.baaf.org.uk

Charity registration 275689

British Library Cataloguing in Publication Data
A catalogue record for this book is available
from the British Library

ISBN 1 903699 12 6

Cover photographs posed by models
Designed by Andrew Haig & Associates
Typeset by Avon DataSet, Bidford on Avon
Printed by Russell Press Ltd (TU), Nottingham

BAAF Adoption & Fostering is the leading
UK-wide membership organisation for all those
concerned with adoption, fostering and child
care issues.

Staying Connected
Managing contact
arrangements in adoption

Edited by Hedi Argent

Acknowledgements

I am indebted to all the authors who have worked cheerfully and enthusiastically, through several drafts, to complete this collection on time; this is their book.

I want to thank Shaila Shah, BAAF's Director of Publications, for her patience, support and inspiration, Susanne Clarke, her assistant, for her unfailing readiness to be helpful, and Joan Fratter, John Triseliotis and Sarah Borthwick for their valued comments on the script.

Finally, the fifteen chapters in this anthology could not have been written without the generosity of families and children who do the real work and share their experiences with us; we are truly grateful to all of them. I would like to say a special thank you to "Liz and Tim" who allowed me to tell their story in *End-piece with Lauren*.

The cases quoted in this book are based on fact but names and situations have been changed to preserve anonymity.

Hedi Argent
Editor

Contents

Introduction

This book is dedicated to all the childcare practitioners and their managers who struggle daily with the problems of maintaining continuity for children who are placed in new permanent families. The struggle is not only to keep children's lives intact, but also to interpret and apply changing orthodoxies and models of good practice, so that contact with birth relatives and other significant people will benefit individual children with different needs. All the contributors to this book are involved in making, sustaining or evaluating contact arrangements and offer examples of varied practice to explore what works and what does not and why.

The assessment of contact needs and agreement about the purpose of contact for each child with each person has to be tackled before the complex activity, described as "contact arrangements", can even begin to be negotiated. We have learned from divorce that the most important single factor for successful contact with the non-resident parent is the level of co-operation between the adults. We are learning from adoption disruptions that unrecognised or unmet contact needs prevent children from making lasting new connections. The task, then, is to allow a child with two families to move between two family circles and to welcome any overlap and withstand any collision. Even permanently absent people can be held in mind within a family circle; a boy of 12 said to his adoptive mother: 'I don't need to see my birth mum because it feels like she's in our family anyway'. His birth mother was a long-stay patient in a psychiatric hospital.

Children who have been in the care system for some time may have collected a few extra segments of several circles along the way. Foster carers will have drawn the child into their own family to varying degrees; if there has been a disrupted adoption placement, there will be segments with jagged edges that hurt but cannot be ignored. 'Does my new grandpa become my old grandpa now or won't he be my grandpa any more?' asked ten-year-old Jade after leaving one adoption placement for another. Having been reassured that she could still visit "new grandpa" but that she would also have two more, she asked in wonder: 'how many grandpas can I have?' The significance of previous carers and their families is sometimes buried under the relief of having achieved stability for the child and the effort of keeping children in touch with their birth relatives. But her relationship with 'new grandpa' was one of the few secure attachments Jade had ever made.

When children have to move between families there is inevitable loss and pain. Unless their continuing contact with the child is clearly valued, foster carers may fear that they could impede the child's transfer to the next family; adopters who consider they have failed the child may think that it is better to withdraw completely. This is an area which needs more formal consideration: it is bad enough if children cannot live with their birth families – we should not compound the damage by allowing them to sustain further losses on their road towards permanence. Children can juggle with several family circles and feel quite comfortable in all of them – in due course, with encouragement and good management, a main circle will evolve and others will recede without being obliterated. The chapters that follow deal with the management of contact arrangements which aim to lead to this end.

There are many statutes and guidelines to point the way: the *1989 Children Act* and the *1976 Adoption Act* (both for England and Wales); the *Adoption Standards for England 2001*; the *Adoption and Children Bill 2002* (England and Wales); the Standards yet to come for inter-country and step-parent adoptions; the *1995 Children (Scotland) Act*; the recent Family Law report, *Making Contact Work*; the guidance to good practice issued by the Department of Health; the *Convention of Human Rights* and the findings of research studies mentioned by many of the contributors. A synopsis of relevant studies can be found in the Appendix.

Hardly anyone today would suggest that children can or should "make a fresh start" when they join "permanent" new families, however traumatic their past experiences have been. As long ago as 1975, Kay Donley warned us that children could not settle into new families while they still had "unfinished business" with their birth family (Donley, 1975). We now know that this business is never finished and that we must make arrangements accordingly. It is no longer a question of whether children should remain connected to their origins but rather how connections can best be preserved and how children can be protected in often problematic circumstances.

Remaining connected can mean anything from being enabled to keep an absent person in mind, like the boy who saw that his birth mother was included in his new family circle, to having face-to-face contact negotiated and agreed between two families or more. The contributors to this collection describe many ways of remaining in touch but they all emphasise the same essential aspects of managing successful arrangements: flexibility and the opportunity to review the arrangements. Situations change, births, marriages and deaths alter family patterns and, above all, children grow and develop. Contact agreements with built-in review systems are generally welcomed. A sample agreement is included in the last chapter, *Orders or agreements?*

All the contributors stress the importance of keeping the interests of the child in the forefront at all times. Knowledge of attachment theory and skill in working with children are considered vital for focused assessment of contact needs; preparation, monitoring and support should accompany the arrangements and, at least, remain on offer until adopted children reach adulthood.

The pendulum is swinging towards kinship care. Many families have always looked after their own and everyone seems to agree that children should say within their families of origin whenever possible. Since the 1989 Children Act and the 1995 Children (Scotland) Act, there has been an "official" line to promote relative carers as first choice, but only recently have a few agencies appointed family placement workers to develop and support placements with relatives. The role of grandparents is becoming particularly topical, as older people in the community are increasingly seen as a potential resource for their own and other people's families. *Is my Mummy coming today? Managing contact arrangements in kinship placements* considers both the advantages and the problems that can arise when contact means "keeping it in the family".

According to the three authors from the *Independent Adoption Service* and the two writers from the *Wandsworth Kinship Care Project*, there is no difference between the needs and expectations of black and white families as far as contact arrangements are concerned. This bears out the findings quoted in *Moving Goalposts* (Department of Health, 1995): 'Neither ethnicity nor gender seemed to have any relation to contact arrangements'. Although it is accepted that there is a cultural base for black kinship care, that is no reason to suppose black families do not require the same level of support as white families with the complex issues that may surface when relatives look after children who cannot live with their parents. Nor should it be assumed that minority ethnic groups manage contact arrangements better without support. Whatever their ethnicity, carers and adopters describe the best arrangements as those where the birth relatives are just like extended family: sometimes it's good to see them and sometimes it isn't but that's families for you!

Although there is an inevitable overlap between chapters, there is also a healthy divergence. The *Berkshire Adoption Advisory Service* and the Post Adoption Centre Contact and Mediation Service take very different views about the management of "letterbox" contact. Both succeed in keeping children connected; it may be that the efficiency and expertise of the workers involved, and their commitment to contact, are at least as relevant as the methods they employ. Readers will be able to draw on the practice that best suits their style and their agency.

The two parents who have adopted from overseas write about quite contrasting perceptions and experiences of contact with far-distant birth relatives. 'How often do children need to visit their country of origin in order to feed their sense of self?' asks one. 'If she becomes fluent in Spanish, she might want to live part of her life in Paraguay' says the other. Both have children who are fully in touch with their original countries and families and cultures.

There are differences between the legal frameworks in Scotland and in England and Wales which affect contact arrangements. These are described and illustrated in *Does the legal framework facilitate contact?* The system of Children's Hearings offers the kind of built-in review before adoption which could, perhaps, be adapted to later stages in the process throughout the UK.

Should contact arrangements be supervised, supported or independent? There are examples here of a variety of different arrangements to fit different circumstances: one little girl in Scotland needs her adopters and her social worker to help her to visit her terminally ill birth mother, another child of the same age in England takes informal, unregulated contact meetings for granted, while the children who see their birth relatives only at the *Child Contact Service*, have to be closely watched for their own protection.

How often, when and where should contact take place? Is it perhaps best to disregard the quantity and to concentrate on the quality and the purpose of the connections? In *Managing face-to-face contact for young adopted children*, the author argues that most children under four will benefit from contact and find it easier to manage than older children, if it is frequent enough to enable them to remember a birth relative between visits. In *Managing contact arrangements for children with learning difficulties*, the author suggests that more than four face-to-face meetings a year can be overwhelming for all concerned. Some agencies advise avoiding significant dates; others encourage joint celebrations. Venues range from formal family centres, where anonymity can be preserved, to open visits in the child's new home. One place is not better than any other, as long as they all work for each particular child.

Who should have contact? *Split up but not cut off: Making and sustaining contact arrangements between siblings* makes out the strong case for keeping links with sisters and brothers; in a recent study of children in long-term foster care (Brannen *et al*, 2000), a boy, in middle childhood, placed the postman on his map of the most important people in his life 'because he brought letters from his siblings'. Many contributors to this collection illustrate the significance of contact with birth grandparents. Grandparents may hold precious family information and memories and may be able to offer continuity and stability through the demonstrable existence of previous generations. The chapter about *contact with contesting birth parents* draws attention to the contribution all birth parents can make to their children's lives, even if they initially opposed the care proceedings and the adoption.

At the heart of the book, and therefore placed in the middle, is *Contact after adoption: What they say and how it feels*. Adopted children and young people and their families are described in case examples throughout this collection, but here they give their own opinions and share their own experiences. Not everything works for them but a great deal does and they illuminate all that can be said about managing contact arrangements.

The author of the chapter *Managing post-adoption contact by mediation* asks: 'Why is contact still such an issue after at least ten years of openness?' In *Orders or agreements?* the writer notes that '. . . in my experience, contact still isn't automatically given any priority as a dynamic part of the agenda . . .'. In their study of direct post-adoption contact, Jeanette Logan and Carole Smith (1999) found that 'agency preparation had stressed the child's need for contact but had neglected to prepare the adopters for the anxieties and the emotional/practical issues associated with managing contact'.

The uncertainty and apprehension that still surround contact with birth relatives can easily result in prescriptive arrangements. Precise, inflexible arrangements may satisfy some Courts and some Adoption Panels and they may make anxious adopters feel more safe, but they rarely serve children's contact needs: a "once and forever family" does not equate with "once and forever contact arrangements". Flexibility has to begin at the recruitment stage; it is more productive to invite prospective adopters to negotiate contact arrangements to meet a child's needs, than to present them with a detailed, carefully worked out contact plan. It is necessary to find adopters who are not merely willing but wanting their children to have continuity in their lives; perhaps adopters can be more open and welcoming and inclusive than they are sometimes given credit for.

Many years ago, it was said that older and disabled children would only be placed with alternative families if professionals really believed they could be placed. It is now time really to believe that adoption does not replicate the nuclear family but offers another way of bringing up children, and that contact with birth relatives and other significant people from the past, preserves every child's right to continuity and connections. The management of contact arrangements can then make contact either desirable or merely endurable.

Hedi Argent
April 2002

References

Brannen, J Heptinstall, E and Bhopal, K (2000) *Connecting Children: Care and family life in later childhood*, London: Routledge Falmer.

Department of Health, Social Services Inspectorate (1995) *Moving Goalposts*, London: Department of Health.

Donley, K (1975) in Sawbridge, P (ed.) *Opening New Doors*, London: Agencies of British Adoption and Fostering Agencies.

Logan, J and Smith, C (1999) 'Adoption and direct post-adoption contact', *Adoption & Fostering*, 23:4.

1 Managing face-to-face contact for young adopted children

Elsbeth Neil

Adoption is predominantly used as a placement option for younger rather than older children. Small numbers of babies are placed at the request of their birth parents but the majority of adopted children have been in the public care system. In 2001, 67 per cent of children adopted from care were under the age of five (Department of Health, 2001). Most pre-school adopted children have either never lived with their birth relatives, or have left the care of their birth family at quite a young age, sometimes months or even years before being placed for adoption. Many adopted under-fives are therefore likely to have quite limited memories of, and relationships with, their birth relatives; for these reasons, face-to-face contact is often not planned for young adopted children. Since 1996 I have been studying contact after adoption for a survey sample of 168 children placed age three and under, and have followed up, with interviews, the placements of 36 of these children who were having face-to-face contact with adult birth relatives (Neil, 2000a, 2000b, 2002).* The mean age at placement of this latter sample was 21 months, and 70 per cent of the children had been in the care system. This chapter, largely based on my research, will explore how birth family contact can work for children in the pre-school age range and will look at what needs to be done to make such contact comfortable and useful for all involved.

What does contact mean to the child?

Additional psychological tasks for adopted children involve the negotiation of issues of attachment, loss, and identity, so it is useful to think about post-adoption contact alongside a consideration of how

---

*Three of the 36 children were of mixed heritage and 33 children were white. All children were placed with white adopters. Two of the birth relatives who were interviewed were of mixed heritage and the remainder were white.

9

children manage these. The capacity of children to make new attachments in adoptive families is largely dependent on the quality and continuity of care the child experienced within previous relationships. Younger children tend to experience fewer difficulties in attaching to adopters than do older placed children (Howe, 1998; Triseliotis *et al*, 1997). Research reinforces what we know from experience: that the younger the child at placement the more adaptable he or she is to the adoptive situation in particular but also to a whole range of wider experiences. Essentially, the better adjusted to the adoptive situation the child is, the more it should be expected that he or she will have the psychological resources to cope with, and make positive use of, post-adoption contact arrangements. In some ways it seems back to front that while face-to-face contact is frequently set up for children placed at older ages (Lowe *et al*, 1999), it is planned only infrequently for the younger children who may manage it more easily (Neil, 2000b).

For many pre-school adopted children the sense of loss precipitated by separation from birth relatives is not overt, but may emerge over time (Nickman, 1985; Brodzinsky, 1990). In my research, only 58 per cent of children had ever lived with their birth relatives. Of these, the average age at which the child left home was nine months and children then usually spent at least a year in foster care before being adopted (Neil, 2000b). For this "average" child the foster carers were in most cases the primary attachment figures at the time of placement for adoption; birth relatives were of less immediate psychological importance. While some pre-school adopted children may have important attachment relationships with birth relatives, in my study it was much more common that birth parents were either strangers or more like familiar known adults than seen as "mummy" or "daddy". My research suggests that social workers tend to think of face-to-face contact as being imperative only when children have established attachments to birth relatives (Neil, 2000a). I propose an alternative view, that the very lack of an attachment between the child and birth relatives may mean that contact is likely to be less problematic for the child, as opposed to a situation where the child has an intense but insecure relationship with birth relatives. This is certainly what we found here at the University of East Anglia when we compared the reactions to contact of older children in long-term foster care (mean age eight years) with adopted children placed age three and under (Neil *et al*, forth-coming). While many of the foster children clearly wanted and needed to see their birth relatives, meetings were often highly charged and children needed help in managing their feelings. In contrast, in three-quarters of the adoption contact cases, adopters reported that their child had either a positive or neutral reaction to contact. In cases where children showed neutral reactions (about half the sample), their relationship with birth relatives was not "special". Children's reactions were as would be expected given their age and personality to any meeting with an unfamiliar adult. Adopters used phrases like, ' . . . *It goes over her head . . .*' '*She has no clue as to who they are . . .*' '*It is just a visit.*' Or '*to him it is like meeting one of our friends really. It's the same situation.*' This fits in with other studies of young adopted children – that the relationship that develops with birth relatives through contact is likely to be more as it would be with an aunt or friend of the family than a close relative or parent (Iwanek, 1987; Rockel and Ryburn, 1988).

About a quarter of the children in my research sample were clearly described by their adopters as enjoying visits with birth relatives. In all such cases the children remembered their birth relative between meetings and they had a positive relationship with them. In some situations the contact sustained an already established relationship, but in others it was used as a means of *building* a relationship. Sometimes children did not fully understand the nature of the links to their birth relatives but they were nevertheless real people to them. For example, Dean was placed for adoption when aged 18 months and his adopters were interviewed about a year later. Dean saw his birth parents in the adopters' home about once every six weeks. His adoptive mother described his reactions:

He likes it . . . Rather than just sit [in the living room] we have got a playroom and they can go in there and I just leave them to it. I may do some housework or something so Dean knows I am here but just to give them some privacy really . . . And when they are here I say to [the birth father] especially, because he is the dominant one in the family, 'you give Dean a cuddle'. And Dean is quite happy . . . He is quite happy if I am around . . . Dean definitely remembers them. He often talks about them. Mainly his birth father. . . He calls him 'Daddy David' and he likes him coming, but he doesn't really understand it all.

11

In all the cases like that of Dean, where children were described as show-ing positive reactions, contact was at least three times a year, but usually more often. Pre-school age children cannot be expected to feel comfort-able with, or even in some cases to remember, birth relatives if the fre-quency is only once or twice a year. Hence if the intention behind contact is to sustain or build a relationship between the child and birth relatives, contact needs to be set up at intervals that suit the child's capacity to remember and feel comfortable with their birth relative. How often this should be is impossible to specify because it will depend on both the age and personality of the child, but adopters should be in the best position to evaluate this.

There are likely to be some situations where children find contact meetings neither wholly straightforward nor positive. In my research, about a quarter of children showed signs of anxiety about meetings with birth relatives, although in all cases there were positive as well as negative factors. Patterns varied. Some children seemed to feel insecure during contact meetings. The adoptive mother of Louis (age 5) said:

> Louis kept coming back to me. He would go off and play with them but he kept coming back to me. He was a little bit concerned about it; you could see it in his face. He enjoyed himself but it was a bit strange for him.

Other children seemed to look forward to meetings and enjoy them, but afterwards they appeared unsettled. This was the case with Freddie, who was placed when he was nearly four.

> He was obviously very pleased about going to see his grandmother but he was just awful and his behaviour was diabolical . . . It was making him revert back to how he used to be. And his behaviour was awful for about two or three weeks. (Adoptive mother)

I found that children who were anxious about contact meetings were those who were older at placement (most were over three years old), who had experienced more adversities before being placed, and who had more emotional and behavioural problems. These children were generally more anxious and unsettled and so it is not surprising that they were more anxious about contact meetings. We do need to ask whether it is productive to invite a troubled child into a further troubling situation and case-by-case assessment is probably the best, if not the only, feasible strategy. However, in my study many adoptive parents felt that even where contact might make children worried, it was still, on balance, beneficial. Such adopters felt that contact meetings did not so much create worries for the child as helpfully bring to the surface pre-existing anxieties. For example, Louis's mother explained how contact meetings helped keep the subject of the birth family open.

> . . . *working up to having the meeting with the birth mother and with his sister, and talking about it afterwards is an opportunity for him to ask to see his photographs and that starts other questions. So I suppose it does provide an opportunity to talk about things and stop us forgetting it, letting it ride, letting it pass without being mentioned. Because it doesn't matter how good your intentions are, time still goes by and you are busy doing other things.*

Contact meetings provided opportunities for adoptive parents to help children deal with their feelings and worries. For example, the following adopters told me how their child wanted contact, but also wanted reassurance about her place within the adoptive family.

> *She said 'you are not going to leave me there?' and I said 'no, we are all going to go together and we are all going to come back together'. She seemed to be reassured by this.*

Given the findings of previous research that adopted people value an environment of openness in discussing adoption-related issues within the adoptive family (McWhinnie, 1967; Raynor, 1980; Triseliotis, 1973), helping create and sustain this atmosphere may be an important benefit of contact meetings.

Contact meetings may trigger a variety of memories for young children and the capacity of adopters to anticipate or detect feelings that the child cannot articulate is important. As one adopter said, 'I do feel you have to tune into the past . . . Because it is there anyway . . . And even if you work terribly hard to suppress it, it's there.'

The place where contact happens may be one aspect for parents to consider. For example, some children may feel more comfortable in the

Family Centre where they have always had contact, but it may remind other children of fraught and unhappy times. There are no rules, except that sensitivity to the child's wishes and feelings is needed. Regardless of venue, seeing birth relatives again may arouse mixed feelings in children and, as in any situation where young children feel worried, the closeness and protection of their adoptive parents is vital. I found hardly any examples of children experiencing difficult behaviours from their birth relatives during contact, and much of the reason for this seemed to be that adopters were almost always closely involved in meetings and were seen as being "in control". In our comparisons of contact in foster care versus adoption (Neil *et al*, forthcoming), we found that sometimes foster children did not have this same security. In the foster care sample (Schofield *et al*, 2000), children were expected to travel in taxis, without their carers, to have contact with birth relatives who had failed to look after them in the past. Such children had no one on hand to help the contact run smoothly or to help them deal with any difficulties. On return to the foster home, carers did not know what had taken place and so it was harder for them to talk to and reassure the child. It is not surprising that in some cases foster carers reported that children were disturbed and upset by contact.

How can birth relatives manage contact?

It is important to remember the normal developmental age and stage of children. It needs to be anticipated that toddlers and young children will probably be wary of unfamiliar adults. When birth relatives are little known, the child may not immediately feel comfortable approaching or being approached by this person. In these respects the post-adoption contact situation is no different to a number of other social situations the pre-school child is likely to encounter. Young children need time to get used to birth relatives before they will feel comfortable with more intimate contact like touching or cuddling. As one adoptive mother said, 'She takes about 20 minutes to warm to somebody . . . You have to back off and let it be on her own terms.' The way that birth relatives manage their approach to the child is likely to be important in determining whether the child will feel comfortable with them. From my interviews with adopters, it seemed that the best approach was one that allowed the child time to warm up, but was also friendly and encouraging. The difference the behaviour of birth relatives can make to the child's feelings of comfort is clearly illustrated in the case of Harry. Harry, aged five, had never lived with either of his birth parents. After adoption he had separate contact with his birth mother and birth father. While he enjoyed visits from his birth father he felt less comfortable with his mentally ill birth mother, as his adoptive mum describes.

He pulls back from Kay. It's like as if there is something there that he knows about. He is wary of her. But then she doesn't give him time to settle. Whereas when his dad comes his dad will give him time to settle and will wait for him to come over and sit with him, she forces herself on him and tries to pick him up and put him on her lap . . . I don't know what it is but he doesn't like get really excited when she is here. And then afterwards he is always a bit more prone to temper tantrums and a bit more on edge for about a day or two afterwards. But then he will chat about mummy Kay. Now he just says 'Kay'. But if you talk to him about his dad he is really happy and chatty about his dad.

Like Harry's birth mother, many birth relatives may lack skills in interacting with their child. In such cases it may be necessary to take an active, facilitative role in helping birth relatives to play and talk with the child. Post-adoption contact is a highly emotional event for birth relatives and there is no blueprint defining what to say or do. With the best will in the world but lacking advice and support, some birth relatives will inevitably get it wrong. In order to avoid this happening there needs to be an acceptance by all that the purpose of contact is not to see what the birth relatives can or will do if left to their own devices, but to assist them to do the best that they can do for the child.

A key psychological issue for birth relatives after adoption is to adjust to their changed role in the child's life, the reality that their child is now also part of another family. The fact that young adopted children are quite likely to act towards birth relatives as if they were strangers can be very painful for those relatives, while it may reassure worried adopters. As one birth mother said to me:

The first contact I didn't really like . . . I didn't know how it was going to be for me to see my son with them, especially when he kept running up to the adoptive father it made me feel, sort of, a bit upset . . . My feelings were quite hurt seeing him with other people and not with me . . . So I felt hurt more than anything else . . . It was seeing him going over there and saying "daddy"; he shouldn't be saying that to other people, he should be saying that to his own dad. That really hurt.

In promoting successful contact it will be important that workers anticipate this scenario and prepare birth relatives in advance of initial meetings. The birth mother below had this kind of help from her social worker prior to the first contact meeting.

The social worker asked me how I feel meeting them and I told her I was nervous. Not worried about what was going to happen, but worried about what they were going to be like, how [my son] was going to react, what to call him.

Support from the social worker also helped this birth mother cope with the ending of the first meeting.

We actually sort of just went where the stairs are. I was in tears. So she [social worker] actually stood there and gave me a cuddle and talked to me about it and then walked me back to the car and then left. Lucky she was there.

Not all birth relatives in my study needed help to maintain contact, but those who could manage alone, or with the help of friends or relatives, tended to be those people without any additional difficulties such as mental heath problems, learning difficulties or interpersonal problems. Some birth relatives will need support to understand the child's perspective. Shy and reticent behaviour may be interpreted as rejecting, or birth relatives may feel that they are not valued by their child (Aldgate, 1980; Jenkins and Norman, 1972; Millham *et al*, 1986). Birth relatives may need to be advised that this behaviour is normal given the child's developmental stage, and that actually it is a healthy sign of adjustment.

It is important that agencies do not assume post-adoption contact arrangements can be self-maintaining. We know enough about the emotional and practical difficulties that face birth relatives to realise that a significant proportion of unsupported contact arrangements will flounder, risking feelings of disappointment and rejection for the child and adopters and a second experience of loss for birth relatives. In contested adoptions, some birth relatives in my study, and in other research (Ryburn, 1994; Charlton *et al*, 1998), describe an inability to work with the agency that placed their child. In such cases the provision of services by a new, independent agency should be considered. In some cases in my research, adoptive parents took on a supportive, almost parental role, with birth relatives. They would connect with birth relatives directly regarding arrangements for contact and would provide the necessary practical assistance to enable them to visit. They would make time to let birth relatives talk about their worries about the adoption, but also about other life issues. Some adopters were happy to "take on" the birth relatives in this way and they seemed to gain satisfaction from this role. In other cases it was plain that adopters felt overwhelmed by the needs of birth relatives, and it is in these situations that agency support is essential.

Contact and developmental factors

If contact is planned because it is hoped that it may help the child in the long term with identity issues such as "who am I?" and "why was I adopted?", rather than for the purpose of maintaining important relationships, then arrangements could be less frequent and managed differently. Adopted children generally have low levels of understanding of their adoptive situation and may show little interest in their adoptive status and other identity issues until they reach middle childhood (Brodzinsky *et al*, 1984). Luke's adoptive mother described this to me as follows:

> *He does not understand a lot of things, does he? If you told him he was adopted he wouldn't grasp any of it . . . He just takes things as they are . . . I couldn't sit down and explain to Luke what adoption is because it would go in one ear and out the other. . . as far as Luke is concerned, he has been here forever.*

With very young children it may seem to adopters that contact meetings are of little point or value to the child as he or she is not asking questions about adoption. What is likely to help such adopters persist with contact is an understanding that the child will need to address questions of identity in the future. In my research, adopters who showed a good understanding of the lifelong needs of their child were more highly motivated to sustain contact as they had a long-term goal in mind (Neil, submitted for publication). Often these adopters viewed contact meetings as an opportunity to build up adult-to-adult links with the birth family, links for the child to draw on or develop later in life. In such cases, there was low emphasis on the interactions between the child and the birth relatives, but a strong focus on the adult interactions. This is actually a model of interaction that many people are quite familiar and comfortable with in other spheres of social and family life: parents will meet with friends or relatives and will take the children along, but there is not a great expectation that the child will be central to this meeting. Adopters often managed this kind of contact successfully by meeting in a place where the child had plenty to interest him or her. Sometimes this was their own home, where not only did the child have his or her toys around but also was in familiar surroundings, adding to the "secure base" effect. Venues away from home included parks, the seaside, amusement parks and play centres. Children could then amuse themselves, the birth relatives had the opportunity to see the child behaving naturally and feel reassured about their wellbeing, and the adults could exchange information and get to know one another. The child thus has the opportunity to gradually develop familiarity with their birth relative without the pressure of being expected to perform for, or interact with, a stranger. Kyle's adopters explained this model of contact.

Adoptive father: *We found a children's activity centre, which Kyle likes a lot. It's not a cruel thing to say, but the birth mother is happy to see Kyle but she doesn't seem to want to get very involved with him. She likes to see that he is happy and running about. Although it is very noisy in there, you can find a spot where you can see what he is doing and you can talk. And she seems quite comfortable with that.*

Adoptive mother: . . . *So the contact is just seeing Kyle and making sure he is OK. At the moment Kyle is happy with this situation, so long as we are going somewhere where he can do something else as well.*

Because adults can sustain relationships over longer time gaps than children, this model of contact can be successful with only one or two meetings a year. If and when the child develops a greater interest in exploring identity issues, frequency can be increased. The child is not starting from scratch, they are increasing contact with a familiar person, and someone their parents have got to know quite well. This may have important advantages over opening up a closed adoption later in childhood or even in adulthood. Thoburn's longitudinal research (Thoburn *et al*, 2000) suggests that it can be very stressful for young people to make contact with birth relatives after a long gap, as often they do so at developmentally difficult times such as adolescence. In addition, they have had many years to build unrealistic fantasies, positive or negative, about what their birth relatives may be like, and reality can bitterly disappoint. Studies of adults who seek contact or meetings with birth relatives also show that, although people usually find the "search" helpful for their sense of identity, the process of searching can be highly stressful (Howe and Feast, 2000).

Understanding the purpose of contact

It is vital that all parties involved share the same understanding of the purpose of contact, and that the arrangements match the purpose. Problems can occur when there is lack of clarity about the aim. For example, Jacquie's adopters had an expectation that the birth-grandparents would want to build up a grandparent/grandchild type of relationship, and so they were waiting for the grandparents to take the lead with the child. The grandparents, however, did not appear aware that this was expected of them. The adopters felt disappointed by the grandparents' lack of interaction, which they interpreted as a lack of commitment.

> Adoptive mother: *The contact visit was like if you imagine in a doctor's surgery. The grandmother will say, 'well how old is she now?' that sort of thing. And Jacquie will be down in the sandpit and the grandmother will just be looking at her rather than getting up and going 'what are you doing, Jacquie, shall I help you build that?' She is only there for an hour. She should make more use of the hour.*

Adoptive father: *The grandmother makes no effort, so Jacquie makes no effort. An adult has got to make the first move. She ain't going to sit on someone's lap unless they put their arms out to encourage her . . . We have knocked the visits with the grandmother on the head, they are a waste of time.*

In other cases the opposite happened; adopters felt uncomfortable with the birth relatives making too direct an approach to the child. In both these situations there seemed to be a lack of shared understanding between adopters, birth relatives, and sometimes the agency, as to what the contact meetings were supposed to achieve and the ongoing role that the birth relatives were to play in the child's life. This suggests that the management of contact starts very much at the planning stage, talking through how it is hoped contact will help the child and what is the best way to meet that aim. The details of the meetings, and any support required, can then be tailored to these aims. If contact is planned without consideration of purpose, then situations can arise in which the tail effectively wags the dog. When initial discussions about contact meetings take place, it may also be useful for adopters and birth relatives to talk over other matters to do with visits. Issues that came up frequently in my interviews were photographs and presents, about which both adopters and birth relatives voiced a whole range of views. What I primarily learned from these con-versations is that blanket rules and policies are unhelpful but that if a good dialogue can develop between adopters and birth relatives, difficulties are rarely insurmountable.

Many adoptive parents will feel nervous about the prospect of having face-to-face contact with birth relatives; their primary anxiety may be that their own relationship with the child will be affected. Yet both my study and other research suggest that face-to-face contact does not detract from the adoptive parent–child relationship, especially for children placed at young ages (Grotevant and McRoy, 1998; Berry *et al*, 1998; Fratter, 1996). I would argue that it is both understandable and normal that prospective adopters should feel fearful of face-to-face contact arrange-ments at the pre-placement stage. But if they can be helped to anticipate the strong feelings that will be aroused, and if agencies are positive and reassuring about contact, they will feel more confident (Neil, 2002). It seems important that adopters are enabled to enter into arrangements willingly and with a positive attitude. I found that plans that were initiated by adopters were the most successful. Arrangements where adopters and the agency were in mutual agreement were also likely to work out well, but situations where adoptive parents felt compelled to go along with a plan that at heart they were not in favour of, mostly did not endure over time. This echoes the large study by Berry *et al* (1998) who found that several years post placement, adopters who had dropped out of contact arrangements tended to be those who felt pushed by the agency into agreeing to the plan.

I found that the most important factor related to the satisfaction of adopters with contact arrangements was not the detail of how the contact was set up, but the belief of adopters in the value of such contact. Much will depend on the message about contact they receive from the agency: in the example above, the agency had warned the adopters that the grandparents would be trouble! I looked at the capacity of adopters to understand the views and feelings of both their child and the birth relatives. Adopters who had high levels of empathy with, or understanding of, other people's perspectives were those who were most likely to keep up contact and feel good about it.

In general, when people are worried about something, it is harder to think rationally about that issue. As well as listening to and containing adopters' fears, support should also be about increasing people's ability to understand each other: as one adopter said, 'Our social worker calms us down, **explains why things happen.**' Because of the feelings contact may generate for all parties, it is not reasonable to expect that all contact meetings will be entirely straightforward. Children may behave in unusual ways, birth relatives may not know what to do or say or may be upset or angry. Adopters need to know why such things happen, as events that are comprehensible are easier to tolerate. The more that adopters can be helped to understand the impact that loss, deprivation, neglect and abuse can have on the development of both their child and his or her birth relatives, the more they will be able to make sense of unfamiliar perspectives and behaviours.

Conclusion

Managing face-to-face contact for young adopted children cannot be defined by a formula. Details of contact arrangements such as where it is to take place, for how long and how often, should not be the first considerations but the end point of a careful process of thinking about the particular needs and feelings of the individuals involved. Because contact is a complicated business emotionally, it can be tempting to try and make things ordered by having a "standard plan". I found that some agencies tended always to suggest a relatively low frequency unsupervised arrangement that maintained the anonymity of adopters and took place on neutral ground. This did not suit all families and, in some cases, led to dissatisfaction and eventual breakdown of contact arrangements. In other cases greater agency input was needed, especially when birth relatives had significant difficulties such as mental health problems. What led to successful, sustained contact, were arrangements that reflected the aims of contact and supported people who needed support without assuming complications where there were not any.

Research justifies a positive attitude towards considering face-to-face contact for pre-school children; benefits may be easier to achieve than for children who are placed for adoption when they are older. There needs to be clarity shared by all parties as to the purposes of having face-to-face contact. If contact is to build or maintain a relationship, then the arrangements must allow for both the young child's sense of time and for any barriers that may stand in the way of birth relatives interacting successfully with the child. If contact is planned to help the child with long-term identity issues, then it is helpful to think about how best to promote the relationship between the adults involved. Arrangements are most likely to succeed when adoptive parents and birth relatives can understand each other and collaborate in a spirit of openness. Post-adoption face-to-face contact is a social interaction with which all parties will be unfamiliar. Yet it may be that the most helpful models to guide such contact are the ordinary and familiar: thinking about how families generally manage young children's relationships with extended family and friends of the family. The presence of adoptive parents as a "secure base", the use of child-friendly meeting places, in some cases including the child's own home, and reasonable expectations regarding how birth relatives and children are likely to react to each other, are all important factors. Finally, children should never be expected to behave in ways that do not match their developmental stage; therefore all arrangements need to be flexible to adjust to the child's changing needs and wishes.

References

Aldgate, J (1980) 'Identification of factors influencing children's length of stay in care', in Triseliotis, J (ed.) *New Developments in Adoption and Fostering*, London: Routledge and Kegan Paul.

Berry, M, Cavazos Dylla, D J, Barth, R P and Needell, B (1998) 'The role of open adoption in the adjustment of adopted children and their families', *Children and Youth Services Review*, 20:1–2, pp 151–71.

Brodzinsky, D M (1990) 'A stress and coping model of adoption adjustment', in Brodzinsky, D M and Schechter, M D (eds) *The Psychology of Adoption*, New York: Oxford University Press.

Brodzinsky, D M, Singer, L M and Braff, A M (1984) 'Children's understanding of adoption', *Child Development*, 55, pp 869–78.

Charlton, L, Crank, M, Kansara, K and Oliver, C (1998) *Still Screaming: Birth parents compulsorily separated from their children*, Manchester: After Adoption.

Department of Health (2001) *Children Adopted from Care in England 2000–2001*, London: Department of Health.

Fratter, J (1996) *Adoption with Contact: Implications for policy and practice*, London: BAAF.

Grotevant, H D and McRoy, R G (1998) *Openness in Adoption: Exploring family connections*, Thousand Oaks: Sage.

Howe, D (1998) *Patterns of Adoption*, Oxford: Blackwell Science.

Howe, D and Feast, J (2000) *Adoption, Search and Reunion*, London: The Children's Society.

Iwanek, M (1987) *A Study of Open Adoption Placements*, 14 Emerson Street, Petone, New Zealand (unpublished).

Jenkins, S and Norman, E (1972) *Filial Deprivation and Foster Care*, New York: Columbia University Press.

Lowe, N, Murch, M, Borkowski, M, Weaver, A, Beckford, V and Thomas, C (1999) *Supporting Adoption: Reframing the Approach*, London: BAAF.

McWhinnie, A M (1967) *Adopted Children: How they grow up*, London: Routledge and Kegan Paul.

Millham, S, Bullock, R, Hosie, K and Haak, M (1986) *Lost in Care*, Aldershot: Gower.

Neil, E (2000a) *Contact with birth relatives after adoption: A study of young, recently placed children*, Norwich: University of East Anglia, Unpublished PhD thesis.

Neil, E (2000b) 'The reasons why young children are placed for adoption: findings from a recently placed sample and implications for future identity issues', *Child and Family Social Work*, 5:4, pp 303–16.

Neil, E (2002) 'Contact after adoption: The role of agencies in making and supporting plans', *Adoption & Fostering*, 26:1.

Neil, E, Beek, M and Schofield, G (forthcoming) 'Thinking about and managing contact in permanent placements: the differences and similarities between adoptive parents and foster carers', accepted for publication in *Clinical Child Psychology and Psychiatry* (forthcoming January 2003).

Neil, E (submitted for publication) 'Understanding other people's perspectives: tasks for adopters in open adoptions', submitted to *Adoption Quarterly*.

Nickman, S L (1985) 'Losses in adoption: the need for dialogue', *Psychoanalytic Study of the Child*, 40, pp 365–98.

Raynor, L (1980) *The Adopted Child Comes of Age*, London: George Allen & Unwin.

Rockel, J and Ryburn, M (1988) *Adoption Today: Change and choice in New Zealand*, Auckland: Heinemann/Reed.

Ryburn, M (1994) 'Contested adoption – the perspectives of birth parents', in Ryburn, M (ed.) *Contested Adoptions: Research, law, policy and practice*, Aldershot: Arena.

Schofield, G, Beek, M, Sargent, K with Thoburn, J (2000) *Growing Up in Foster Care*, London: BAAF.

Thoburn, J, Norford, L and Rashid, S (2000) *Permanent Family Placement for Children of Minority Ethnic Origin*, London: Jessica Kingsley.

Triseliotis, J (1973) *In Search of Origins*, London: Routledge and Kegan Paul.

Triseliotis, J, Shireman, J and Hundleby, M (1997) *Adoption: Theory, policy and practice*, London: Cassell.

2 Managing post-adoption contact through mediation

Sally Sales

I have been spying on you all my life.
A seven-year-old adopted boy on seeing his birth father for the first time since he was two.

We will never remember anything by sitting in one place, waiting for the memories to come back to us of their own accord. Memories are scattered all over the world. We must travel if we want to find them and flush them from their hiding places.
Milan Kundera *–The Book of Laughter and Forgetting*

. . . the souls of those whom we have lost are held captive, until the day when we happen to pass by the tree or to obtain possession of the object, which forms their prison. Then they start and tremble, they call us by our name and as soon as we have recognised them the spell is broken. Delivered by us, they have overcome death and return to share our life.
Marcel Proust – *In Search of Lost Time*, Vol 1

I want to begin by writing about a visit I made to see a nine-year-old white girl, whom I shall call Sharon. I had just taken on the support of this girl's twice-yearly contact with her birth mother, a woman with profound mental health problems. This was the first time I had met Sharon, but she was very clear why I was there and immediately produced her life story book, eager to talk to me about her early life. I was struck by the painstaking way she went through the book, explaining to me in great detail the events leading up to her current adoptive placement. Her adoptive mother joined us after about half an hour and at that point Sharon closed up her book. She then proceeded to talk to me about her current life – school, a forthcoming Brownie camp, her recent summer holiday. Here was a girl who had learnt to move between the distinctive histories that made up her identity. I was left with the strong impression that Sharon felt there wasn't room for all her histories together; that her birth history had to be shut away, closed up in the context of her current life. And yet I knew that her adoptive mother was very open and supportive about contact.

I think this story encapsulates a fundamental contradiction within open adoption, which I want to explore as an introduction to the work of the Post Adoption Centre Contact & Mediation Service.

Why does open adoption continue to be such a controversial phenomenon in adoption practice? Why, after more than a decade of openness, do we still require more research-based evidence of its validity? What does this caution and concern speak to?

I believe that the whole notion of open adoption unsettles and upsets our deep belief in a very particular form of family life that is dominant in Western culture. This kind of family is private, self-enclosed, with a strong sense of its members belonging. The sense of belonging is based on sameness, a sameness transmitted through the blood tie and represented by the emphasis and importance placed on the possession of similar physical and psychic features: 'you have your mother's eyes, your father's temper, your grandmother's stubbornness.' In this form of family organisation, to belong is to be the same as, not different from; it is difference that sets us apart and potentially makes us outsiders.

Maybe this works well enough for biological families, but I think it becomes enormously problematic when applied to adoption. Adopted children bring with them complex histories that do not fit neatly into this culture's prevailing concept of family life. These children have often moved through many different families or institutions and have a profoundly plural sense of their identity. They bring with them unsettling and disturbing differences that cannot be neatly tied up into a "forever family" fantasy. Unless these differences are permitted, talked about and kept alive through contact, I believe it will be very difficult for adopted children to establish a secure sense of belonging to any substitute family.

The current debate that continues to rage around the issue of contact – whether it is good or bad, what form or frequency is best for the child – I understand as a direct consequence of a difficulty in revising our views of family life for adopted children. It is almost as if we need to come up with an exact measure of contact that might contain our fears in the face of the challenge that contemporary adoption makes to the beliefs we have about family and what it means to belong. I think it is critical that we shift our focus away from how much and what kind of contact and consider instead the question of how to support, manage and sustain a child's link with his birth history over time – to keep open a child's differences and simultaneously allow him or her to belong. The service that the Post Adoption Centre has developed over the last eight years has been framed within this perspective.

The Contact & Mediation Service

The Contact & Mediation Service was originally inspired by the approach used in family mediation, where mediation helps divorcing or separating families to reach decisions in a non-adversarial forum. Family mediators have long recognised how children suffer when caught between parents in conflict; through helping the adult parties reach agreement, children are removed from a position of divided loyalties. The Centre saw the benefits of transferring such an approach into the field of open adoption. Mediation could be used to bring adoptive parents and birth family together in an independent setting outside the adversarial adoption process, where they could be helped to negotiate decisions about contact.

A number of principles have underpinned the development of the service:

- co-operatively negotiated agreements help the child at the centre of the contact issue feel more secure and more able to move between his or her different histories;
- adults concerned about a child's welfare have the capacity to negotiate and reach decisions together;
- agreements between birth parents, birth relatives and adoptive parents are more likely to last than arrangements imposed by an outside authority;
- contact arrangements need to be reviewed and renegotiated to meet the changing needs of the developing child over time.

At the heart of the Service is a belief that the parents – both birth parents and adoptive parents – can make and manage decisions about contact themselves. The role of the mediator is to facilitate and support dialogue and negotiation, not to assess or to impose their view about contact. This central belief runs counter to prevailing adoption practice, where parents are often subjected to decisions made by either the local authorities or the courts.

It is not surprising, then, that the Service has struggled to establish its approach with local authorities, which, particularly in the beginning, believed it was neither responsible nor safe to let parents themselves reach decisions about contact. They wanted any mediation work to be informed and framed by their own views about contact, views often based on the history of the child protection concerns. The problem with this approach is that it always designates birth parents as "bad", "failed" and "inade-quate" and the child as needing a compensatory and reparative family experience. Thinking about the child's welfare in terms of continuity with the past becomes impossible within this framework. The Service believes that a distinction has to be made between birth family as parents and birth family as participants in a child's life. Because a birth parent could not parent does not mean they cannot make an important contribution to a child's need for continuity.

The Contact & Mediation Service now always undertakes an initial consultation with local authorities, so that the involved professionals can draw parameters around the basic questions of contact: for example, whether there is to be face-to-face contact and which people are to be involved in arrangements. The Service prefers professionals to make as few stipulations as possible, so that families have a wider and freer scope for negotiation. The parameters are defined for all parties at their individual interviews, making it clear from the outset what is a negotiable and what is a non-negotiable issue for discussion.

The Service places a central emphasis on establishing an effective channel of communication between all the significant adults in an adopted child's life. We think this is fundamental whether the contact is letterbox or face-to-face, as it will be the quality of the adults' relationship that will be the primary factor in how well contact is both sustained and renego-tiated over time. The current emphasis that local authorities place on the form and frequency of contact post placement is misguided. It is far more important to focus on *how* the involved adults will meet to discuss and review contact than to fix and impose an arrangement at the point of placement. Such an approach does not promote or foster the kind of dialogue that both adopters and birth family members will need to have if contact is going to address children's changing needs. The experience of the Centre – supported by some contemporary research (Neil, 2000; Fratter, 1996) – is that decisions the parties themselves make are not only more long-lasting, but are more reflective of, and responsive to, children's changing needs.

Case example

Jake, a boy of African descent, was fostered as a baby because his birth mother had severe mental health problems that meant she was hospitalised for long periods of time. He was fostered by a white family, with no plan for this becoming an adoptive placement, but the local authority was very slow in finding Jake an alternative permanent home. By the time he was four he was so attached to the foster carers that moving him was out of the question. The foster family adopted him and agreed to very frequent visits with both his birth mother and other members of her extended family, recognising the enormous importance of this within a transracial placement. However, they were not given any support in managing the visits with the birth mother, whom Jake found very demanding if she was unwell. In spite of real doubts, the adoptive mother felt she couldn't change arrangements put in place by the local authority.

Eventually, when Jake was nine, she approached the Post Adoption Centre for support with re-negotiating the contact. Jake was now saying much more vociferously that he wanted to see his birth mother less and that the weekly telephone calls with her were sometimes upsetting. The Service convened a number of meetings with the adoptive mother and the birth mother to help them reach a new decision about visits and telephone calls that would be more reflective of Jakes' needs and wishes. Jake now sees his birth mother less frequently, but still speaks to her regularly on the telephone. He has a better understanding of why the calls are sometimes "strange". The arrangements will now be reviewed annually with the support of the Contact & Mediation Service.

From its inception, the Service had been aware that the voice of the child was not independently represented at mediation meetings. During the last year, we have employed a child consultation worker whose role is to consult with children about their wishes regarding contact. The worker attends the mediation meeting to represent the child's views and these views inform the negotiations. This has been a very welcome addition to our work, particularly in cases where the birth family have not always trusted what adopters are saying about their children's wishes and feelings. It has also greatly enhanced our work with older children, who can now actively participate in the decision-making about contact. In the example above, Jake was able to speak to the consultation worker about his difficulties with contact and these were communicated to the mediation meeting. The birth mother found it easier to accept what was being said because it was coming from an independent worker and not the adoptive mother.

Negotiating contact

Letterbox

Letterbox is often viewed as the easy end of the contact continuum, with face-to-face meetings considered to be the more demanding to both negotiate and sustain. This is not the experience of the Contact & Mediation Service. The negotiation and sustaining of an apparently simple letterbox has often proved to be an enormously demanding task for all parties involved.

We always recommend that any letterbox arrangement is reciprocal, so that birth parents give, as well as receive information. If the information is only one way – still sometimes the case with many letterbox arrangements – then the child's sense of his or her birth history remains frozen in time. A life story book may have been compiled at the point of placement, but unless this is a living record, continuously updated and renewed, it remains a dead archive for the child.

The Service is sometimes in a position where it is co-ordinating a letterbox for families. In these cases the letters are always forwarded unopened to both birth family and adoptive parents. If either party is upset about an inappropriate communication, the Service will convene a meeting with the parties to discuss what went awry. The Service does not monitor or censor any correspondence, not even that from birth parents to adopters, trusting that adopters are competent to assess whether a letter is appropriate to be given or read to their children. Parents know they can ring to talk through any concerns they have about a letter. Birth parents sometimes call because promised information has been missed out. Recently, adopters rang because they had received a rather "bizarre" letter from a birth parent, who was unwell at the time of sending it. The availability of support to parents is what is critical in the setting up of any letterbox system.

In mediation meetings where a letterbox is under discussion, parents are encouraged to address the following questions:

• Who will be writing to whom?
• What do birth parents write about themselves? What do they say about their history with the children? How do they talk about painful or difficult events, for example, their mental health problems, their children's removal, a long break in visits?
• How do birth parents refer to themselves? How do they sign off letters – "lots of love" "love you forever" "from"?
• How do they answer difficult questions asked by the children?
• What kind of information would the birth family like in letters? Would they like to know whether their children ask after them?
• What kind of presents? How many? Which birth family members will send them?
• Will birthday and festive cards be reciprocally exchanged?
• Will photographs be sent? Will this also be reciprocal?

Moving towards direct contact

It has become very clear during the work of the Service that letterbox arrangements do not remain static. As children develop and mature, the regular flow of letters frequently stimulates questions and a desire for increased or different contact. This is the point where there is a vital need for a forum where arrangements can be reviewed and renegotiated. The

Service has been working with some families for between five to eight years and during that period there have been many changes that have had to be discussed and negotiated. It is, of course, not only children's lives that change, adults' lives change too – they separate, change partners, have more children, become ill, move house, change sexuality. It is important that the impact of such changes can be considered for the children who will be living through them.

Managing the shift from letterbox to face-to-face contact is not an easy experience for parents. Mediation meetings at that point are an excellent opportunity for both adopters and birth parents to talk through the anxieties, fears and insecurities that such a change evokes. The meetings are also used to discuss how to prepare children. Sometimes birth parents write a letter about the forthcoming contact and include an up-to-date photograph. One adoptive family telephoned the birth mother, so that the children could speak to her prior to the meeting. Another adoptive family felt their son needed some therapeutic preparation and they spent a day at the Post Adoption Centre together, working through their fears about the meeting.

In situations where the face-to-face meeting is the first after a long break, adopters are encouraged to write to the birth family to tell them how the children were afterwards. Some adopters encourage the children to write a letter too. Sometimes there will be another mediation meeting to plan for future contact immediately following the first visit. It is clear that managing the transition from letterbox to face-to-face contact needs support in the initial stages.

Direct contact: Some frequently-asked questions

Where will it happen?

For first meetings or when there has been a long gap, a quiet and private place is suggested. The Service tends not to recommend local authority offices or family centres, as they can be resonant with negative memories for both children and birth family. In situations where face-to-face contact has been ongoing, there may be a need to discuss new venues, as children often report boredom or frustration. Six months between visits can be a long time in the life of a young child and birth parents sometimes need help in considering what is commensurate with the child's age and abilities. A birth mother who had been seeing her son for some years found it very difficult when he became older and wanted more energetic activities. She had enjoyed the quiet meetings in a mediation centre, drawing and colouring, with him sitting on her lap. She struggled at first when the meetings changed to bike riding and skating in a local park.

The Service has not usually worked with adopters who have offered their own homes for visits. We have one case where contact takes place in the birth grandmother's house; this has been going so well that the adoptive family are now considering having some of the visits in their home. We have had a few cases where foster parents have adopted and the pattern of visits to the foster home has continued post adoption.

Who will be present?

The Service always recommends that everyone meets together with the child. This gives the child permission to move between their two family lives, without feeling disloyal or in conflict. During a recent contact meeting, three children were together with their adopters and their birth mother and father. All three children happily moved between their two families, referring to both sets of parents as mum and dad, something that didn't confuse them for a moment. They were quite clear who their first mum and dad were and who the mum and dad they live with day to day are. Their adoptive parents were very comfortable with sharing this highly symbolic designation, having discussed it beforehand in a mediation meeting with the birth parents.

How long will it last?

The Service encourages parents to be clear about time limits, particularly when it is a first meeting. If there has been an interruption in direct contact, even if not for a great length of time, it will impact enormously on relations between the child and both his/her birth family and adoptive parents. Most children will have sustained regular contact with their birth family prior to their adoptive placement. A break in this routine may evoke disturbing thoughts and fantasies; for example, children may think that family members have died, abandoned them, become dangerously ill or moved away and forgotten them. It will be difficult for children experiencing such a reaction to make attachments to their new parents. It will also be confusing, bewildering and possibly shocking, to then reintroduce contact at some later point. In spite of these potential repercussions for the child, it is still often the case that direct contact is stopped while children "settle" into their adoptive families, continuity of contact not being understood as a positive factor in helping children adjust to their new homes. This is contrary to our experience and contrary to the outcome of recent albeit limited research (Fratter *et al*, 1991; Fratter, 1996). In many of the cases referred to the Service, direct contact has been terminated or suspended once children have been permanently placed. Our work then lies in helping parents re-open or re-establish visits after a period of great psychological and physical turbulence in the child's life.

Case example

The Service negotiated the re-opening of contact for two children of mixed English/Iranian heritage. They were aged six and eight when placed with white adopters, having been unable to stay with their birth mother, who had a long mental health history. The birth father has had no involvement in their lives. Their visits with their birth mother had been suspended when they moved to their adoptive placement and they had not seen her for six months.

The local authority referred the case because they felt they needed the help of an independent agency, as the birth mother would not co-operate. She was very upset about the break in contact and no longer trusted the local authority. Originally, the plan had been for quarterly visits post adoption. However, by the time of referral the local authority no longer had a fixed position about frequency of contact. The overriding concern was to re-establish the birth mother in the children's lives without conflict.

The Service saw the adopters and the birth mother separately and then convened a mediation meeting. In the meeting the three parents decided to make the first contact short, as the children had been through a time of great change and were very unsettled. It was agreed to re-open the contact at the Post Adoption Centre, with the option of going on to a park if the meeting went well. The older child had asked to call her birth mother before the contact, as she felt very anxious and confused about where her mother had been. This telephone call was a great help to her and afterwards she wanted to buy her mother a huge bouquet of flowers to take to the visit. The contact went well and reassured the children both that their birth mother was all right and that she hadn't forgotten them. They began to settle much more quickly with their adopters following this contact and regular, longer meetings were planned for the future with their birth mother. Clearly, the interruption in contact had had an adverse effect on the children's capacity to settle with their new parents. Significantly, the older child could only begin to express her anxieties about her mother once contact was again in place.

The children had been placed without emphasis on their paternal ethnicity, presumably because their only significant attachment was to their white mother. As their birth father has disappeared, their dual heritage could not be kept alive through contact.

What will happen?

The Service always supports families in setting up meetings that feel "natural" and unforced, which can be difficult outside the familiar surroundings of a home environment. In mediation meetings adoptive parents suggest activities that the children currently enjoy or offer to bring activities from home that will help to make the children feel more relaxed.

A common complaint from adopters is that birth parents overload meetings with expectations – they want their high energy six-year-old to sit and talk; they want exclusive play with their children; they want to take too many photographs. It seems that it can be difficult for birth parents to appreciate that the significance they have for their child does not depend on the intensity of time they spend together.

Case example

For the last five years the Service has been supporting a birth mother on her annual visit with her son, Steven. He is nine and lives with his adoptive parents, who also have a birth son about his age. The meetings take place in a London park and usually last about three hours. The adoptive mother always brings both boys, who appear to get along very well. The two families eat lunch together and then arrange an activity – children's zoo, skating or whatever suits the mood and the weather. The boys bring their bikes and ride around together, very caught up in each other's company.

The birth mother often complained to me that Steven didn't sit with her and chat and she wondered whether he really wanted to see her. It certainly seemed to be a matter of indifference to Steven and it seemed likely that he continued to come out of duty. However, this was far from the case. Following a visit last year, the adoptive mother rang to say that Steven wanted to see his mother more frequently and had requested a visit to his previous home where his birth mother still lived. His way of negotiating his relationship with his birth mother could not be easily read, but the meetings with her were clearly very important to him and were helping him to make sense of, and sustain, his history with her.

Will birth parents have time alone with children?
Birth parents often have an anxious concern that they won't be able to spend time with their children on their own during visits. In mediation meetings this is openly discussed, and if adoptive parents have a difficulty about it, they are encouraged to be clear about why they feel that way. Birth parents need to understand if their behaviour or comments are inappropriate, so that there is the opportunity for change.

Case example
The Service supports a Guyanese birth mother, who has profound mental health problems, with her twice-yearly visits with her nine-year-old daughter, Sharon. Sharon lives with her single carer, a Jamaican woman, who places great importance on Sharon keeping links with her Guyanese heritage. The visits are supported because the birth mother will sometimes engage in very inappropriate conversations with Sharon. In a mediation meeting the birth mother requested to go swimming with Sharon, which would have meant time on her own in both the changing room and swimming pool. The adoptive

mother explained that this wouldn't be possible as Sharon became upset by the questions that the birth mother asked her sometimes when they were on their own, particularly the questions about sex. The birth mother was obsessed that someone was interfering with her daughter and constantly wanted to check this out. The adoptive mother was sufficiently empathetic with the birth mother to see her behaviour as a way of showing concern for Sharon, but she also needed to communicate how distressing Sharon found her questions. The visits were not stopped, but supported in a way that could enable Sharon to enjoy her mother's company without upset and embarrassment.

What questions are children currently asking?

Birth parents need to know what kind of questions they may be asked by their children so they can prepare themselves – particularly if the child is going through a time when certain moments have acquired significance. Steven in the example above wanted to ask his birth mother about a fire in the flat where he used to live – he thought he had caused it. Another adopted boy wanted to know whether his birth mother would cuddle him when they met, as he was fearful he had been given up because she didn't want him. In both cases the two families could discuss these questions together and work out the best way of responding to the children. We think it is important that children grow up with a full sense of their birth history and why they were adopted. This may mean helping birth parents answer difficult or upsetting questions about why they couldn't look after their children.

What about presents?

Bringing presents can be a controversial issue and mediation meetings always address how people feel about this. Some adopters prefer to keep present giving separate from the actual visits; some adopters don't mind a few agreed presents and some just accept whatever birth parents feel moved to give. The most important point is that there should be an agreement about it and that everyone is comfortable with what then transpires.

Case example

Grace was placed at five for adoption, having been removed from her mother's care at three. Her mother suffered from severe clinical depression and was unable to provide Grace with consistent parenting. With the help of the Service, the adopters and the birth mother set up a letterbox arrangement that continued for the next four years.

In a review meeting, when Grace was seven, the adopters agreed that the birth mother could buy one small present for Grace's birthday. The birth mother was very disappointed, as she had bought the complete set of Encyclopaedia Britannica, but the adopters refused to allow such a present.

When Grace was nine she began to ask to see her mother. At the annual review meeting this was discussed and it was agreed to extend the contact to include visits. The first visit took place on a hot June day at a mediation centre in south London. Everyone met together for about half an hour and then Grace went off for lunch with her birth mother. At the next review everyone agreed that the visit had been a great success and that at least two visits a year should take place. Another contact was planned for the autumn, possibly a cinema trip. The birth mother asked whether she could now give Grace the Encyclopaedia Britannica; the adopters immediately agreed. I think this became possible for two reasons: the adopters felt more secure in their parenting of Grace and the birth mother was now beginning to have a more significant relationship with Grace, within which such a present felt appropriate.

A case for mediation

In conclusion I want to document a case from referral to post-mediation to illustrate how the Service supports families and children. This case was referred post placement by a London local authority.

Three white children, Katherine, 11, Sarah, 8 and Tom, 4 were placed together for adoption with a white childless couple. The birth mother had a long psychiatric history and could only live in the community with support. Notwithstanding this, the two older girls had a close and warm attachment to her and worried when they did not see her. Tom had only lived with his birth mother for a short time and did not manifestly have the same close attachment to her.

The referring authority was very concerned about a dispute with the birth mother regarding their plans for post-adoption contact. They were recommending direct contact twice a year, but the birth mother wanted four visits and to include the children's grandmother, aunt and cousins. The birth mother and the prospective adopters had not met because of this dispute and the birth mother was withholding her consent to the adoption. The three different birth fathers were not involved.

The first meeting was a professional consultation with the local authority and the Guardian ad litem at the Post Adoption Centre. We persuaded the local authority not to get entrenched in a battle about frequency, but to allow the parents themselves to meet and decide arrangements. The local authority agreed to withdraw conditions about face-to-face contact, although they were anxious about ceding such control. They understood that they would not be involved in the mediation work, but that they would be sent copies of any agreement that was reached by the parents.

A fortnight following the professional consultation, we held initial separate interviews with both the birth mother and the adopters. The birth mother came to her interview with her mother. She was very agitated and angry with the local authority and insisted she would contest the adoption, if she didn't get the contact she wanted. However, she agreed to attend a mediation meeting, liking the idea that 'I'll get my say at last'. It was suggested she bring someone to the meeting, so she didn't feel out-numbered by the adopters.

At their interview, the adopters also agreed to mediation, but were very nervous about meeting the birth mother. They clearly felt over-whelmed by what they had heard about her wishes regarding contact. They said they didn't feel able to take on the children's extended birth family during visits, although they were open to "some" contact with the birth mother.

The mediation meeting was held a fortnight after the interviews. We asked people to arrive at separate times, so they did not bump into each other on the doorstep of the Centre. The birth mother brought her housing support worker.

The meeting began with the mediator explaining the purpose of mediation – to reach an agreement about contact arrangements – and setting out the ground rules of the process. In our experience, participants feel safer and more contained if they know both what to expect and how the meeting will be facilitated.

As this was the first time the adopters and the birth mother had met, some time was given to introductions. Because the children were the focus of mutual interest and concern, there was an immediate point of conversation. The adopters spoke about how the children were settling in and they asked the birth mother some questions about her early life with the girls.

The meeting then moved on to consider the issue of contact. The local authority's view was reported – that there was to be direct contact to be agreed by the parties. The birth mother said she wanted quarterly contact and to include her mother, her sister and her nieces. The adopters responded by underlining the importance to the children of seeing their birth mother, but voiced concern that this would get lost if other relatives were included. The birth mother felt very strongly about the children keeping in touch with their grandmother at least. The adopters suggested that the grandmother could come for one of the visits every year, which the birth mother accepted. The adopters also felt that four visits might be too much and proposed two, with an option of a third if the children wanted it. The birth mother was disappointed, but she did not fiercely contest this proposal. We reassured both families that any arrangement was subject to an annual review and renegotiation. This seemed to make it easier for the birth mother to accept a compromise. She asked to have a letter and photographs, if the third visit didn't take place, and the adopters agreed.

The parties agreed the practical arrangements for the next two visits – dates, venue, duration, meeting place. The adopters did not want to be too restrictive and agreed that the visits could include presents for the children. The Service would be supporting the birth mother during the contact, as she found the experience of parting with her children afterwards very distressing.

An agreement was written up and distributed to the parents, the local authority and the Guardian ad litem. The birth mother did not contest the adoption once the contact issue had been agreed.

The agreement formed the basis of the contact for the next three years. The families would meet twice a year (October and Easter) at the same venue, a London park, and spend half a day together. The grandmother always came on the Easter visit. There would be an activity – ice-skating, adventure playground – and sharing lunch. Neither party felt the need to review the arrangement in this three-year period, although they both accessed telephone support from the Service from time to time. The birth mother was happy with the meetings and no longer felt so concerned about having them more frequently, in part because the length of the visits had been informally increasing over the years. The adopters too seemed happy with the contact, except on one occasion when they discussed not bringing Tom. They felt he was getting "the least" from the visits, but after talking it through with the mediator, decided that contact was a "family occasion" and not to bring him would be divisive.

The Service continued to support the visits, primarily because the birth mother needed to talk afterwards. She liked to talk through a range of concerns: how the contact had gone, how the children seemed, how she felt with the adopters and how to deal with any information the children had given her. For example, on one visit Katherine had talked about having a boyfriend and the birth mother got the impression that the adopters did not know about this. She needed some help with working out how to approach the adopters with the information, as she was very nervous about upsetting her daughter. We finally agreed that the Service would pass on the information to the adopters by telephone and contact the birth mother with their response and Katherine's response. In fact the adopters knew about the boyfriend, although Katherine had been very secretive about him. They appreciated that Katherine wanted to have some secrets with her birth mother, whom she continued to miss in spite of settling in well with her adoptive family.

In the fourth year of the arrangement, Katherine was starting to request extra time with her mother. She also wanted to meet with her extended birth family. At the October contact the adopters mentioned this to the birth mother, who was delighted. It was thought that it needed further discussion, but not with the children present. Everyone agreed to get together for another mediation meeting the following summer.

Holiday commitments meant that the Easter visit was deferred until June. This visit went really well, everyone seemed very relaxed and Tom was noticeably more at ease with his birth mother. The adoptive mother had prepared a picnic, which everyone enjoyed together in the sunshine. The ease and informality of the atmosphere made having a post-lunch activity unnecessary and the time was spent in conversation, with the girls having time apart with their birth mother.

Tragically, a few days after this contact, the birth mother committed suicide. The Service was contacted almost immediately by the community project where the birth mother lived and we were able to speak directly with the adopters. We spent a lot of time on the telephone talking through the best way to tell the children about their mother's death. Once they knew, the children all wanted to go to the funeral and Katherine and Sarah wanted to participate in the service. The birth mother's sister was in charge of arrangements and she liaised directly with the adopters about including the girls in the funeral ceremony in the way they had requested.

The children now have informal visits with their birth mother's extended family, which have been an enormous help to them, both in making sense of suicide and living through the loss of their mother.

Losing touch with familiar places and familiar people may feel like another kind of death for adopted children, throwing them into a state of grief that makes settling down with a new family a very difficult undertaking. The Contact & Mediation Service is committed to lessening the severity of such loss through helping parents manage and sustain contact arrangements for their children. The adopted children we support are growing up with a rich and full sense of the complex emotional legacy of adoption by keeping connected with significant people from their birth histories.

References

Fratter, J (1996) *Adoption with Contact: Implications for policy and practice*, London: BAAF.

Fratter, J, Rowe, G, Sapsford, D and Thoburn, J (1991) *Permanent Family Placement: A decade of experience*, London: BAAF.

Neil, E (2000) *Contact with birth relatives after adoption: A study of young recently placed children*, Unpublished PhD, Norwich: University of East Anglia.

3 'Is mummy coming today?'
Managing contact arrangements in kinship placements

David Pitcher

'You see,' Wendy said complacently, 'our heroine knew that the mother would always leave the window open for her children to fly back by . . .'

For the three children in Peter Pan (Barrie, 1911), knowing that their mother had 'left the window open' was what made the difference between feeling angry and forgotten and being able to 'stay away for years and have a lovely time'. This is no less true for any other child who is placed away from his or her parents. Recent research (Richards, 2001) tells us that the majority of children placed with their wider family do continue to have an ongoing relationship with their mother or father, but this can be stressful and carers generally feel ill-equipped and poorly supported in dealing with such contact.

As a social work practitioner, I am regularly involved in making and supporting placements for children with their wider family members. I also run a support group for grandparents caring for their grandchildren, where the relationship with parents is often on the agenda for discussion. Thus, in my daily work I cannot escape either the vital importance, or the potential for difficulty, of contact. In this chapter, I shall explore the issue of contact from a practitioner's perspective.

How contact helps children

Contact with parents is important in promoting a child's wellbeing in many ways (Triseliotis, 1989). Most significantly, it can reassure him or her that they have not been abandoned, and that their mother or father is happy about the attachments they are making. If they recognise the child's achievements, this will increase his or her confidence. It is also important that a child's picture of her parents is reasonably realistic – neither over-idealised nor exaggeratedly bad (Littner, 1975). All this should work for children in kinship placements but good quality contact rarely "just happens", especially when a child is placed at a time of family crisis, confusion or abuse. It is the adults' job, and perhaps especially the social worker's, to ensure that contact becomes a constructive and integral part of the child's life.

To achieve this, those caring and planning for the child need to adopt an outlook that always includes the birth parent. It is this, rather than the amount or style of contact, which will be decisive. Without being able to continue their attachment, albeit in a readjusted form, the child or young person will be likely to develop difficulties that could well threaten the placement.

But is it always so simple? Often, the effect of contact is to unsettle, or even to frighten, the child (Phelan, 1995), or to undermine his or her new relationships. Parents may be difficult or inconsiderate (Littner, 1975). It is in just these situations, where the temptation is to write off the parents, that the social worker must use his or her skill to make contact successful. The birth parent, who will be feeling grief, shame (Fratter, 1996) and perhaps a strong sense of resentment, can be enabled to accept the new form their relationship has taken and new carers too can be helped to understand the parent's importance to the child in their care.

Contact in kinship placements

When a child or young person is placed with a family member, this may provide a special opportunity to build or maintain a good relationship with his parent or parents. We must, however, avoid easy assumptions. My own small-scale study of a group of grandparent carers (Pitcher, 2002) gave me a number of clues about aspects of contact in this setting.

- Children often behave in a "disruptive" way before and after contact with their parents, and this makes carers less inclined to support it.
- Poor reliability can be a major issue, and this makes carers feel angry that their grandchild's parent has "let them down".
- Grandparents are able to recognise the importance of contact to their grandchildren, and may seek out parents in a way that foster carers may not.

- Grandparents are highly committed to the placement, not just for the sake of the children, but also to keep matters "in the family".
- Despite initial shock and disbelief, grandparents almost invariably agreed with Social Services on the need for protection. Although there were some cases in which a protection plan was compromised by a grandparent's inability to accept the seriousness of the risk posed by their son or daughter, it was just as likely that they would feel the social worker was being "taken in" by a persuasive parent.
- Grandparents try hard to find a sensitive way of telling their grand-children about why they are living with them or why the contact arrange-ments are as they are, such as 'mummy is not very well again today'.
- Some grandparents deal with the pain of the situation by becoming severely critical of their son or daughter: 'She's a druggie, not my daughter any more'.
- The vast majority felt that their son or daughter was pleased that they were caring for their child, but many felt that this allowed the parents 'off the hook, to do as they liked, knowing that they could see the child anyway'. In a few cases, this led to resentment or condemnation greater than is expressed by non-relative carers, creating a situation in which the child is exposed to a very negative perception of the parent which would inevitably become a considerable barrier to contact.
- Many grandchildren felt inhibited about mentioning their parents in their grandparents' presence. The fear of disloyalty was as great as for children with non-relative carers.
- Parents greatly valued opportunities to contribute to their relatives' and children's lives, even if this was only in indirect or practical ways. It made a big difference if they were consulted about how their child was being brought up.
- A consistent, reliable social worker can help kinship carers to think about, and feel safe about, contact.

According to a much quoted American study, it has to be understood that not all grandparents are the same and that they hold many different beliefs about what grandparenthood is, or should be (Neugarten and Weinsten, 1964).

In a helpful analysis of family dynamics in kinship foster care, Roger

Greeff (2001) asks how the changed family situation affects a mother or father's sense of parenthood:

Will she see herself (and be seen by their child and the grandparents) as continuing to parent her child, or will her status as parent be temporarily or permanently suspended?

An excluded parent who feels their identity and status as parent – which is integral to their sense of self – have been taken away is likely to behave very differently from an included parent who feels that he or she has a role to fulfil, even if it is a changed or restricted one. This can be mirrored in how relative carers feel about their task.

Research also shows that in kinship placements, carers receive less support than do non-relative carers, feel less certain about their role, and are less clear about the nature of the placement (Le Prohn, 1994) Children, too, feel less clear about their situation, and this correlates directly with their feelings of wellbeing (Liddy, 1970). Relatives are likely to have a more complex set of feelings and relationships with the parties involved, and be less well-trained to understand those emotions and their effects.

Four case examples, all from my current practice, illustrate some of the issues involved.

Sue and Jane: contact within boundaries

Sue and Jane were sisters. As children, they had made a pact with each other that, if either of them had children and anything happened, they would look after each other's. Later, Sue was "happily" married with three children; Jane also had two children, Jack (9) and Sophie (7). Jane's partner was violent towards her, and they were both involved in heavy alcohol use. Their home was not clean, and Jack and Sophie were often described as "dirty" and "unkempt". Sue and her family used to have Jane's children to stay with them for a while, and they felt very protective towards them. Often, Jane's partner would suddenly demand them back, or alternatively fail to collect them for several weeks.

Suddenly, following a Police Protection Order, Jack and Sophie were brought to Sue. Over the following weeks, it became clear that things at home had been much worse for Jack and Sophie than anyone had suspected. In addition to neglect, there had been deliberate physical and emotional abuse, and Jack and Sophie had been sexually abused by a visitor to the house. Sue and Jane's mother could not believe that the sexual abuse could have taken place. Care proceedings were started, and Sue and her partner were assessed as kinship carers.

Jane was very keen for Jack and Sophie to go to her sister Sue, saying that she knew they would be in safe hands. She also hoped that Sue would allow her frequent contact with them. Weekly contact was set up, and supervised by Social Services in a Family Centre. During contact, Jane felt awkward and was observed not to be relaxed with the children. She would hint to Sophie that she would 'get you back' by saying things like: 'What wallpaper would you like in your new room?' She also promised them presents, which she did not always bring. Jack and Sophie often returned from the contact in an agitated mood, and were similarly agitated for about two days before the next meeting. Sue felt that contact was having an adverse effect on them. Jane went to prison for six months for assault and after her release it was agreed that contact should be re-established at once a month.

Prior to the admission to care, both Sue and Jane would regularly drop in to their mother's. Now, Jane spent most of her time there. Social Services said that Sue could not visit with Jack and Sophie, as Jane might be there. This was difficult, as her mother had been one of Sue's strongest sources of support. She felt that she could handle this situation, but the social worker was insistent that there should be no informal contact.

Sue commented: 'Jane was expecting me to be a bit more flexible with contact, but I won't be. The Care Order and the Social Services plan seemed a bit harsh at first, but it helps us all to know where we are. Jane co-operates because she's terrified that if she doesn't they would go to strangers. If the contact were not so tight, it would intrude too much into the rest of my life and I'd find it too much to cope with. The biggest issue for me is the loss of being able to see my mum when I want. I wish Social Services could leave me to make that judgement.'

Jane told me that she was grateful to Sue, but also expressed resentment towards her sister for having 'sided with Social Services'. Over time, however, Jack and Sophie's social worker was able to encourage Jane to attend the reviews, and she felt much more positive about being able to contribute to decisions. She was also able to use some of the "contact" time to help Jack with his spelling and reading, which resulted in him trying harder at school and wanting to produce work 'to show mum'.

- Social Services were firmly in control in this situation, and treated it similarly to any other foster placement.
- The clear plan made by the authorities created boundaries that protected Sue from being overwhelmed by pressures from her sister.
- Jack and Sophie's experience of being accommodated was less stressful than for children entering non-relative care because they not only knew where they were going, but felt positively welcomed.
- Jack and Sophie kept in touch with most of their wider family on their mother's side, as these relationships were also shared with Sue and were maintained naturally.
- All family members lost, as well as gained, roles and relationships. Sue felt that she could not support her sister, and that her own and her children's relationship with her mother suffered. Her own children lost their role as "the baby of the family" and "the only boy".
- Jane's contact with Jack and Sophie became much more constructive when she began to feel part of their lives, rather than just "having contact".
- When, two years after the placement, the social worker questioned whether the Care Order had become unwieldy (for instance, Sue had to ask permission from Social Services every time the children went to stay with other relatives or friends), Sue said that the compulsory framework it provided helped Jack and Sophie to feel safe.

Jamie: tensions within contact

Kelly's parents had separated when she was very young and she barely knew her father, John, who worked abroad for a big company. John had remarried, and when Kelly was 15, after a row with her mother which was never resolved, she started making contact with him and his new wife Anne. She was excited about finding her 'long lost dad'.

Kelly had a baby, Jamie, when she was 16. Her partner, who had several convictions for violent behaviour, injured Jamie when he was eight months old, and Jamie was admitted to hospital. John and Anne came forward offering to care for Jamie, as Kelly would not leave her partner.

Kelly was unsure about her father's offer. She was worried about being "controlled" by a parent again now she had left home. She also remembered some family stories about her father's violent temper. At the same time, she secretly hoped that it would give her an opportunity to get to know him. After a three-week period with foster carers, Jamie was placed with John and Anne. There were no restrictions about how often Kelly could visit but she felt uncomfortable whenever she did: 'Anne just wants to do everything herself. Anybody would think he was her baby!' Her father was openly critical of Kelly's boyfriend, and contemptuous of Social Services' plan to offer him 'a bit of counselling'. After a while, Kelly began to visit Jamie less frequently. John and Anne felt that she was losing interest in Jamie, and that there should be no plans for rehabilitation. Kelly told her social worker that she was frightened of her father, and could not talk to him about it. She also felt that Anne was trying to treat her as a daughter, which she resented. Later, in a counselling session, Kelly said: 'My dad was never there for me. Now he's all over Jamie and I'm out of it again'.

The social worker arranged a family meeting at which Kelly, John and Anne were able to talk a little more openly, and contact improved for a while. Despite frequent discussions, however, Kelly continued to report that Anne would jump up and see to Jamie, rather than letting her attend to him. Anne also told Kelly that she was not making Jamie's drinks correctly. Anne said: 'Kelly had her chance. The baby's needs have got to come first. When he cries, Kelly's never there quickly enough, and he deserves to be cared for properly now.' Kelly reported to her social worker: 'Why should I bother then?'

- Jamie's story illustrates the fact that kinship does not guarantee warm or close relationships. Jamie's grandfather tried to protect him by hardening his attitude towards Kelly and her partner, and making sure that Jamie was cared for "properly".

- This placement meant that Jamie could have a permanent home, so that strong unbroken attachments could begin to be made.
- Hopefully, Kelly would have lifelong, informal contact and might be in a position to resume the care of Jamie at some stage in the future.
- However, sadly, Kelly felt that she was not respected as Jamie's mother, and that her role had been taken away from her. This caused Kelly to give up trying.
- The negative attitude John and Anne displayed towards Kelly's boyfriend meant that Kelly could not relax when she was with Jamie. Kelly also felt that his grandfather's attitude would be picked up by Jamie as he grew older. Kelly felt that Jamie's foster carers had been more neutral, and did not criticise her.
- Kelly's comment about hoping to get to know her father again, and then her experience of rejection, is a dynamic that occurs in different guises in many kinship placements.
- The social worker was concerned that relationships could deteriorate further and set up four family sessions to enable Kelly, John and Anne to express their feelings. During these sessions, Kelly explained how angry she was with Anne who, as a step-parent, had no right to act in such a familiar way. She felt that John was supporting Anne rather than her, which John accepted. Anne felt angry that Social Services was listening to Kelly's views more than to theirs, when they were doing all the work. These sessions led to some improvements in relationships but the situation was never relaxed.

Simon: informality or safety?

Michelle had learning difficulties, and had always lived with her parents. She began a relationship with Terry, a tenant in the same block of maisonettes, and became pregnant. Social Services told Michelle and her parents that Terry was known to have committed sexual offences against children, although he had never received a conviction. Michelle's parents found this difficult to believe, as Terry had been very helpful to them in the past, but they agreed not to allow him contact.

When Simon was born, Michelle's parents obtained a Residence Order. Michelle left home and married Terry, and she visited Simon every day while Terry was at work. Sadly, her mother died, and Michelle's daily help with Simon became essential. There was no contact with Terry. After two years, Social Services ceased their involvement. Simon's grandfather, who was aged 64, expressed some fears about how he would manage in years to come.

Four years later, it came to light that Simon's grandfather had been allowing some contact with Terry. This was always strictly supervised, he insisted, but 'everyone deserves a second chance'. He maintained that he would never risk Simon being left with Terry on his own, but he also said, 'Social Services don't always have their facts right'.

Social Services convened a case conference, at which it was decided that Simon would be placed with foster carers away from the area.

- Simon's early experiences were of a natural family arrangement which involved little confusion of roles or social stigma.
- Michelle felt positive about the arrangement as she could see Simon whenever she wanted to, and she knew she had a valuable role to play.
- In the new arrangement, Michelle will continue to see Simon, but she will not be able to do as much for him as previously.
- Simon's grandfather said he hoped Simon would have more opportunities with a younger family, but questioned whether they would have the same love for him.
- It would be hard for Simon to understand this move. He had not experienced any abuse, and the disruption might well carry with it serious risk indicators for the future.
- This situation illustrates how hard it can be for a grandparent to police a relationship without a formal framework. Dangerous adults do groom the carers of their children, but there may also be cases in which risk is wrongly suspected.
- Social Services believed that Simon really was at risk from Terry but could not persuade the grandfather to take the risk seriously. Following Simon's removal, his grandfather was referred to a group, by an

independent professional, which helped him to develop a new "grandfather" relationship with Simon.

Jonathan: uncertainty within contact

Janice, a single mother, had mixed feelings when she learned that her daughter Sarah was pregnant. She knew that Sarah, 17, and her boy-friend were drug users. After baby Jonathan was born, they left Janice to "babysit" on many occasions, often not coming back when they had promised. Once, this was for seven days. Janice felt sorry for Jonathan and gave him lots of treats to 'make it up to him'. Jonathan was observed to be significantly overweight. Sometimes, Sarah and her boyfriend went through stable periods, when they cared for Jonathan well. Then they became homeless and came to live with Janice. They went out a lot, and after a while it seemed to Janice that it was she, not her daughter, who was bringing Jonathan up. Jonathan often got quite upset, and refused to sleep in his own bedroom, asking to 'cuddle with nanny'. Janice had a strong family, many of whom lived locally and helped her out. Janice admitted that she was a little afraid of Sarah and her boyfriend, and would not be able to stand up to them if need be. She also admitted that she sometimes felt angry that Sarah should have so much freedom while she was left to care for Jonathan. Yet she said, 'I can't let Jonathan down. So what else can I do?'

Jonathan looks forward to being taken out by his parents – who usually 'take him round town' and buy him a treat. If they stay away too long, he becomes difficult. What Janice finds hardest is that he takes it out on her, and never blames his parents. A friend has advised her to get professional help, but Janice is anxious to "keep it in the family".

- This was a private placement. The grandmother attended a grandparent support group but Social Services was not involved.
- Many kinship carers are unclear about their role in a child's life. This may be coupled with considerable anxiety on the part of the child, the carer and the parents.
- Jonathan has a clear view about who his parents are, and they feel they are 'in the picture'. Janice feels that they value her as a carer for

Jonathan, and that they appreciate the attachment between grandson and grandmother.

- There would be clear advantages if Janice could feel in a more confident position with regard to Sarah and her boyfriend.
- The family's anxiety about revealing secrets, perhaps fearing that Jonathan could be removed by "the authorities", presents a problem. It may be that the family could use a professional service with a high level of confidentiality (such as mediation). But all professional agencies should give out positive messages about valuing and wanting to support kinship arrangements.

Discussion: maximising the benefits of contact

Placement with relatives presents undoubted advantages for many children, but if we are to offer adequate support, and to carry out accurate assessments prior to decisions about placement, we need to recognise the great complexity of the issues involved. Of the advantages that kinship care offers, promoting good quality long-term links with a child's mother and father must be one of the greatest; but it is here too that the complexity can be at its greatest. If we are to learn from what works best in our existing practice, as illustrated in the four case studies, we might identify two dimensions for success in contact.

1. All adult parties (the parent, the carer, and the agency) should feel valued and respected and be confident that they have an important role to play in the child's life. Even if children have been removed because of ill-treatment, everyone should be able both to express their views, and to listen to views that the others express. Informal, relaxed contact arrangements can be the great strength of placements within the family. Where there is the requirement for a policing role, such as for Sue in the first case example, this benefit is lost.

"Contact" should not be about a parent exercising a right to see a child, or even allowing a child the right to see a parent, but about doing something useful and uniquely valuable (which can include seeing the child). If a parent cannot find a way of being useful, he/she is likely either to opt out, or to subvert the process of contact. We might call this the dimension of *power*.

2. All adult parties (the parent, the carer and the agency) should agree that the care arrangement is in the best interests of the child, and that accommodation is necessary. This should be based on trust, and go beyond acceptance of a form of words. There should be agreement on the way the story is told to the child, what the child calls the carers, on the boundaries to be observed, and the reasons for them. A kinship placement that is working well has within it great potential for this mutual respect and understanding to develop. However, families are also places in which criticism can be keener than elsewhere, and in these cases a kinship placement will be less likely to achieve this measure of trust. This highlights the need for accurate assessment in each case, rather than a blanket position about kinship placement. We might call this dimension that of *acceptance*.

Using these two dimensions, we could construct a practice model to help us to understand contact situations:

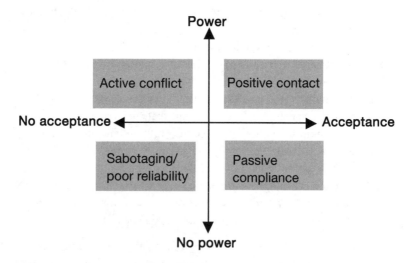

If we are to help children, their parents and their kinship carers to achieve positive contact, Social Services must play a role that is not *just* about ensuring safety, or deciding who has contact when and for how long, but also about the following:

- Explaining, if necessary over and over again, *why* something is decided. What is "obvious" to a trained social worker may not be "obvious" to Michelle's grandfather or Kelly's father, in the case examples.
- Offering ongoing help to negotiate relationships and roles. For Janice, in the last case example, this may include what Jonathan is told about why his parents are away so much. This might involve discussions with the social worker, or the use of an impartial mediator. Open communication is so often the first victim of stresses within families.
- Offering individual, independent help and support to parents who are not caring for their children. This can help them to see the positive role they can play in their children's lives, and the positive messages they can give. This support should also be given to carers, so few of whom have access to "link" social workers as foster carers do:

  When children are placed with kin, child welfare agencies should support both the birth parents and the kinship parents in their respective roles as nurturers, protectors and teachers of the children in their care. (Child Welfare League of America, 1994)

Making contact arrangements work requires vision and commitment and, however great our efforts, there may not be rewards in every case. But when children know that their parent has "left the window open" while they live safe, confident lives within their wider family, there is the power to heal.

This chapter is dedicated to Lord Michael Young of Dartington (1915– 2002) who supported and inspired our work with children and their extended families.

References

Barrie, J M (1911) *Peter Pan*, London: Hodder & Stoughton.

Child Welfare League of America (1991) *Kinship Care: A natural bridge*, Washington DC: CWLA.

Fratter, J (1996) *Adoption with Contact: Implications for policy and practice*, London: BAAF.

Greeff, R (2001) 'Family dynamics in kinship foster care' in *Kinship Care: The placement choice for children and young people*, Lyme Regis: Russell House Publishing.

Le Prohn, N S (1994) 'The role of the kinship foster parent: a comparison of the role conceptions of relative and non-relative foster parents', *Children & Youth Services Review*, 16:1/2.

Liddy, L V (1970) 'The self-image of the child placed with relatives', Smith College Studies in *Social Work*, 40:2.

Littner, N (1975) 'The importance of the natural parents to the child in placement', *Child Welfare*, Vol. LIV No. 3.

Neugarten, B L and Weinstein, K K (1964) 'The changing American grandparent', *Journal of Marriage and the Family*.

Phelan, P (1995) 'Incest and its meaning: the perspectives of fathers and daughters', *Child Abuse and Neglect*, 19:1.

Pitcher, D (2002) 'Placement with grandparents: the issues for grandparents who care for their grandchildren', in *Adoption & Fostering*, 26:1.

Richards, A (2001) *Second Time Around: A survey of grandparents raising their grandchildren*, Family Rights Group.

Triseliotis, J (1989) 'Foster care outcome: Review of key research findings', *Adoption & Fostering*, 13:3.

• • •

3a Managing contact arrangements in black kinship care

Hilary Galloway and Fiona Wallace

For centuries black kinship care has been one of the oldest traditions in rearing children, but it appears to be a new phenomenon for professionals working with children and families. Hegar (1999) traces cultural roots of kinship care to 'ancient and traditional societies in many parts of the world'.

The Children Act 1989 Section 23 (6) places a duty on social workers to consider placements with family and friends as one of the choices for a child who is not able to live with their birth parents. Historically, for black families, slavery often meant the dispersion of a parent; usually it was the father who was sold. The mother and/or kinfolk cared for the children. This enabled the children to remain within their family culture. The more recent phenomenon of workers finding employment some distance from their homes, including, of course, in other countries, has also resulted in children being brought up by their mothers and/or extended family members. It is not surprising that, when black families emigrated to Britain, the tradition of children living with their extended family network continued because it was an established cultural practice (Hegar, 1999).

There is a prevailing belief that once a black child[1] is placed with their kinfolk, the issues of identity and family links are addressed, and therefore managing contact does not always receive the amount of attention it deserves. This belief may be reinforced by the family's reticence in asking for support, either emotional or practical. The effects of institutional racism, which make black families wary of authority, can leave black kinship carers feeling isolated and abandoned. They may give out signals that they do not trust Social Services and social workers may accept the signals too readily without offering specific support or giving clear messages about how to access future services.

It would seem from the feedback from kinship carers in the Broad study (1997/1998) that they feel there is a tendency for social workers and their managers to have an "all or nothing" approach, and partnership involving a light touch of support from the local authority is difficult to achieve. The power and control issues that exist between family members

---

[1] Ince (2001) defines "black" as children from African and African Caribbean families; it is also used to refer to children of mixed heritage backgrounds with one parent who originates from Africa or the Caribbean. She goes on to say that the definition does not in any way devalue other cultural groups.

and the local authority influence the relationship, often adversely; this may be particularly marked if the family is black.

The emotional impact on the child, the main carer (who is either grandmother, aunt, uncle, sibling) and on other children living in the kinship household, may then be ignored in the whole process of setting up kinship care placements. Yet serious role conflicts can arise for all kinship carers who have to cope with their own emotions, demands from the child, parents, and extended family.

The question is, does anyone hold the power to control what is best for the child, parents and carer? Wheal (2001) suggests that contact with parents varies from case to case but is often difficult to manage. It is a very sensitive issue, which continually requires careful monitoring. She goes on to say that there are no guidelines for contact in kinship placements; guidelines would help but they would have to be flexible, otherwise black kinship care could become bureaucratic, with social services taking control and leaving the family carer powerless.

Family Group Conferences

The use of Family Group Conferences has provided a model of working in partnership with the extended family. Family members take the lead in making decisions about their children and request resources to support their plan for where the child will live, and with whom. The local authority remains responsible for child protection issues. In Wandsworth, a high proportion of kinship care placements are made following a Family Group Conference. Broad's study (1997/8) in Wandsworth found that the greater proportion of kinship carers were African, African-Caribbean or of dual heritage.

If the child stays in the family as a result of a Family Group Conference, then a black family will usually wish to control and manage the contact arrangements; after all, one of the reasons for kinship care is to keep the child connected to parents and out of the care system. There is a danger that everyone will breathe a sigh of relief: the kinship carers will be glad to be left to get on with it while the social workers will be only too glad to stand back and let them do it. But no matter what has been agreed, there is no guarantee that the contact arrangements will work as planned just because the family is black. There is a good reason why the child cannot live with the parents and we cannot make the assumption that the parents will be able to abide by any agreements, however they have been made, especially if kinship care re-awakens old family conflicts or sibling rivalries.

Case Study

One auntie says: 'Where is Social Services? On the fringes looking in. When the social worker visits, she wants to know about Marcus (who is 14 years old, on a Care Order to the local authority), his education, health and whether he has had contact with his parents but there is more to Marcus and his family. When my sister visits she turns up any time of day or night, demanding to see her son. This behaviour affects my children too, and what do the neighbours think? Sometimes we are able to laugh, other times we become angry at the situation we find ourselves in.

My last resort could be to call the police. This is a real dilemma for me, given the relationship the black community has with the police. What would the rest of my family think anyway? I do believe that Marcus should have contact with his mother because it is his mother and I know deep down she does care about him. She promises that she will visit on an agreed date and will bring him a gift and he then waits and waits and she does not come for months. Is this good for his emotional development? I don't know. I think he gets used to it because his attachment and memories of his mother are strong'.

It is very tricky to strike the right balance, from the beginning, between helping carers to identify issues that might arise and seeming to put barriers in the way. Marcus's auntie has settled for the situation as it is; she doesn't believe that anything will make any difference and doesn't want to have another Family Group Conference to discuss it. The case study shows how difficult it can be for social workers and kinship carers to manage contact between children and their parents that can affect all individuals who are living in the home with the child. There is a conflict of interests for the main carer because she has a bond with both child and parents. Even if social workers have left the door open, as Marcus's black worker did, and families feel confident in asking for help, it may not be possible to agree a more formal contact plan. Marcus's social worker was inclined to make contact less frequent, more prescribed, and she wanted to move it to a neutral place. But many black kinship carers, like auntie, would feel very guilty if they limited or formalised contact arrangements with parents – and they would feel they had betrayed the whole family if contact had to be controlled by Social Services. In the end, sometimes kinship carers know best what can and what cannot be changed in the family.

> Auntie says: 'The difficulty is that I can't, and Social Services can't, organise contact because my sister doesn't keep to any agreements.'

> Marcus says: 'When I see my mum I feel great because I know she is alright. We talk about places she used to take me and visit. She encourages me to do well at school. I love my mum. Living with my auntie is great and I know the reason why I am not living with my mother. I get to see other members of my family as well, I feel a whole person. I feel secure and very confident and don't feel that I have a label, because I am not in foster care.'

In living with his maternal aunt, Marcus has retained and, in some instances, regained contact with other aunts, uncles, cousins, and an older brother who was never in local authority care. Marcus is very much part of his family's culture, attending family functions and church. Marcus has siblings who are in "same race" foster care and the children's contact usually goes well. It is organised between the foster carers and auntie and everyone is pleased to see each other; it is not a dramatic experience.

Some of the challenges of kinship care

While every effort to keep children in their own families and communities should be applauded, there are specific difficulties that need to be recognised by social care experts: for instance, should emphasis be put on placing a child of mixed ethnicity with black relatives? And if not, why not? Complexities must be teased out when looking at kinship placements; what works in one case may not necessarily be the solution for another as the very essence of kinship care is the uniqueness of each family. Every ethnic group will have its own culture and views about children in society. It is not possible to use one model to fit all minority ethnic families. Ince (2001) states that 'Professionals need to have a positive attitude towards methods of child rearing different from their own and to work from a *"cultural competence"* which takes a holistic approach to family life'.

The number of black kinship carers not only reflects the disproportionate number of black children in the care system, but also a general increase of interest in kinship care. Local authorities need to recognise that black children who are placed with their kinfolk should receive the same services as *all* children who cannot live with their parents. It is not acceptable if, as soon as a black child is placed with kinship carers, the social worker is allocated another case. There is a need for continuing support, monitoring and evaluation.

Managing kinship contact in black families should not be given lower priority than managing contact between other children and their birth parents when Social Services workers are involved. The fact that social workers are involved indicates that there have been concerns about the care and welfare of the children above the threshold that the family can resolve on its own. Complex intra-familial emotions surface when all four parties (children, parents, kinship carers and social workers) bring their different perspectives to the planning of contact. Some of these are based on the history of the working relationships between the parents, social worker and carer and the roles they play, and have played, in decision-making. Nobody is neutral in kinship care placements! Stranger carers can start from a neutral base. But when setting up a kinship contact arrangement for any child, black or white, attention needs to be paid to how these difficulties and conflicts will be resolved. There will be as many different resolutions as there are differences in family culture.

References

Broad, B (1997/8) *The Child and Placements with Relatives and Friends – Research Project*, De Montfort University in partnership with London Borough of Wandsworth.

Hegar, R and Scannapieco, M (1999) *Kinship Foster Care: Policy and practice and research*, Lyme Regis: Oxford University Press.

Ince, L (2001) 'Promoting kinship care: preserving family network for black children of African origins', in Broad, B (ed.) *Kinship Care: The placement choice for children and young people*, Lyme Regis: Russell House Publishing.

Laws, S and Broad, B (2000) *Looking after Children with the Extended Family: Carers' views*, De Montfort University in partnership with London Borough of Wandsworth.

Wheal, A (2001) 'Family and friends who are carers: a framework for success', in Broad, B (ed.) *Kinship Care: The placement choice for children and young people*, Lyme Regis: Russell House Publishing.

4 Through the letterbox:
Indirect contact arrangements

Alison Vincent and *Alyson Graham*

It is important that all those concerned in indirect contact should be clear about its purpose and what it entails; this calls for preparation, negotiation and, in some cases, monitoring.

Adoption Now: Messages from Research
(Department of Health, 1999)

History of the Information Exchange Service

The Berkshire Information Exchange Service* was established in 1994. When local government re-organisation occurred, Berkshire split into six unitary authorities. The Berkshire Adoption Advisory Service (BAAS) was established at the time of disaggregation to offer facilitation of training, joint adoption panels, consultation and the Information Exchange Service. The Information Exchange Service has continued to operate from one central point and has had continuity of both process and personnel for a number of years.

The central operation of this service has several significant advantages. There are now 266 children from a range of backgrounds and cultures involved in letterbox exchanges; this represents just under 1,000 exchanges per year and thus enables the development of expertise and experience in a specialised area. The Letter Box Co-ordinator is a qualified social worker with many years experience in the field of adoption and fostering and there is also an administrator who offers clerical support to the service. With limited personnel involved, it has become clear that those who participate feel more comfortable when contacting the service

---

*The Berkshire Adoption Advisory Service operates the Information Exchange Service on behalf of Bracknell Forest Borough Council, Reading Borough Council, Slough Borough Council, West Berkshire District Council, Wokingham District Council and The Royal Borough of Windsor & Maidenhead.

as they know the names of the staff and are usually able to speak directly to them with little, if any, delay. The "independent" nature of the service can also be less intimidating for all those involved, especially birth family members. The court process may have placed the birth family in an adversarial relationship with the local authority. This relationship can be acrimonious, stressful and one from which it can be difficult to move forward positively. BAAS gives the opportunity for the issue of ongoing indirect contact to be removed from the arena of conflict and offers the possibility of a "fresh start".

Preparation for establishing an exchange

To underpin the process of setting up and running such a service there are clear written guidelines for workers, leaflets for participants, written arrangement forms and guidance for writing letters for both adopters and birth family members. In addition, training on the Information Exchange Service and contact issues in general is regularly included in adopters' preparation groups. Training for workers on the same theme but with a slightly different emphasis is also offered.

When considering the detailed arrangements for indirect contact, the work with the adoptive family and members of the birth family is usually completed by the link worker for the adopter(s) and the worker for the child respectively. The role of these workers is pivotal in the future functioning of the exchange. The Letter Box Co-ordinator can also be called upon for advice and or mediation.

In one particular case, agreement had been difficult to achieve and a joint visit to the birth family with the social worker was arranged. The birth family remained angry with the social worker as they viewed him as the instigator of the children's removal. The involvement of someone from BAAS incorporated an "independent" element and someone who could also draw on experience of the working service to explain the process. It also gave the birth family the opportunity to meet the Letter Box Co-ordinator so that they would know through whom they were sending their letters and who to contact if problems arose.

Throughout the process the child remains central:

Contact arrangements should centre on the benefits for the child, while acknowledging the adults' wishes and feelings and meeting these as far as is consistent with promoting the child's welfare. (BAAF, 1999)

In their book, *Supporting Adoption: Reframing the Approach* (Lowe and Murch *et al*, 1999) the authors summarise their chapter on contact with the following paragraph:

Finally, the child's needs must always be the priority when planning for contact. Sometimes, the needs of the child get confused with the needs of birth parents, especially when the same social worker is allocated to both. Granting birth parents contact to alleviate their loss, or to persuade them to agree to the adoption, can have negative implications later, and can cause conflict at other levels.

Though by no means unique, there are certain features of our service which help in its smooth operation, making it responsive and flexible.

* There is no limit to the number of exchanges that can be established for each child, nor is there a limit on those who can participate. If a certain level of contact is thought to be in the best interests of a particular child, then the service will accommodate this. Each child and their particular circumstances must be taken into account. Workers are encouraged to remember that indirect contact may open up other connections in the future.

* Indirect contact is not to be used as a bargaining tool with birth family members nor does it replace the vital counselling work with the birth family in helping them understand the process and deal with their loss.

* The arrangements that are written down and signed (first names only) are between the birth family, the adopters and the social worker, not between the birth family and the child. It was considered important that this be an intrinsic part of the service. Although not legally binding, it empowers the adopters and enables them to share the information at a time and stage appropriate to their child's needs. It allows the birth family to send information, such as news about the birth of another child or medical information, knowing that it may be more appropriately given to the child at a later date or that it may remain with the adoptive parents only.

One such example was a letter to adopters that included information about a genetic condition, recently diagnosed, affecting a birth family member. The adoptive parents and the birth family then had an ongoing dialogue via the Information Exchange Service to ensure the child received the most appropriate medical support. When the investigations were complete, the adoptive family communicated the results to the birth family via our service. All parties felt this to have been very valuable; a good example where the services of the exchange and a continuing indirect contact arrangement left the door open for information that could be, and was of significance to the child. This was not a child who had been relinquished but one whose removal and placement had been contested. However, the letterbox had been established for some considerable time and had worked very well before the medical condition posed a potential risk to the child.

- Many adoptive parents encourage their children to be involved by sending drawings, paintings and cards; this can develop over time. One birth mother we visited, decided to have the drawings laminated as table mats so she could see them daily. She felt that such things gave her a closer insight into the child's world and was delighted to have them. We have had several instances where, as children get older, they take more responsibility for the information sent. In one particular situation a young man, then aged 14, took over total responsibility for the indirect contact and although the response is now made directly to him, he knows that his adoptive parents are also sent copies.

- If a birth sibling who remains within the birth family wishes to be included in the exchange, independent of their family, an arrangement would have to be made with a responsible adult on their behalf, because the protection the exchange offers to adopted children should be afforded to all children. In one case, a 12-year-old girl moved to live with her birth father. Her half-sibling, not the child of her father, was placed for adoption. The girl had memories of this child as they had previously lived together with their birth mother. The girl wished to hear news of her brother but her father refused to become involved. This was resolved by including her grandparents in the indirect contact on her behalf.

- The timing of letterbox exchanges should relate to the child's understanding. The purpose of contact for children is multiple but essentially it can help a child to develop a positive identity, be reassured about his/her birth family, provide more knowledge about that family both historically and currently and maintain their sense of "connectedness". For a very young child, with no conscious memory of their birth family, the exchange of information around a birthday and Christmas may be unsuitable, however much a birth family member wishes it. For an older child, this could be quite different as the child may need the reassurance of the card that they have always had. Another difficulty that has emerged with exchanges around birthday and Christmas times is that often only cards are sent which include no "information". Thus the child gets a card but has no sense of what is happening in the birth family, which only partially fulfils the purpose of indirect contact. If contact at such times is considered to be in the child's best interests, then consideration should be given to an additional exchange at another time of the year so that the valuable two-way "information" does not get forgotten.
- It was always intended that letters, cards and photographs only would be exchanged and that gifts were not to be enclosed. In a very small number of cases, gift vouchers have been included in the arrangement but this is usually for an older child who might be confused and feel rejected if grandparents, for example, did not continue to send presents as before.
- Once the arrangements have been agreed by all parties, the arrangement forms are signed and all participants are given a copy of the document. It is often helpful for this to be signed if and when the two families meet during introductions. It is, however, vital that any negotiation or mediation has been completed beforehand to avoid potential conflict and difficulty face-to-face. If it is possible for the form to be signed at such a meeting, a joint sense of ownership is often engendered. If the two families are given the opportunity to meet, the exchange of information becomes more meaningful and is much more likely to succeed and continue. There are some birth family members who feel unable to cope with a meeting at the time of placement and this is quite understandable. Such one-off meetings

can, and have, been offered by our service at a later date once the child is in placement.

A non-operational letterbox

Although indirect contact for children placed for adoption is becoming the norm (it may operate in addition to direct contact), there are a small number of children for whom no contact arrangements are established. In these situations, workers are encouraged to set up a "non-operational" letterbox. The forms with the basic information are completed but the arrangement forms are not signed. The reasons for not having any indirect contact are explained and the circumstances in which it could be activated are detailed. This is very useful as it is written contemporaneously with placement events and any subsequent request for contact can then be more easily addressed.

A child with a life-long disability was placed with adopters and his birth parents felt unable to engage with the exchange at the time of placement. Their decision to relinquish their son had been a very painful one and although they indicated that they did not wish for any contact, the door was left open for them should they change their minds. Two years later they had a change of heart and work was done with them to help establish contact.

We have also had a number of non-operational letterboxes where one or both of the birth parents felt too angry to make an arrangement. When a period of time had elapsed and they were more able to deal with their loss, they asked us to set up contact. In all but one case this has been successful. In the one unsuccessful case, the adopters felt unable to consider contact and it appears that this was because the preparatory work at the time of placement had not been fully understood.

How the information exchange works

Once the arrangements are agreed and signed by all the parties, the worker (usually the child's social worker but sometimes the family placement worker) will complete the confidential forms necessary for BAAS to operate the exchanges. These forms will have names, addresses and telephone numbers of the participants and a little background information, such as the reason a child was placed for adoption, whether or not the adopters and the birth parents met, and details of sibling relationships.* This information is particularly helpful when, as is often the case, families contact the Letter Box Co-ordinator and expect them to know their situation. Some workers have commented on the length of the forms but such detailed information is needed if it is to be a responsive and informed service.

Upon receipt of the forms, the Co-ordinator writes to the participants, thus establishing the contact point and giving them a name should they need any help in the future. A separate file is opened for the child and this eventually becomes part of their adoption file, although it is held separately from the main adoption file while the information exchange is in operation. The files are all retained in the child's birth name, as this is the name that is known to all the parties. They are kept in a locked fireproof cabinet in line with regulations.

Basic information is also kept on a database, mainly for statistical purposes but it can also be used to write to all or some of the participants. In addition to the database we have two index files that cross-reference the child's birth name and their adopted name. This has proved very helpful when letters come in without it being clear who they are intended for or who has sent them – something that has caused problems in recent years as the numbers have increased so markedly. If we were to be setting up the system now, we would consider giving everyone a reference number to quote on all correspondence, perhaps sending them a sheet of address labels with their individual reference number included.

When a letter is received, it is opened, copied and copies are placed on file. The information given to the participants makes it clear that this will happen. Photographs and gift vouchers are colour copied on a scanner. Keeping copies has proved very valuable as there have been several

---

*Ethnicity is recorded. Most of the children are white and have been placed with white families. There are only a few children with dual heritage or from minority ethnic backgrounds who have mainly been adopted by families which reflect their ethnicity. As numbers are limited, it is difficult to quantify the impact of ethnicity on the operation of the exchange. However, in our experience it has not had a significant effect.

instances where, particularly birth family members, have lost, mislaid or had their photographs and letters stolen. In one case, the birth mother had all the information stolen and destroyed while she was in a halfway house. We put copies of everything into a new "booklet" with spaces for further additions and sent it to her. On rare occasions letters have been lost in the post and again, we could either copy our copies or ask the sender to replace them. We also had one very sad case of adopters who never shared information they had received. When their son reached the age of 18 and requested access to his adoption file, he discovered letters from siblings he had not seen before. This caused great distress and he needed considerable support but contact with his siblings was re-negotiated successfully.

All the letters are read and checked for identifying information and they are always acknowledged. The question of "vetting" is complex and should not be seen as purely scrutinising the information sent from birth family members. We recently received a letter from an adoptive mother that could have made the birth mother anxious for it mentioned unresolved medical and behavioural problems. The link worker was still involved, and she was asked to visit the adopters and discuss the letter. This was the first letter in the exchange and the adoptive mother acknowledged that she had found it difficult to write; she gladly accepted the support offered and readily changed it. Often a little intervention at an early stage helps to establish the exchange and enables it to run smoothly. In general, information will always be sent in its original form but addresses will be removed and recently an email address that was included in the body of a letter was deleted. Addresses are removed from all letters because we think it important to take an even-handed approach and to avoid unnecessary pressure on each of the parties.

It is only in exceptional circumstances, if information could cause significant distress or anxiety, that intervention may become necessary. In such instances the Letter Box Co-ordinator will consider each case individually and may contact the sender or recipient but will always try to act with compassion, respect and flexibility. In our service this is seen as a social work task and not an administrative one. We are not in a position to make decisions about what may or may not be in the interests of a child; only their adoptive parents can really do this. However, there are occasions when some support and guidance are offered to help parents deal with sensitive issues.

In one instance, where the children had been relatively recently placed, the birth mother's letter only contained phrases expressing her loss, her sadness and her wish to have the children returned. The older child had a very anxious attachment to his birth mother and needed her "permission" to attach to his new family while still knowing she cared about him. As the birth mother had written first, i.e. before the adopters, it was suggested that she might, in future, like to reply to the adopters' letter giving news of the children, rather than writing first. This prompted a very caring letter from the birth mother, which the adoptive parents felt much more able to share with their child. They have kept the first letter for when the children are a little older and more settled.

This kind of intervention should not be seen as too paternalistic or the local authority being unwilling to "let go". On the contrary, we have had very positive feedback from adopters and birth parents who value the responsive involvement we can provide.

We try to be flexible and we do operate one exchange where both parties prefer us not to open or copy the correspondence. The arrangement form indicates this and, as far as possible, we are happy to comply. Occasionally it has not been possible when the outer envelopes did not make it clear who had sent them or for whom they were intended. In this particular case, the adopters requested that the letters should not be opened as they felt that the birth mother would write more openly if she knew her letters were not being read first. The birth mother and the local authority were in conflict and the adopters wished to distance themselves from this antagonism.

Who should write first is a question we have long debated. Over the years we have come to the conclusion that the exchange works better when it is clear that the adoptive parents write first and the birth family replies. For many birth family members, to write a letter in isolation, maybe only once a year, is a very difficult and emotive task. It can prompt letters that give little information or insight into their lives as well as letters that are highly emotional. To respond to news about the child can help birth family members to give similar sorts of information and this has proved to be more meaningful for children as they can see that their birth parents and other relatives have heard about their activities. There are several birth parents who have limited abilities and we try to offer them support in writing their letters. It is often necessary to visit them or, if they live at some distance, an initial meeting is agreed and any follow up is by telephone. We believe that it is important to make an initial visit so that people can begin to build a relationship; they are then more likely to request help when they need it.

A visit to a birth mother living some considerable distance away was recently made as she was having difficulty writing about herself. Her life during the last year had been very stressful; she had suffered a relationship breakdown, her health was fragile and her accommodation insecure. She was anxious to write to her children who had been placed for adoption and wanted to be honest but did not wish to worry them.

We would also offer the opportunity to birth parents with literacy difficulties to send their information in another way, perhaps using audio tapes. It may be that English is not the first language of birth parents or adopters. In those cases we would engage interpreters to support the families and to enable us to understand the communication. We would keep a record in English and include a translation for the child.

Birth parents as well are likely to find difficulty in knowing what to write, either to their children or to the adoptive parents. Written agreements about such matters go only so far; the parties to them may need help in their realisation. (Department of Health, 1999)

Reviews of individual arrangements

When the letterbox exchange scheme was established, no formal reviews of the arrangements were built in. The form states that if any party wishes to change the arrangements, they should contact the Letter Box Co-ordinator, who would then offer a review.

A child or young person's need for contact and openness is not static – arrangements need to take account of each individual's changing needs and circumstances. (BAAF, 1999)

A service with no formal review could result in not meeting the child's needs. Such regular reviews, however, would be time consuming and have considerable resource implications and, if due at specific intervals, may not be sufficiently responsive. We have recently been giving thought to this issue and are considering reviewing individual arrangements at particular developmental stages related to the child's possible under-standing of the adoption process. This could be based on the work of David Brodzinsky *et al* (1992). It is important to bear in mind that any changes should reflect the child's best interests. That is not to say we would not consider a request from a birth family member, but the child remains the focal point. Lowe and Murch *et al* (1999) comment: 'Written contact agreements can be useful because, unlike contact orders or conditions for contact in the adoption order, they do not give inappropriate messages about the rigidity of contact agreements. Building a clause into the agreement which says that it is variable will remind families of this and may help prevent families from straying from agreements.'

In one instance, when the adopted young person reached adolescence, he requested increased letterbox contact with his birth grandparents. These grandparents, although very much against his placement for adoption, had always been active, co-operative and sensitive in their exchanges. This request, via his adoptive parents, prompted us to visit the grandparents who were delighted to respond. This contact has led to direct telephone calls and the exchange of videos via our service. One such video was of the area in which the young person was born and bought up prior to placement as he felt he had too little knowledge and memory of it, having been placed some considerable distance away. The confidentiality of the placement remains intact. It seems likely that, in time, limited face-to-face contact may follow and, in the interests of continuity, this would probably be facilitated by our service.

Audit of the service

In 1999/2000 we undertook a wide-ranging audit of the Information Exchange Service. This included questionnaires to all users and workers who had been involved. There were two main aims: firstly, to ascertain the overall perception and value of the service to all users and, secondly, to gauge opinion from adopters and adopted young people about what they wished to happen when the young person reached the age of 18. We did not ask birth families this question as we considered that the decision should rest with the adopted young person. There was an excellent response from users, 55 per cent from adopters, and 52 per cent from birth family members. The adopters were generally pleased with the service, felt it was responsive and well managed. Many said that the arrival of information at various times in the year gave them the opportunity to talk about adoption and to update their child's life story book. Several adoptive parents indicated that it helped to put worries and questions into perspective and helped the child to keep in touch with his/her heritage. However, several expressed sadness and concern that the birth family did not actively participate in the service or had ceased to send news regularly, as this could cause distress and confusion for the child. In one or two cases adopters commented that it reinforced their sense of rejection by the birth family.

Particularly pleasing was the positive response from birth family members, many of whom had opposed the placement of their children for adoption. The majority of the birth family respondents felt that the service was helpful and that they would approach the Letter Box Co-ordinator if they encountered problems. This is borne out by the number of phone calls for help and advice. Most birth family members said that the main difficulty was what to write; although guidelines for writing letters were available, many birth families had not been given them by their social workers and we were able to rectify this as a result of the questionnaire. A few birth parents did report feelings of sadness and distress at the time of the exchange but none of them considered that this was negative, it was just reality.

What should happen to the information exchange when the young person reaches the age of 18?

When the service was established, it was thought that the exchange should operate for some time before reaching a conclusion on this issue. In formulating future policy, all the views of those who responded to the questionnaire were taken into account. Most adopters indicated that they would like the option of extending the service beyond the age of 18. However, the overwhelming number of comments reflected the need for flexibility and the necessity of having a service that could respond to individual needs, with the offer of counselling if required. Interestingly, those adopters who said that the exchange should cease at the age of 18, were those who had very young children and had used the information exchange for a relatively short time. It was clear from the responses that most parents considered that receiving information was of benefit to their child but that continuing support and advice also had to be available. Indeed, as children in the information exchange reach adolescence, this may have to become more focused. Several of the teenagers we are in contact with have needed further life story work at this stage. The staff within BAAS have been able to offer this service. Children's needs will change over time and we must be responsive to those changes if we are to help those young people move towards independence.

We are aware that many of the children who are placed for adoption today have had a disrupted, fractured and sometimes abusive history and as a result can take a very long time to settle, form attachments and mature. For such children, the age of 18 may not be an appropriate time to either stop indirect contact or to offer direct contact as the only other alternative. In the light of the responses and current research evidence, the following policy has been adopted by all the six unitary authorities on behalf of whom we operate the Information Exchange Service. In the year preceding the young person's 18th birthday, a letter will be sent to the adoptive parents enclosing a letter for the young person. These letters will identify the options available:

- To stop the letterbox when the young person reaches the age of 18 and for the letterbox file to be closed and placed with the child's adoption file and retained, in line with regulations, for 75 years.
- To offer the young person the opportunity to extend the information exchange in their own name, subject to the wishes of the birth family. This option also includes the offer of counselling for both parties.
- To offer counselling to the young person and their family to help them to make a decision about what course of action to take.
- To negotiate with the birth family if the young person chooses to establish direct contact.

Extended contact would be facilitated up to the age of 21, but in exceptional circumstances this could be further extended until the age of 25. If the young person and their family wish to discuss the options, then this will be arranged by our service if they remain within relatively easy travelling distance. However, if they live too far away then we would undertake to identify local support.

We hope that this defines a clear policy while retaining the flexibility requested which enables individual responses. There are obvious resource implications but we feel that the policy adopted by all the unitary authorities shows the commitment to the young people they placed for adoption. It also goes some way to acknowledge the lifelong impact that adoption has on all those involved.

Conclusion

The key message for information exchange schemes is that they have to be flexible. While exchanges are primarily for the benefit of children, if well thought out and responsive they can also meet the needs of adopters and birth relatives. Arrangements that are detailed and clear to all parties are an essential component of a successful scheme. Most of the difficulties experienced in managing the scheme have been the result of arrangements that have been poorly set up and where some or all of the parties have received inadequate preparation and/or support. However, we are consistently encouraged by the generosity, empathy, and understanding shown by all parties which allows a mutually respectful relationship to develop despite the sensitivities inherent in the situation.

An element of independence within schemes is also key to ensuring the co-operation of all parties who are then able to put aside old adversarial relationships and move towards positive communication.

With the change in the profile of children placed for adoption during the past 10 years and the likely increase in the numbers placed, information exchange becomes more complex. Many adopters will have difficult and sad stories to tell their children, and these children will need to see their birth relatives as real people whose own lives have often been traumatic.

Placing older children for adoption carries with it a responsibility to ensure that their needs are met into adulthood and beyond, and in doing this successfully it may be necessary to step outside the traditional boundaries and extend indirect contact arrangements beyond childhood.

In the future we may well see an increase in reunification work with children and their birth relatives. It is hoped that, by ensuring that the communication and exchange of information is sensitively and compassionately addressed, we can avoid some of the distressing scenarios experienced in the past when adults attempted to trace their birth relatives. There should be no shocks or surprises for adopted children if an information exchange has been successful.

The dearth of research into how contact affects children is of concern as we can only work to ensure that information is exchanged and support adopters in sharing it with their children. However, to have access to information about one's past can inform one's future. It is, therefore, vital that all parties in a letterbox exchange are nurtured and accepted, supported and enabled, in an effort to help children deal with experiences as they grow and mature into adults with a sense of understanding about their past and a hope of completeness for their future.

References

Department of Health (1999) *Adoption Now: Messages from research*, London: Department of Health.

BAAF Good Practice Guide (1999) *Contact in Permanent Placements*, London: BAAF.

Brodzinsky, D M, Schechter, M D and Henig R M (1992) *Being Adopted: The lifelong search for self*, New York: Doubleday.

Lowe, N and Murch, M *et al* (1999) *Supporting Adoption: Reframing the approach*, London: BAAF.

5 Split up but not cut off:
Making and sustaining contact arrangements between siblings

Shelagh Beckett

In recent years the significance of peer and sibling relationships has begun to attract more attention. Professional debate and the findings of research studies have started to recognise that sibling relationships are complex and need to be addressed when planning services – nowhere is this more so than when planning permanent placements. Children entering public care and subsequently joining new families are at risk of losing contact with some or all of their siblings. For example, in their study of permanent placements, Rushton *et al* (2001) found that:

- half of the placements were made without any plan for sibling contact;
- of those who had contact with some siblings, many children would keep in contact with fewer of their siblings after permanent placement;
- new families were broadly committed to maintaining inter-sibling contact but there were often practical problems which needed addressing e.g. venue, timing, costs;
- ensuring that contact occurred and was positive, required active social-work intervention;
- there was little consideration of indirect means of maintaining sibling links e.g. letters, telephone calls (these tended to be used only when there was also direct contact).

The finding that so many children are placed without any plans for sibling contact is perhaps surprising. The Children Act 1989 in England and Wales and the Children (Scotland) Act 1995 stress the need to place a child with his/her siblings so far as possible and guidance such as that contained in Local Authority Circular *Adoption: Achieving the right balance*, LAC 98(20) para 58 (Department of Health, 1998) stresses the importance of continuing contact:

In the exceptional case where siblings cannot be placed together with the same family, it is important for agencies to ensure that contact arrangements with other siblings are given very careful attention and plans for maintaining contact are robust.

The law, human rights considerations and relevant guidance to local authorities should underpin planning and decision-making. The recent National Adoption Standards for England (Department of Health, 2001) also recognise the significance of placing a child with his or her siblings. Furthermore, the Standards make it clear that, in the event a child is separated from siblings, direct work should be undertaken so that children can be helped towards an understanding of why this decision was reached:

Every effort will be made to recruit sufficient adopters from diverse backgrounds, so that each child can be found an adoptive family within the timescales ... which best meets their needs, and in particular:

a) which reflects their ethnic origin, cultural background, religion and language;

b) which allows them to live with brothers and sisters unless this will not meet their individually assessed needs. Where this is the case, a clear explanation will be given to them and recorded.

In respect of contact, the National Adoption Standards also state that adoption plans will include details of the arrangements for maintaining links between placed children and birth relatives who are significant to the child. The Standards emphasise that adopters should be involved in discussions as to how they can best maintain those links identified in the adoption plan. The Social Services Inspectorate (Department of Health, 1995) has drawn attention to the importance of negotiation between the parties when drawing up written agreements:

The study found without doubt that the process of negotiation leading to the preparation of written contact agreements, and the agreements themselves, proved invaluable in reducing conflict, establishing a clear understanding of the expectations of all parties and forming a basis for subsequent review and where necessary, amendment. Use of such agreements should become a standard element of agency procedures. (p. 33)

The process of meeting and starting to form constructive relationships that focus on how best to address children's needs is crucial. Such meetings can reduce the potential for any confusion; early planning is central to achieving workable contact arrangements. However, research (Lowe and Murch *et al*, 1999) has shown that agencies were less likely to use written contact agreements in respect of inter-sibling contact than they were for contact with birth parents and grandparents. This finding may suggest that, when contact is planned, agencies tend to assume that inter-sibling contact is generally "more straightforward". While this may be the case for many permanent placements, clarity about arrangements remains an important issue for all parties. The Standards stress that children's '. . . needs, wishes and feelings, and their welfare and safety are the most important considerations . . .' when making plans for maintaining links. Children and families' contact and support needs are likely to change over the years and a framework for planning, reviewing and renegotiating contact is therefore essential. Clearly it will be important for adoptive parents to be able to access support and to have confidence that plans for maintaining contact and/or links, can be reviewed. Children and young people are also likely to find this reassuring and, depending upon their age and understanding, may want and need to attend these planning or review meetings.

The experience of regular albeit not frequent contact with significant members of the birth family can ease the transition of older children into their permanent new family and promote placement stability (Borland *et al*, 1991; Fratter, 1996). Research has also found that adopters are more likely to support inter-sibling contact and to view this positively than they are contact with birth parents (Barth and Berry, 1988); this is particularly so when birth parents have been abusive (Berry, 1993).

While the majority of children are likely to benefit from sibling contact, a minority may be unable to make progress when sibling contact continues. Sibling relationships may have become so distorted by earlier abuse that contact exposes them to damaging and abusive experiences or memories that are too painful. Most of the children needing adoption placements will have had disrupted and difficult early lives, which have all too frequently included significant child protection concerns. Local authority policies should arguably be based on a presumption of inter-sibling contact but recognise that assessments must always take account of each individual's history and needs, and that needs change. A child who cannot cope with sibling contact when placed as a nine-year-old may need to check out shared history with siblings during the teenage years.

Does the child understand why they are not going to live with some or all of their siblings?

Direct work with children in respect of placement and contact plans should build on earlier work that has begun to help the child make sense of their evolving life story. It is sadly the case that many siblings have been separated in the past without this work having been done; such gaps in practice will inevitably make it harder for the child to understand what is happening and why. In the absence of information, fantasies can develop which can "spill over" into inter-sibling contact; for example, one sibling may blame another for entry into local authority care. The decision to place a child apart from one or more of their siblings should have been explained in a variety of ways and on more than one occasion. How best to help the child achieve a reasonable understanding will depend upon age, cognitive development and circumstances, but will often include the following elements:

• direct work sessions with the individual child and with his/her siblings;
• involving the child's foster carers so that as far as is possible they are able to reinforce the same message to the child;
• birth parents and other significant relatives may also be able to take an important role in preparing the child, for example, by helping the child to avoid blaming him/herself for the separation;
• explanations contained in the child's life story book;
• talking with the child about future contact and the ways in which links can be maintained;
• explanations contained in "later-life" letters for when the child or young person needs a more detailed and sophisticated understanding.

Case example

Brandon Walker aged nine had taken an active role in caring for his two younger siblings, Ryan aged five and Suzy aged three. Brandon had endured physically and emotionally cruel treatment from his mother's co-habitee; his mother had presented as powerless to protect him owing to her own fear of violence from her partner. Brandon and his siblings have been looked after for almost a year and the Care Plan now is adoption for Ryan and Suzy. Brandon is placed in a foster home on his own whereas Ryan and Suzy are placed together. Brandon, in contrast to his younger siblings, retains a strong, albeit complex relationship with his mother. He is fiercely loyal and protective of her. He has consistently denied or minimised the role that his mother had in the children's abusive past and has been anxious to retain a high level of contact with her. The two younger siblings appear less affected by whether or not contact takes place with their mother but look forward to seeing Brandon. The local authority is concerned that the children's mother, Mrs Walker, would undermine an adoption placement if any direct contact continued post adoption. Brandon often appears angry with his social worker, seeming to blame her for the break up of his family. Little or no direct work has been done with the children as the social worker has said that Brandon is resistant to it and Ryan and Suzy are 'too young to understand'.

Key issues that will need to be addressed

- Has an adequate assessment of the children's sibling relationships been undertaken?
- What type of contact might be feasible between Brandon and his younger siblings once Ryan and Suzy join a permanent family? This assessment should consider the risks and benefits of maintaining, changing or severing contact both in the short and the longer term.
- Explanations for all three children regarding decisions made about their future. This should include the reasons why different and separate placement plans were made.

Children's ascertainable wishes and feelings

Children's perceptions about their siblings – including their understanding of any differences between them – are likely to impact on their views about contact. For example, parental favouritism tends to increase hostility between siblings. Children who have felt emotionally rejected by parents and siblings may react by expressing reluctance about the prospect of future contact or conversely want contact to continue in the sometimes forlorn hope that past wrongs can be put right. Sometimes children may want contact but 'only if . . .' for example, 'only if it's going to be nice'.

Case example

Tammy aged five had been physically and sexually abused by her stepfather, Wayne, although the latter abuse was not known at the time that she came into local authority care accompanied by her two older half-siblings, Conor aged nine and Liam aged seven. Tammy had effectively been scapegoated by Wayne and subjected to differential treatment. Her relationship with Conor and Liam reflected the complexity of the children's family life. In foster care Tammy ranged from sometimes being anxious to please her brothers to physically lashing out at them when they teased or taunted her. Conor has been especially rough towards Tammy and episodes of physical aggression occur on a daily basis. The foster carer has noted that Conor and Liam often make derogatory comments to and about Tammy and seem to be 'generally negative about girls and women' including herself. For example, talking about girls being 'bitches' and their mother 'asking for it' when referring to incidents of domestic violence at home. It is anticipated that Conor and Liam may go to live with their paternal grandmother and that Tammy will be placed for adoption outside of the family. Direct work has recently started with Tammy to prepare her for adoption. In thinking about the prospect of moving to an adoptive family, Tammy has said that she would like to see her brothers but only when they're nice to her.

- Children's feelings of responsibility and concern for siblings may have a considerable impact on their need for contact. For example, an older child living with birth parents may be anxious about the wellbeing of younger siblings placed elsewhere, while they in turn may be concerned as to whether their sibling is "safe" at home.

- The significance of any established roles within the sibling group should be considered as this may impact on children's perceptions and behaviour when together. Some roles will have been functional in one setting but appear less so in another – for example, a parenting child helping to care for siblings at home may subsequently be discouraged from behaving in the same way when placed in foster care. The parenting child may feel displaced and experience loss of self-esteem. Different societies attach different meanings to parenting behaviour in children; for example, some cultures place greater value on caregiving siblings. It is important to understand the overall context in which behaviour has developed, the ways in which behaviours have been reinforced, and the meaning that certain behaviours and roles have for each child within the sibling group. For some children, their most significant attachment may be to an older sibling.

- Highly aggressive, destructive and sexually abusive patterns of behaviour within sibling groups will need to be carefully observed. Outwardly it may seem that the children are not particularly close but superficial behaviours may belie the strong bonds of loyalty, shared past and a powerful sense of being connected. Placing children in separate homes will not in itself resolve problems; safe care issues are relevant not only when planning placements but also in respect of arrangements for contact.

Plans aren't always "agreements"

In reality we know that what some children and adults may want and what is achievable may not match. It is best to be clear that not all parties may "agree"; sometimes, for example, an adult birth relative or older sibling may not be entirely happy with the level of contact proposed. Nonetheless all parties need to know what is planned and why. Everyone should be encouraged to focus on the importance of trying to make the planned contact work in the interests of the children involved. When there are significant differences, the potential consequences of causing avoidable distress and not respecting the boundaries of planned contact are aspects that need to be addressed.

In other instances children may want a higher level of contact than is thought to be feasible or may want contact with siblings where this is assessed to be too risky. The reasons for reaching such decisions need to be shared with the child, together with an acknowledgement that this is counter to their expressed wishes. For example, it can be helpful to do this in tangible ways such as drawing up a simple list that includes the child's views and recognises that there may be problems. Sarah aged six was being prepared to join an adoptive family where she would no longer retain direct contact with her elder brother Jo who remained within the birth family:

Things that would be good about seeing Jo	Things that might cause problems if I saw Jo
We could go to the park together	*He doesn't think I should get adopted*
I'd be able to talk to him about what I'm doing	*He might get us into trouble if he took me out nicking things like before*
He's fun	*He might try to get me to go home*

If the child finds it difficult to identify any problems, then another list could be included to go alongside the child's list of the 'good things about contact'. For example:

Worries that the court and your social worker have about contact

If you saw Jo you would probably not be safe because he has taken you with him when he has stolen cars.

He is not old enough to drive cars safely.

Jo does not understand why you cannot go home.

Whatever the reasons for separation, circumstances change and children should be assured that the arrangements for contact can also change.

Key issues in assessing and planning inter-sibling contact

- The child's individual needs as well as relationships within the sibling group must be assessed. For example, the roles children may have had within their family of origin such as a parenting child used to taking care of and "organising" their siblings, a child who "keeps the lid on" family secrets, or the child who has disclosed abuse.
- What can we learn and reasonably anticipate from the children's background histories, their previous and current behaviour? For example, if there has been a history of sexual abuse within the family, what impact has this had on how a child perceives and relates to his or her siblings?
- What is the purpose of contact? Everyone should be clear about the reasons why contact is being planned. For example, it is important to consider not only the children's current relationship but also to recognise potential benefits in respect of direct and indirect contact, over the long term. Some siblings may not appear very close now but part of the rationale for maintaining links is to allow the relationship to develop over the years. Similarly, issues of identity, talking about shared family history, etc., may become more important as children mature and "recycle" aspects of their earlier experiences in their family of origin.
- Are there any specific risks and how can these be managed and minimised? For example, establishing safe care practices should be integral to planning contact between abused siblings exhibiting sexualised behaviour.
- Do some but not all of the children have contact with adult birth relatives? If so, what are the potential implications of this contact?

Case example

Bina, a seven-year-old Asian girl with mild learning difficulties, entered local authority care at the age of five after concerns about long standing emotional abuse followed by a serious physical assault which resulted in facial scarring. While in foster care, Bina had approximately monthly, though sporadic, contact with her mother and

younger brother Amerjit. Upon placement for adop
ago, Bina's direct contact with her birth family ended
Asian parents have expressed concern that Bina seems
Amerjit and is anxious about whether he is being hurt
says that she wants to see him to see whether he's got
face. The adoptive family has been told that direct contact \
is not feasible because the birth parents will not allow it. Bi_ ..as little
understanding of why she cannot see Amerjit and the adopters have no
explanation that they can talk through with her.

A maternal aunt who sees Amerjit regularly has been asked to provide
reassurance of Amerjit's wellbeing through letterbox contact. However,
this only occurs twice annually. A recent letter received by the adoption
agency from the aunt has referred to the fact that Bina's mother is
pregnant – the contents of the letter have not been shared with Bina.
More frequent social work visits to the birth family are part of a child
protection plan. Bina and Amerjit's birth mother is expecting her third
child soon.

Issues to consider

- The difficulties for Bina and the adoptive family of not having a clear
  understanding as to why Bina cannot see Amerjit.
- Both families are Asian but do they share the same cultural views of
  adoption and contact?
- Could and should any information obtained by social workers visiting
  the birth family be shared with Bina and her adoptive family?
- The adopters have asked for advice because they are unsure about
  whether Bina should be informed about the prospect of having another
  birth sibling, and if so, how and when this should be done.

Issues to address when drafting written contact agreements for siblings placed with different families

- Purpose of contact.
- Type of contact and frequency.
- What information are families happy to share? For example, in the case
  of direct contact, are adopters prepared to exchange addresses and

telephone numbers, to keep in touch between visits? Bear in mind that young children may find it especially hard to retain significant relationships when direct contact visits take place only several times a year. Their timescales and capacity to remember are important factors to take into account. It is helpful to consider ways of keeping memories alive between contact visits, for example, telephone calls, making use of photographs and video material.

- Who will make the arrangements? This may be as simple as being clear about who will telephone whom to set a date, time and venue, but in the absence of clarity, each party may be left waiting to hear from the other.

- Geographical location of the adopters – a mid-way, accessible location may be preferred. If not, arrangements need to be seen to be fair rather than one set of adopters always expending more time, effort and expense to attend contact meetings.

- Adoptive families and siblings – identify any significant areas of compatibility and areas of difference. Half siblings of white and mixed ethnic heritage may be placed with families matched to them but therefore not to each other; being aware of the potential for cultural, dietary and other differences to exist and to develop is important. Also, consider ages and the age spread, the individual needs and interests of all the children. For example, what type of activities would they enjoy and how might this change as they grow older?

- Do any of the prospective adoptive families already have children? If so, it will be important to consider their involvement and status. For example, if they are adopted, do they have birth family contact and how has this progressed? Is it envisaged that they would attend any contact meetings with the family?

- Wherever possible encourage the adults to meet before the new child or children are placed. Be clear in identifying each of the families' views and any strong preferences they have expressed about the draft contact plans.

- Do any of the children who are being placed have special or additional needs? Racial, cultural, religious, linguistic and dietary aspects that may be relevant in planning meals, locations to be visited and so forth.

- What sort of contact venues would be appropriate? Prepare a list of ideas and suggestions for the adopters (local authority Leisure and Amenities sections and/or the local Tourist Board should be able to help). Give consideration to any venues that should be avoided and the reasons for this – for example, meeting for a session at a swimming pool may be unsuitable for siblings who have a history of sexual abuse. Is it possible now, or may it be possible later, to have contact in any of the adopters' homes?

- Practical and financial aspects.
- Who will provide support to all parties?
- Arrangements for reviewing and, when necessary, changing the contact plan.

Matching and linked placements

When two or more adoptive placements are being sought for siblings, matching the families should be considered so far as is possible. Sometimes the limited number of suitable families will make this difficult to achieve in practice. However, issues such as geographical proximity, similar lifestyles, a shared sense of humour, family values, socio-economic status and aspirations, may increase the likelihood of families establishing some common ground between them. The experience of having attended the same set of preparation groups may also provide opportunities for prospective adopters to make links with others.

Case example

Linda and Steve Hendon attended the same preparation groups as Pat and Tim Squires. Linda and Steve were involuntarily childless whereas Pat and Tim already had a grown up family. Although different in many respects – and perhaps not an obvious match "on paper" – the two couples quickly struck up conversation. They found that they shared an interest in attending weekend car boot sales and had a similar "whacky" sense of humour! Their adoption agency was able to build on this developing relationship when planning the placement of three siblings. The elder child, Ricky aged seven was placed with the Squires family, while Jacey and Candice aged four and three were placed with the Hendons. The local authority felt that as Ricky had learning difficulties and was sometimes physically aggressive to his younger sisters, placing them together would be too much for one family to manage.

The process of planning and arriving at a contact plan was made much easier because the two couples had already met and felt comfortable with each other. This, together with the families living in the same county, contributed to a relaxed attitude to joint contact meetings. Ricky, who had been angry about the prospect of being separated from his two young sisters, was gradually able to relinquish some of his angry behaviour as regular contact meetings took place. Both sets of adopters felt that it was crucial for Ricky to see that Jacey and Candice were happy and well cared for. However, they also felt that what had helped Ricky was that he could literally see that his new family and that of his younger sisters, really "got on". This was perhaps summed up by Ricky's comment on the return car journey after a contact day, when he said 'They're OK – Linda and Steve – aren't they?' To which his adoptive parents could respond that they agreed with Ricky, and felt similarly, that Linda and Steve were indeed OK.

Providing support and reviewing contact arrangements

Contact plans may need to be reviewed for a range of reasons. Sometimes plans will have to be adapted to take account of problems that develop. On other occasions, changes may be required simply to better meet children's changing needs as they grow. All parties to a contact plan or agreement should know that they can ask for arrangements to be reviewed. Ideally, adoption agencies should take a proactive approach when significant changes suggest that a review is needed. These would include:

- placement disruption for one or more siblings placed elsewhere;
- siblings resuming contact with birth parent/relatives;
- children asking for more or different contact with siblings;
- children asking for no contact or for less contact;
- carers expressing concern about contact arrangements;
- child behaviour management issues arising during contact meetings;
- significant changes in the birth family's situation;

- inappropriate information being conveyed in written material or shared during contact.

Case example

Lucy and Tom Farndon are the white adoptive parents of Kyle, aged three and Lucy aged five, both also white. It was planned to continue twice yearly direct contact with Mandy, their eight-year-old elder sister, who is in a long-term foster placement with the possibility that it may lead to adoption. Mandy is of mixed parentage and is placed with Therese, a single black carer.

The Farndons are an affluent couple who have not only been able to provide Kyle and Lucy with a high level of emotional security but also clothes, toys, holidays and outings which match their lifestyle. Exchange of Christmas presents between the children left the foster carer feeling unhappy about the expensive gift that the Farndons had given Mandy. Therese felt that 'too much money had been spent' by the Farndons. The contact during the school summer holiday had also led to some resentment on the part of Therese. The Farndons had suggested meeting at a theme park approximately mid-way between the two families. While "successful" on many levels this proved an expensive day out. Mandy was keen to go there again 'next time' as she had thoroughly enjoyed the day and the venue. She had taken a great liking to the Farndons who insisted on treating her to several rides, ice cream and drinks. Therese had asked the local authority about financial help towards the cost of contact and had been told by Mandy's social worker that only travel expenses would be reimbursed.

Therese has recently shown some reluctance about the next contact visit saying that she and Mandy are going to be quite busy during the following major school holiday. The Farndons have expressed the view that Therese does not seem keen on contact but they are sure that the children do want to see each other.

Issues to consider

What actions could have been taken to minimise the potential for any difficulties arising between the two families?

Some actions that might have helped

- Arranging a pre-placement meeting between the adoption agency, adopters and the foster carer to discuss arrangements for contact.
- Clarity about the local authority's role in promoting contact; including agreement to finance contact costs up to a certain level for each contact meeting.
- Agreeing the approximate amount (or establishing an upper limit) for money to be spent on exchanging presents between the children; recognising that Mandy's carer will be purchasing two sets of birthday and Christmas presents whereas the adopters only have one to buy for Mandy.
- Confronting the ethnic, cultural and socio-economic differences in family life styles.

What can be done to help resolve the differences now?

Possible actions might include

- All parties having access to a named support person to discuss any concerns about contact.
- Holding a review meeting to consider those aspects of contact that are working well and those that might need to be changed.
- The local authority discussing with Therese what level of finance would be reasonable to support contact meetings and the cost of purchasing presents for Mandy's younger siblings.
- Discussing with both parties the suggestion that a trip to a theme park is a once-a-year treat to be planned during the school summer holidays and that the second contact meeting should comprise a more "every-day" and lower cost activity.

Maintaining links – indirect contact

For a minority of children it may be assessed that the risks inherent in maintaining direct contact outweigh the potential benefits. Recent research (Rushton *et al*, 2001) quoted earlier in this chapter, found that indirect contact tended to be used predominantly to supplement direct contact between siblings. There was little consideration of indirect means of maintaining sibling links and the range of ways in which such contact could be promoted, but for some children indirect contact will be the only type of contact that can be maintained.

Helping to promote and maintain links

- Adopters should receive preparation that introduces ideas about indirect contact. Even when there is no direct contact, siblings living elsewhere can be "held in mind". Prospective adopters can benefit from the experience of other adopters about different ways that they can include and talk about the child's absent siblings.
- Appropriate use of new technology opens up more ways of keeping in touch. The widespread availability of home computers, use of e-mail and mobile telephones present opportunities but also make it harder to maintain confidentiality and anonymity of placement. For example, is it known whether the placed child already had access to birth relatives' mobile telephone numbers prior to placement?
- Even children who cannot read or write can contribute ideas to include in letters and cards 'What shall we tell Lucy about what we did this summer holiday?' Sending cards which mark significant times such as birthdays and celebrations, or a postcard sent while on holiday can keep vital connections alive.
- Photographs – even very young children can be involved in helping their carers select photographs to be sent.
- A child can be encouraged to enclose a recent drawing or painting when letters or information are sent to siblings.
- Audio cassette tapes are good communicators. For example, one set of adopters included a cassette tape of two young children giggling and correcting each other as they sang *Old MacDonald Had a Farm*, a song that they had only recently learned. Their older sibling was pleased to receive this tangible evidence of the children's progress.
- Children should be involved in selecting and sending presents – for example, making a special trip to go to shops and the post office. Sometimes gift vouchers may be more practical. If children are too young to sign it, adults can help the child to draw a cross for a kiss. Such small efforts can still mean a lot.
- Video material – a video that features sibling(s) living elsewhere can

be played many times. When direct contact is also occurring, a video camera recording of some aspects of meeting, can be used to reinforce memories between visits.

- Life story books can be updated with the adopted child to include more recent photographs of siblings living elsewhere.
- The child should have a manageable choice about where a photograph of a sibling is displayed 'Would you like to put this here, in your bedroom or on the family noticeboard in the kitchen?'

Summary

The complexity of children's experiences within their family of origin will have had, and will continue to have, a significant impact on children's sibling relationships. The experience of loss on entering the looked after system is also likely to have influenced the quality and nature of sibling interactions and contact. Becoming separated from siblings is an additional loss – broken contact with siblings could prove to be the most far-reaching, damaging blow. Planning permanent placements and considering children's contact needs within these, is demanding of practitioner time and skills. However, early investment in planning and preparing children and families for contact is crucial and is likely to contribute to placement stability.

Human rights considerations, the National Adoption Standards and our increased awareness of the importance of sibling relationships all require us to give much greater attention to promoting sibling links, including contact. Even in those cases where children's relationships may have been distorted by parental abuse or neglect, inter-sibling contact can provide an important source of continuity, shared history, identity and support throughout life. The complete severance of sibling links carries profound consequences. Children are entitled to know what arrangements will be made to maintain their relationship with siblings living elsewhere and for such arrangements to be reviewed as needs change. All adoptive families and foster carers should receive preparation and support that assists them in valuing and promoting children's connections with siblings.

References

Barth, R and Berry, M (1988) *Adoption and Disruption: Rates, risks and responses*, New York: Aldine de Gruyter.

Berry, M (1993) 'Adoptive parents' perceptions of and comfort with open adoption', *Child Welfare*, Vol. LXX11, no. 3, USA.

Borland, M, O'Hara, G and Triseliotis, J (1991) 'Placement outcomes for children with special needs', *Adoption & Fostering*, 15:2.

Department of Health, Social Services Inspectorate (1995) *Moving Goalposts – A study of post-adoption contact in the North of England*, London: Department of Health.

Department of Health (2001) *National Adoption Standards for England*, London: Department of Health.

Fratter, J (1996) *Adoption with Contact: Implications for policy and practice*, London: BAAF.

Department of Health, *Adoption: Achieving the right balance*, LAC 98(20), London: Department of Health.

Lowe, N, Murch, M, Borkowski, M, Weaver, A, Beckford, V and Thomas, C (1999) *Supporting Adoption: Reframing the approach*, London: BAAF.

Rushton, A, Dance, C, Quinton, D and Mayes, D (2001) *Siblings in Late Permanent Placements*, London: BAAF.

6 Managing and valuing contact with contesting birth families

Maureen Crank

Introduction

Continuing contact with birth families for children and young people adopted from public care gives rise to many and wide-ranging debates. Much of this derives from five flawed assumptions about adoption which many people never challenge, and which have a huge impact on contact decisions and practice. These are:

1. Adoption is a perfect solution to three of society's most vexing problems: providing families for children who need them, meeting the needs of adults who want to parent but cannot, and relieving parents who have given birth to children but are unable to rear them.
2. It makes no difference whether a child is adopted by, or born into, a family.
3. Adoption is a one-off legal event.
4. If a young healthy child is placed with a "good adoptive family", the adoption will have no complications.
5. Adoption can and should be kept secret.

Our experience at After Adoption suggests that each of these statements is problematic. This is not to deny the value of adoption as a social intervention which can be beneficial to children and their families, provided practice respects that adoption is a life-long adventure, not a once and for all solution.

Adoption rearranges family boundaries in a way that ties together the birth family and the adoptive family and complicates the narratives of those involved for the rest of their lives.

There are, then, three major challenges facing those working in adoption. The first is to confront the loss and subsequent pain at the core of each adoption. The second is accepting and negotiating the complexity of the relationships for children who will have to integrate both families into their sense of identity. The third challenge is to create an adoption system that supports the needs of the older children and their families who are a part of today's adoption process. In other words, high standards in adoption practice, a whole range of pre- and post-adoption services, and good access to information about each particular adoption as and when needed. This involves planning and supporting contact.

Contesting birth parents

After Adoption was set up eleven years ago to offer a post-adoption service to children and their families. From very early on in its operation, the agency was approached by birth mothers losing their children to adoption through contested proceedings. These birth parents often came to us long before the adoption order was made or even shortly after the adoption decision had been reached. They needed independent support and help for themselves – quite separate from anything offered to their children – and not from the social services they were in conflict with.

In 1993 we set up a pilot project, "Before Adoption", to work with contesting birth parents. This was funded by the Nuffield Foundation and was modelled on the groundbreaking work of "Parents without Children" in the North East. Both projects were the subject of the book *Still Screaming* (Charlton *et al*, 1998). A second "Parents without Children" project, funded by Henry Smith's Charity, followed on here in Manchester to develop the work further and to convince local authorities of the benefits of providing this service on a regular basis. Back in 1990, letterbox contact was common though face-to-face contact was rare. During the last ten years, we have seen a growth in all types of contact and a large part of the work of our "Parents without Children" project has been to support, negotiate and review contact arrangements.

In order for birth parents to continue to be a resource to their child or children, they need both emotional and practical support in their own right. Almost all of the hundreds of birth parents we have worked with have been able to focus on the needs of their child once some of their own needs have been met. Their needs are often for someone to listen to their story (witnessing), to clarify the adoption processes for them, and to support them in any meetings. An early meeting between birth and adoptive families can be of enormous value to the child as it may help a contesting parent to agree to adoption. When they see the adoptive family they may be reassured and consent to the order. One birth parent said to me following such a meeting: 'If I can't have Clinton then I am glad he will live with Ellie and Tom. I don't want Clinton to have any more distress, so I will consent to his adoption by them.'

Birth relatives often require practical help to provide written information for their child including regular postings through letterbox systems. When they have face-to-face contact, whether supervised or not, all birth parents should have access to a comprehensive support service.

Some guidance about contact

I have listed some extracts from legislation and guidance for contact on which practice needs to be based.

From guidance to the Children Act 1989

'Contact, however occasional, may continue to have a value for the child, even when there is no question of returning to his family; these contacts can keep alive for a child a sense of his origins and may keep open options for family relationships in later life.'

From the Adoption & Children Bill 2001

'The court or adoption agency must have regard to the following matters (among others):
- the child's wishes and feelings;
- particular needs, age, sex and background;
- the likely effect on the child (throughout his life) of having ceased to be a member of the original family and becoming an adopted person,
- any harm the child has suffered or is at risk of suffering;
- the relationship the child has with relatives, including wishes and feelings of relatives.'

From the National Adoption Standards for England, 2001

'**A10** The child's needs, wishes and feelings, and their welfare and safety are the most important concerns when considering links or contact with birth parents, wider birth family members and other people who are significant to them.

A11 Adoption plans will include details of the arrangements for maintaining links (including contact) with birth parents, wider birth family members and other people who are significant to the child and how and when these arrangements will be reviewed.'

From the draft practice guidance to the Adoption Standards, 2001

'All adoption plans should consider the appropriate level of contact to meet the child's needs and set out arrangements for maintaining this.'

(There is the proviso, however, that in certain cases, no contact at all may be in the best interests of the child).

The guidance goes on to say that the adoption plan should set out:

* 'the people who should have contact with the child;
* timing of such contact;
* place of contact;
* nature of contact.'

From the guidance to the Adoption (Scotland) Act 1978 as amended by the Children (Scotland) Act 1995

'An assessment of whether any form of contact should be retained must be based solely on what is likely to be in the child's interests, both at the point of placement and in the future.'

From the Adoption (Scotland) Act 1978

'Courts and adoption agencies shall have regard to all the circumstances but –

* shall regard the need to safeguard and promote the welfare of the child concerned throughout his life as the paramount consideration; and
* shall have regard as far as practicable
  i) to his views (if he wishes to express them) taking account of his age and maturity; and

ii) to his religious persuasion, racial origin and cultural and linguistic background.'

From the National Care Standards for Adoption Agencies in Scotland

Standard 7 (for children and young people):

'You have contact with people who have been important to you in the past if this is in your interests.'

Standard 17 (for birth families):

'You can be confident that all contact arrangements will be based on the best interests of your child.'

All of this, like the whole process of adoption, must take into account the lifelong adventure that is adoption. As the child develops, their needs change, so may their need for contact. I often suggest to people that a helpful way to consider links and contact is in the context of normal family relationships.

We all see:

* some members of our families regularly, e.g. daily, weekly or monthly depending on geography, time and a variety of circumstances;
* we see some relations only at family events, e.g. weddings, funerals, religious rituals or celebrations;
* some we rarely or never see but keep in touch by exchanging festive and birthday cards or by notifying a change of address, a birth or a death;
* there are some who, as a result of a family conflict, we have no contact with whatsoever.

In terms of adoption this can mean:

* the two families have full access to each others' address/telephone numbers and meet regularly;
* face-to-face meetings are organised through a third party;
* they exchange occasional information through a third party;
* they meet once;
* the two families never meet and know nothing about each other.

Contact in contested adoptions

In contested adoptions the vast majority of the children are older and have clear memories of people in their past, particularly their birth parents, and situations arise where adopted children have reopened their own adoptions. They know their birth family's names and where they lived. One 12-year-old we were working with took it upon himself to visit his grandmother whom he had last seen when he was eight years old. Often the birth and adoptive families in contested cases are just like "normal" families who have had a serious conflict. Where there is violence or danger they will not see, or have any contact with, each other.

A history of violence or abuse in a contested case often ensures that the adoption remains tightly closed or, if there is organised face-to-face contact, it will be heavily supervised. An exchange of information through a letterbox system is also often supervised. Letters may be checked for content in order that "nothing" disrupts the placement. A 14-year-old girl attending an After Adoption group was incensed that her letters from her birth mother were always opened in social services and scrutinised:

Why do they do this? I lived with Eileen for my first eight years – I know better than anyone that she lies sometimes. I know it's because she feels she let me down and it still hurts and sometimes she is just plain stupid. It hurts me too, but not as bad as someone I don't know opening my letters all the time.

This girl's outrage shows that letterbox agreements, like all contact agreements, have to consider the voice of the child.

Letterbox contact is the most common way to preserve continuity in contested adoptions. We know that good practice is about information and keeping all those involved in an adoption informed about each other. A letterbox arrangement can do this and ensure safety for the particular child. The letterbox can keep that child and the adoptive family informed about other birth family members and will replace speculation and fantasy with facts and help children come to terms with difficult aspects of their history (e.g. mental illness).

If adoptive families embrace the information, the child's attachments are enhanced. This in turn can lead to a healthier sense of entitlement for the adoptive parent. Given that almost all contesting birth parents experience high levels of social, economic and psychological disadvantage, then letterbox contact may well be the best that some can manage and there may even be a measure of reassurance in knowing that contact must be limited.

When the adults involved in adoption, exchange information about the child, it is not uncommon for that child to want it to stop. Teenagers often say that they do not want their photographs or news passed on without their permission. It is understandable that they want to control what is said about them and it may be suitable for the young person to take over responsibility for sending information at an agreed point.

We have found that, in contested adoptions with any level of contact, including indirect letterbox exchanges, children make better psychological adjustments and have fewer identity problems in adolescence. However, it is crucial that letterbox arrangements, like all contact arrangements, are carefully monitored and adjusted to match the child's developmental needs.

We must always take note of the child's attachment patterns and age and the capacity of both families to want to make contact work.

Case example

Joanna was six years old and had been in foster care for two years. When an adoptive family was found for her, she had not had any direct contact with her mother, Anna, for over a year. Protracted and acrimonious care proceedings had left Anna too angry to have anything to do with social services and thus with her daughter.

Anna was aware of the adoption plan – a freeing order having been made alongside the care order. When Joanna began introductions to her new family, her social worker contacted us asking for help. She sensed a reluctance in Joanna about visiting the new family's home. She got distressed and said she had tummy ache prior to each arranged introductory visit. Joanna had a life story book and had been looking forward to moving to her new family but was persistently asking questions of her foster carers about Anna and how Anna would feel or manage without her.

An independent worker from After Adoption began to work with Anna; she enabled Anna to write a letter to Joanna telling her that she was glad a new family had been found and that she wanted Joanna to have a good and happy life. This letter reassured Joanna and she became more settled. It also reassured her adoptive family who agreed to meet Anna. Anna was then helped to make a videotape for Joanna explaining in appropriate language what had gone wrong and how she would be there should she ever be needed, but explaining that she wanted Joanna to have a family and 'be happy'.

Some 18 months later, the adoptive family approached us wanting another meeting with Anna. They had many questions that needed answers for their daughter. This second meeting went well and they brought a videotape of Joanna. A year later, secure in their relationship with Joanna, they requested face-to-face contact as this was what Joanna now wanted. She had more questions for Anna. The families now meet approximately once a year; they make the arrangements themselves and enjoy a day out together. We see Anna after these visits as she needs some support and reassurance for herself.

The period between Joanna being removed into care and having regular direct contact was about four-and-a-half years. During this time Anna had some psyciatric help and some counselling at After Adoption to address her own feelings of loss and abandonment by her mother and her relationship difficulties – she has had many short-term violent relationships. She clearly loved her daughter and wanted her to be happy. The information she received about Joanna helped her settle and become resigned to her position. She was able to acknowledge that she had not been the 'best possible Mum' to Joanna. Anna's acceptance of the status quo makes the contact possible. The fact that Joanna's adoptive parents began to feel empathy towards Anna also played a part in moving things on.

Joan Fratter (1996) suggests that the success of contact between children and their birth parents is related to the adjustment of the birth parent. This ties in with the story of many of the birth parents we work with, and in particular, Faye.

Case example

Faye was referred to After Adoption by her children's local authority social worker when the adoption plan was made. The social worker felt that Faye needed support for herself. During all of the care and adoption proceedings, Faye had an independent social worker from After Adoption. Since the adoption order, she has had several periods of counselling from the same worker. Faye has supported other birth parents in similar positions by sharing her own experiences.

Faye had serious mental health problems when her son and daughter were removed from her and later adopted. The heavily contested care order, and eventually the adoption plan, included face-to-face contact two or three times a year between Faye, her children and their adoptive parents. Initially the meetings were in an office under supervision; Asok, the adoptive father, did not always attend.

The reason for the contact was to reassure the children, particularly her daughter aged eight at the time of the adoption, that their birth-mother was well. As Faye's children were black African Muslims placed with a black family of a different religion, Faye felt it important for the children to keep in touch, even in a small measure, with their Muslim background. It was agreed, therefore, that Faye's parents should be included in the contact meetings.

On one occasion Faye dropped into our office for us to send on a birthday card to her daughter. She had a cup of tea with a member of staff and started to write the card. As she finished she shouted, 'I've done it!' People crowded round to see what she had done. She explained, 'I have called myself Faye, not Mummy Faye, but Faye. It will give Myra (the adoptive Mum) a proper chance to feel that she is their Mum.'

Six years later, Faye, her children and their family manage their own contact and Asok, the adoptive father, has joined them and grown more comfortable as time has gone by.

Faye often sees a worker before and after the visits. She needs this time to help her prepare for the meetings, and afterwards to make sure that she has not said 'anything stupid'. Faye says that she often thinks it would be less painful not to see her children at all as she feels she loses a month before and a month after each visit with worry, anxiety and not sleeping. Faye says she revisits her loss twice a year. She could not stop now as she feels her children need to see her, but if the children want to stop for a time, then that will be fine by Faye.

During counselling sessions, Faye acknowledged openly that she would never have been able to parent her children. She had no family or community support, her parents were elderly and she was aware of her illness and its effects on her children. Faye grew to like the adoptive family and wanted them to succeed in parenting her children. Faye has her own individual worker whom she has been able to trust. On the final day of the adoption hearing, Faye and her worker went for a walk in the hills. She didn't want to hear the judge's words – she said she could say them for him. In the hills the worker helped Faye prepare a letter for the children about their family history.

Faye feels that by helping other birth mothers, she is putting her own experience to a positive use. She has been involved in groups for contesting birth parents and has helped to run them.

Some myths about contact

- *Face-to-face "direct" contact is necessarily more difficult to manage than indirect contact.* Faye's story above clearly shows that this is not always the case, even when there has been serious conflict about the adoption.
- *Contact is only appropriate for older children who have "meaningful" relationships with the birth relative.* Contact and links provide information that is important for *all* adopted children. Information empowers and can help provide that child with a sense of identity. Ongoing exchange of information helps even very young children to understand their adoption.
- *A final "goodbye" is appropriate whenever children are to be adopted and especially if birth parents have been unco-operative.* This process at times appears barbaric. Birth parents and children who have been put through "goodbye" visits remember them as one of the most traumatic

experiences of their lives. In *Farewell Behind Bars* (Charlton, 1999), a birth mother describes watching her children crying and being dragged by the social worker down a long prison drive and out of the huge metal gate. Did this help anyone? A video or letter may have been less destructive.

Preparation

Birth relatives, like all parties involved in contact arrangements, need careful preparation.

Birth parents in contested proceedings are exceptionally vulnerable. Unlike parents who have voluntarily relinquished children, these birth parents have been deemed by society to be unfit to care for their children. There is little sympathy for them and they are often portrayed in the media in a totally negative and unsympathetic way. The birth parent will have been involved with social services over a period of time; often, unsuccessful attempts will have been made to prevent the child becoming looked after or to rehabilite the child with the parents. When the decision is made that adoption is in the child's best interests, the social worker's job is to present a case to the court in support of the plan. This involves using what has happened to build up the "case". The social worker may well have formed a good relationship with the birth family but it is exceptionally difficult to maintain this from opposing sides of a court room. It is not unusual for the birth parent to feel abandoned and betrayed by the social worker. One comment from a birth parent in such a situation was:

> Not only would Liz [her social worker] not talk to me about Robert [her child] but she would not talk about any of the things we used to talk about, not even music – we both liked Van Morrison and when she used to give me a lift to contact that's what we talked about.

Most, if not all, of these birth parents live in poverty and on benefits. Many are addicted to drugs or alcohol and many will have little or no family support. Some have been abused or neglected themselves as children. Some also have mental health problems and/or learning difficulties. Almost all birth parents have very "low self-esteem" and those involved in contested adoptions are even less confident.

These birth parents, more than most, need their own worker, who is not employed by the adoption agency. They need to know that what they tell this worker will not be used in court against them. One birth mother who had been abused and raped by her father as a child did not want this information given to the court. The information was relevant to her situation but she felt it was not relevant to the two children she was losing now. The birth parent's worker must be able to remain independent. After Adoption has clear criteria for working with contesting birth parents.

1. Allow time for the expression of grief and anger, validate their feelings, and let them "tell their story". Acknowledge the pain of knowing someone else is raising their child and explore attitudes towards the adoptive parents.

2. Be aware that supporting the birth parents may well lead to an exploration of issues from their own past e.g. abuse and poor parenting they themselves received. This may be necessary in order to come to some acceptance of why they have been unable to parent.

3. Emphasise that they will always be the birth parent and no one can ever change that.

4. Be clear that they are a "non-parenting parent" but stress that they are still a valuable resource for the child.

5. Be clear about the purpose of the contact.

6. If supporting a birth parent regarding indirect contact, be clear about the process e.g. letters will be read by the letterbox administrator. Explore the best way of communicating with their child:
   - Take notes while they talk then draft a letter, using their phrases, for their approval.
   - They write the letter after discussing what would/would not be desirable/acceptable.
   - Write the letter together.
   - Prepare a video together or help the birth parents to make their own life story book for the child.
   - Use pictures/collage, especially for birth parents with learning difficulties.
   - Encourage birth parents to send letters and cards in their own handwriting where possible.

7. When preparing a birth parent for face-to-face contact with their child:

- be clear about boundaries; who will be there/where and when contact is taking place/travel arrangements/what can or can't be said/given/bought for the child;
- discuss how to handle the situation if birth parent or child gets upset/child misbehaves.

8. Use mediation skills if both families can meet to discuss or role play the absent adopters.

Tensions in contact

According to Schaffer's research (1990) young children are capable of attaching themselves and loving more than one set of carers at the same time. Studies of step-families suggest children fare better if adult relationships continue with the non-resident parent. However, powerful societal criticism and blame of birth parents, especially those whose children have been adopted from public care and where there has been neglect and/or abuse, make the process of ongoing contact unpalatable to many adoptive families. We know that often adopters have little in common with the birth family other than the child, but that is actually a "huge" connection. If the child's needs can be kept central, then many families can maintain links or indeed have some regular face-to-face contact in spite of the clash between family lifestyles. One adoptive family commented: 'If I couldn't find something to like in Jane's birth family then it would be harder to give Jane a positive sense of identity'.

Grotevant *et al* (1998) showed in their research that adopters benefit less from continued contact than other parties. They saw a difference between adoptive mothers and fathers. Often adoptive mothers can relate more easily to the birth parents' loss and want to support contact; fathers find it harder. However, they may also find that contact is a constant reminder of the birth parents' pain which can lead to stressful feelings of guilt. This could be why, in Faye's situation, Asok found contact easier as time went by.

Our experience at *After Adoption* is similar to the findings of Berry *et al* (1998). Their studies showed that, over time, in adoptions where contact arrangements are set up, the trend is for these to decrease or end. We see very many families, birth and adoptive, whose contact has stopped altogether. It could be that the child's needs have changed and were not reviewed. It is our view that all contact arrangements, even indirect letter box exchanges, are too challenging for birth parents and adoptive parents to sustain without help.

Birth parents who have contested an adoption find it especially difficult to maintain any contact unsupported. If letterbox contact has been set up, and even if a reminder has been sent, they often struggle to know what to write. Faye, in the previous case study, was a well-educated woman but she still needed help to put pen to paper. One birth parent, who had not maintained her twice-yearly contact for three consecutive years, eventually came to see us after breaking down at work on the birthday of her daughter. She was by then in another relationship and was successfully parenting a son. She didn't know how to tell her daughter about this or whether she should. She was afraid the social services concerned would want to investigate her present situation. She had moved over the border to another local authority to have her next child. The same psychosocial and economic reasons which led to the adoption of their children also affect these birth parents' ability to sustain contact arrangements without support and guidance.

Conclusion

Contact can work in situations where children and young people have been adopted from public care even if the adoption was contested. If all the adults can learn to co-operate for the sake of the child, then it can work well. Sometimes birth parents cannot agree to have their children adopted but it should not be supposed that they do not want to do the best they can for their child or that they would undermine the adoption if they had contact.

Case example

Rosie was a child born to a couple, Johnnie and Freda, who both had learning difficulties. By the time Rosie was a year old, it became clear that Johnnie and Freda were not coping. Rosie's development was very delayed and on several occasions she had some unexplained bruises. She was placed in foster care in order that a full assessment could be made of her needs and eventually she was made the subject of a full care order. Rosie remained with her foster carers for the next three years, still with serious developmental delays. During the first two years of Rosie's stay in foster care, Johnnie and Freda visited weekly and Johnnie often popped in midweek on his own as he worked nearby as a street cleaner. Freda's learning difficulties meant that she could only visit with Johnnie's help.

When it became apparent that Rosie would not be returning to them, Freda stopped visiting regularly but Johnnie continued. When Rosie was five years old, her foster carers, Tim and Betty, adopted her. Johnnie and Freda did not consent. Johnnie said in court that he believed Rosie should live with Tim and Betty but he couldn't 'sign her away' as she would always be his daughter. By this time Rosie was attending a mainstream school with additional professional help. She remained in mainstream education until she left school at 16.

Johnnie went on visiting throughout Rosie's childhood, popping in approximately once a week and staying about 10–30 minutes for a cup of tea. Rosie always knew who he was and referred to him as 'Da'. Tim and Betty were 'Mum and Dad'. About once a year Johnnie brought Freda. Rosie knew her as Freda, her birth mother.

Rosie now has her own home and baby. Johnnie, who has retired, still calls to see Rosie. Freda died some years ago. Johnnie also visits Betty and Tim regularly.

This case shows how both Johnnie and Freda knew intuitively that Rosie was happy and well cared for by her parents Betty and Tim. Through contact, they were supporting Rosie and helping her understand why she was adopted. Rosie was always sure of her identity and Betty and Tim clearly felt entitled to be Rosie's parents. Other disabled non-consenting parents can also, with support, contribute to the life of their birth child. It is important for the worker to take steps to ensure that, whatever the disabilities, birth parents can be helped to communicate.

A large research study in America was carried out by Ruth McRoy (1999) over five years with 720 participants including 190 adopters,

169 birth parents and 171 adopted children who all had some level of contact. The findings were:

- many of the fears and concerns about openness are without foundation;
- the level of openness has to be decided on a case-by-case basis;
- adoption is an ongoing process;
- adult parties in fully open adoptions are not confused about who has parenting responsibilities;
- fears that birth parents would intrude into the lives of adoptive families are not borne out in open adoptions;
- providing information does not confuse children or lower their self-esteem – more information was related to high levels of understanding of adoption;
- in fully disclosed adoptions children do not struggle with divided loyalties.

McRoy (1999) says:

> *When children were removed under child protection procedures, little attention was sometimes paid to the maintenance of family links and as a result the relationships between parents and children were impoverished. It may well be that issues of contact are viewed less favourably when the child has been removed for reasons of abuse and neglect; but children who were denied access to important family members suffered unresolved feelings of loss and guilt.*

In Joan Fratter's book, *Adoption with Contact* (1996), she suggests that, with goodwill, a child-centered approach and skilled negotiation, positive contact for children and young people adopted through the care system, can work. And this is what I truly believe.

The case studies in this article are evidence in themselves of how contact with contesting birth parents can work and that all children and young people require an assessment of their contact needs which will form the basis of individual arrangements for that particular adoption.

The multiplicity of losses for birth families and children, compounded by their experiences of the care and court process, make the words of Claudia Jewett in *Adopting the Older Child* (1978) so significant:

> *The fewer people you lose the better.*

References

After Adoption (2001) *Good Practice in Contact*, After Adoption Manchester.

Berry, M, Calvazos Dyalla, D J, Barth, R J and Needell, B (1998) 'The role of open adoptions in the adjustment of children and their families', *Children and Youth Services Review*, 20:1/2.

Charlton, L, Crank, M, Kansara, K and Oliver, C (1998) *Still Screaming*, After Adoption Manchester.

Charlton, L (1999) *Farewell Behind Bars*, After Adoption Manchester.

Department of Health (forthcoming) *Draft Practice Guidance – The Adoption Standards 2001*, London: Department of Health.

Fratter, J (1996) *Adoption with Contact: Implications for policy and practice*, London: BAAF.

Grotevant, H, McRoy, R, Elde, C and Fravel, D (1994) 'Adoptive family systems dynamics: Variation by level of openness in the adoption', *Family Process*, LXIX (3)

Jewett, C (1978) *Adopting the Older Child*, Harvard, Massachussetts: Harvard Common Press.

McRoy, R (1999) *Special Needs Adoptions: Practice issues*, New York and London: Garland Press, Taylor Francis Group.

Schaffer, H (1990) *Making Decisions about Children's Psychological Questions and Answers*, New York: Blackwell.

7 Contact after adoption:
What they say and how it feels

Patricia Swanton

In 1990, Adoption UK (then known as Parent to Parent Information on Adoption Services) surveyed its membership on the issue of contact. The idea of adopted children keeping in touch with birth parents, brothers and sisters or other significant people, was fairly new then, but was becoming increasingly important. We wanted to know what adoptive parents thought and what their experiences were. Not surprisingly, there was a wide range of answers, and many people's views about contact were directly related to their personal experience of it. Very few people were in favour of no contact at all, but the majority expressed the view that contact should be regulated by the adoptive family, and not be too disruptive to family life. People wanted "openness" in adoption, despite being wary of exactly how this would impact on their families. These responses occurred during a time of transition, when contact was a newly introduced idea, untested and unfamiliar to many.

Now, more than ten years later, we have again been asking adoptive families – parents and children – what they feel about contact. What has the real experience been like? How has it affected family life over the years? Has it been as beneficial, or as problematic, as people thought it would be?

Our sample was small and, in the main, self-selected – that is, I was only able to talk to those who responded to our invitation. The children ranged in age from those just starting school to those at university. Most had had contact of some kind since placement. We did our best to include families across the ethnic and cultural range of Britain, but of the 16 families who responded, 15 had two white parents; 11 of these families had adopted children whose birth parents were white, and five had adopted children of mixed ethnicity and nationality. Specific issues of ethnicity were not addressed.

The children and young people's experiences

For many children, contact seemed to be taken completely for granted, as an integral and normal part of their lives. For a few others, the experience has been ambivalent, and for some it has been confusing. A number of responses came from young people in their 20s and 30s, some of whom had had contact during their childhood while others, who had not had any contact, still had some very strong views.

Leon, adopted eight years ago at the age of six, whose adoptive mother initiated direct contact with his birth family, says how 'weird' it was when he first got back into contact because he could hardly remember them. 'At first,' he said, 'I didn't know what to say, but after a while I got used to them and I can't wait to see them whenever I'm meant to go.' When Leon, now 14, was placed, his adoptive family had letterbox contact with members of his birth family (his birth mother died soon after his adoption). Leon needed and wanted more information and was sad that the letters sent by his adopters were never reciprocated. His adoptive mother, Sarah, knew where Leon's birth aunt worked and made contact through a third party, explaining tactfully that Leon was distressed at never receiving letters and that he very much wanted to see his relatives. From this approach, Leon's aunt, to whom he was very close before he went into care, and his grandmother have resumed regular contact, including visits for Leon of several days during the summer holidays, weekends before Easter and Christmas, and phone calls. Leon tried initially to play his two families off against each other. His adoptive mother commented that this was no great problem, since 'it's no different from grannies and parents in most families'. Leon's birth family have in fact been very supportive to his adoptive family: Leon suffers from severe attachment disorder, and his birth aunt has accompanied him and his adoptive family to a therapy centre, where she was able to answer questions for which his adoptive parents had no answers. The birth family has also consistently included Leon's older, adoptive sister (who has no contact of her own) in their attentions. She is appreciative of this, although it continually reminds her that she has no contact with her own birth family.

Three young people who had not experienced contact spoke out strongly against it. **Rosie**, 17½, felt contact would have confused her, though she did admit to wanting more information. **Zoë**, both in teenage and now, at the age of 30, considers she would have 'played one mother off against the other' and is glad she did not have contact. She is quite open about adoption, traced and met her birth parents when she was 23, and discusses her adoption in a matter-of-fact way with the rest of her family and with her own two young daughters. **Jane**, also 30, has seen a much younger adopted sister suffer confusion and disappointments as her contacts with birth parents waxed and waned, and, although she has recently made letter contact with her own birth mother, she is certain she would not have wanted this in childhood.

Lisa, now 25 and a mother herself, said that her one-off meeting with her birth mother at the age of 16 answered a lot of questions for her about her own identity, about why she had to be adopted, and why her birth mother had had so many children. She also gained some additional information, some of which, she said, 'wasn't very nice'. Lisa looked on this visit as a chance to say a proper goodbye, as she and her brother had been taken from their mother in the night. Lisa also commented that she might not have been 'so horrible to live with' if she had been able to meet her birth mother sooner.

Sasha, now 22 and at university, saw her birth mother, Jill, once every two years from the time she was placed with her adopters at the age of 18 months, until she was 16 and it was left to her to decide whether she wanted contact to continue. Sasha always knew whom she was meeting: 'I knew what was going on, that she was my natural mother; however, I don't think I thought much more about it than that, and just had a good day.' When Sasha was 21 and hadn't heard from Jill for about four years, she went to find her – discovering then that Jill had lost her address and was renewing efforts to get back in contact. While Sasha feels that she remains in touch partly for her birth mother's sake, she knows also that she doesn't herself want to lose touch: she looks forward to Jill attending her graduation and meeting her (eventual) grandchildren. However, she admits that, 'The older I get, the harder it is to relate to her. I don't know whether to treat her as a parent, a friend, a sister. We don't have much in common apart from genes.' Seeing her birth mother's lifestyle has also shown Sasha the greater opportunities she has gained in education, travel and leisure activities through her adoptive family.

Patsy, aged 14, has enjoyed contact with her elder sister and thrown herself happily into her sister's relationships. At the time I spoke to her parents, Patsy's sister had just broken off her engagement and Patsy was very upset. Consequently, she has not wanted to talk to anyone about contact and what it means to her. Her parents feel that part of her sadness is the way in which she hears news like this: both Patsy and her parents know that if she and her elder sister lived together they would have shared confidences and the news would not have been such a bolt from the blue. 'It is often hard for the children, being so close and yet so far from those they still love,' Jo, her adoptive mother, said. 'But we hope by keeping contact alive, we are paving the way, so that as adults they can be as close as they want.' (This family had, for 11 years, been sending updates to Patsy's birth father, which had neither been acknowledged nor reciprocated. A chance remark from the older sister – 'Dad says thanks for the letters, he loves getting them but never has any news to share . . .' – made them glad they had persevered with what had seemed at times a thankless task.) The meetings between Patsy and the elder sister upset Becky, a younger half-sister of Patsy and a member of the same adoptive family. She decided she wanted no more information about herself sent to any of the birth relatives, including parents, siblings and grandparents, who received annual letters from her adoptive parents. However, after reading a letter from her birth parents in which they said they respected her wishes, she decided that it would be acceptable for them just to be told that she was 'alright'. Jo, her adoptive mother, says, 'What was wonderful for one child was awful for another. We have learned from this that there are no set rules.'

The adoptive parents' views and experience

How adoptive parents feel about contact is influenced by a number of different factors. The impact on the specific child is perhaps the most important of these, but several parents are troubled by the negative impact that one child's contact has on other children in the family. While most parents would regard their own feelings as the least important, some admit that they find both the practical and emotional aspects of contact difficult. Others are able to look on contact with their child's birth relatives in much the same way as they regard contact with their own extended family. Where there are friendly feelings and sympathy between the adoptive and birth families, the experience of contact can be positive for everyone involved.

Diana has mixed feelings about the contact her 13-year-old son, **Ben**, has because she sees it brings him as much sorrow as pleasure. The letters and photos he receives are infrequent, and the letters difficult to decipher. One photograph, showing his birth mother with his younger half-siblings (all in care), upset him as it emphasised the fact that they have the face-to-face contact that he has been denied. He has had behaviour problems at school, and talking to a counsellor revealed that adoption issues are very much on his mind. He has said that he likes to hear from his birth mother, but it is a sensitive issue for him and he gets tearful and upset when talking about her. Diana values letterbox contact for the information it provides and for helping children to feel they have not been rejected by their birth families, but sees its potential for confusion and insecurity. She feels it needs to be well regulated and efficiently organised if it is to succeed.

Suzie's adoptive mother, **Janet**, describes how Suzie, at three years old, had just got used to visiting her birth mother in prison, at which times she also met her maternal grandparents, when the birth mother decided a clean break would be better for everyone. Janet recalls how confusing this was for Suzie, and how difficult it was to explain. Contact then continued for the next five years in the form of 'bigger and bigger Christmas and birthday presents with more and more effusive, loving messages' from a "Daddy" whom even the birth mother did not acknowledge as Suzie's father. Suzie's adoptive mother considers her daughter was seduced to the point where she began to write "love letters" back and to ask for more and more expensive presents. The adoptive family feel that the loss of Suzie's first social worker and the fact that no one else 'picked up the thread of our story' added to their problems, and it was not until a social work student investigated the background that the family began to receive help for Suzie. Suzie's mother believes she remains very confused, and continues to equate love with expensive presents.

Keith and Ella say that their son, **Jeremy**, benefits from seeing his birth father, but find their face-to-face contact three times a year stressful and difficult. This is mostly because the birth father, John, is nearly always 'under the influence of alcohol to a greater or lesser degree', and has a tendency to make comments that are not really appropriate for a 10-year-old to hear. Keith feels that the contact enables their son and his birth father to reassure each other that they are alright: when first placed, nearly four years ago, Jeremy used to imagine that his birth father had died, and still has some unresolved feelings of guilt, blaming himself for allegations he made that led to his removal from his father (which he now claims were "fibs"). However, once father and son have met up and fondly greeted each other, the birth father prefers to chat to the adoptive parents rather than spend time with his son, and they have to facilitate almost all the communication between the two. Farewells are "sweetened" for Jeremy by a gift of money from his birth father. Keith and Ella organise the meetings themselves by telephoning the birth father, and are always present. Although they have not needed any involvement from social services, they like to think that if any problems arose they could discuss them with their social worker, and count on her help to find solutions. The meetings were held at neutral venues for the two years before the adoption order was made, and since then, either at the birth father's home or their own. John has never attempted to make contact in between the arranged visits. Since the adoption, Keith and Ella have felt more secure in their position as legal parents, which helps them to cope with the difficulties of the meetings. They feel that the meetings give Jeremy a realistic picture of his birth father and help him understand why he cannot live with him.

Another adoptive mother, **Sandra**, has noted her eight-year-old son **David's** tendency to place greater value on the presents he gets from his birth mother than on actually seeing her. David, placed at four years old, has said that he might not want to go on seeing his birth mother. The family have letterbox contact with his birth mother as well as the twice a year face-to-face contact, and letterbox contact with three siblings, two adopted into different families who have no contact with their birth mother and one sixteen-year-old permanently placed with grandparents, who sees her mother every day. David's grandparents do not reply to any of the letters they receive from Sandra: they are supportive of his birth mother, once bringing her to a contact meeting when she was late, but not staying to see David. When I asked Sandra about the benefits of contact for David, she felt that contact 'does him no harm' but is not very meaningful for him. He helps choose the photographs that are sent to his birth relatives but is not ready for any further involvement. David has some learning difficulties, and in many ways operates a few years behind his chronological age. Sandra is currently considering inviting David's mother to visit them at home, rather than meeting in public places as they have been doing. Sandra does not find keeping contact going a problem, and has seen positive enough benefits for David, to agree to a similar type of contact arrangement (letter box and face-to-face contact twice a year) with the birth mother of four-year-old Helen, who was placed with Sandra this summer. However, Helen's birth mother's mental health problems and her vulnerability mean that there will always be a social worker present at the meetings.

Lawrence and **Kate**, with two sisters of eight and nine newly placed, are ambivalent about the value of contact. Letterbox contact is in place with the girls' birth mother, with whom Lawrence and Kate have a great deal of sympathy. The birth father, who had care of the girls for a number of years, has asked for a similar service, but since the girls suffered abuse and neglect while living with him, Lawrence and Kate are reluctant to comply with his request. The children remember difficult and unhappy experiences with their father and have said they do not want contact with him; his request is currently "on hold". The first letter to the birth mother proved harder to write than Lawrence and Kate expected, compounded by the fact that the older girl, **Sophie**, wrote an accompanying letter to her birth mother declaring her to be 'the best mother in the world' whom she loved very much and didn't want to leave. Kate was upset, particularly as she and Sophie had been growing very close. Since Sophie had not lived with her mother for several years and had also used similar expressions in a letter to her former foster mother, Lawrence was sure that Sophie was writing 'what she thought she was supposed to write'. He talked to her about her letter, telling her that she had upset Kate and that he also thought that it might upset 'Mummy Jane' if she thought that Sophie was unhappy. Sophie's immediate reaction was to tear up the letter and refuse to do anything at all. Eight-year-old **Sarah-Jane** drew and coloured a picture for her mother.

Sally, herself adopted, and her husband **Colin** have a six-year-old adopted daughter, **Ashley**. Ashley knows that they write to Vicky, her 'tummy-mummy', and helps to choose photographs to send, but Sally feels that, although Ashley is interested in her own history and asks a few questions, the contact is going on 'over her head'. Adoption is an open subject in their family, and Ashley talks to her grandmother about Sally's adoption. Although Ashley knows when a letter has been received from her birth mother, she has not yet seen one. Sally does have some concerns as to what Ashley will think about her birth mother's handwriting: her birth mother's learning difficulties mean that her handwriting is not even as good as Ashley's. She also feels inhibited about taking Ashley to the nearby town where Vicky lives. There is face-to-face contact with a 12-year-old half-sibling, adopted into another family, who has no contact with her birth parents. Both girls enjoy this contact which, after being initially set up by the social worker, is now left in the hands of the two families. Sally is grateful also for good, continuing contact with former foster carers who had taken photographs of Ashley as a baby and of the birth parents and other relatives during visits. When Sally herself was adopted, her adoptive mother made the decision that it would be better for her not to have any direct contact with her birth mother while she was growing up, although the fact that the two mothers themselves kept in touch made it easier for contact to be resumed when Sally was adult. When Sally and Colin began their preparations for adoption, neither was in favour of contact during childhood: however, during their assessment, they began to realise the benefits of contact and to feel more comfortable with it. But they cannot see very much in it for Ashley at the moment; rather they feel they are storing up information for the future.

Carol and **Daniel**, adoptive parents of 22-year-old **Sasha** and her 23-year-old brother, have always appreciated the birth mother's sensitivity towards the adoptive family. It was the birth mother, Jill, who had decided on a two-year break in contact when the children were first placed (at 18 months and nearly three years) to enable them to settle into their new family, and who never subsequently abused her knowledge of where they lived. Contact continued with letters exchanged and meetings every two years until the children were old enough to take control of the arrangements. A son was born to Carol and Daniel after Sasha and her brother were adopted, and was always included in any presents that Jill brought on her contact visits. (Currently 18, he did not want to add any comments.)

The family really like Jill, although Carol is aware that Jill is more relaxed with Daniel than with her, and wonders whether this is to do with personal "chemistry" or with her role as mother. Carol says, 'Contact has been a very positive factor in helping our children live with being adopted'.

When **Kay** and **Tim** adopted **Andy**, placed at the age of 13 months, and his sister **Lily**, placed at the age of eight months less than a year later, annual letterbox contact was agreed with birth parents and direct contact with a half-brother placed in another adoptive family. The birth parents have since separated, and their current whereabouts are unknown. Two other half-siblings had already been adopted into different families, and another lives with the extended birth family. Although Kay and Tim were aware of these other three children, the issue of contact with them was 'never discussed'. Indeed, the face-to-face contact with the half-brother was negotiated by Kay and Tim, as he was adopted by a local family whom they met on the preparation courses and have remained friends with. Once Lily was securely adopted, Kay and Tim asked for a letter from them to be placed on the children's files to say that they wanted to be informed if any other significant birth family members expressed interest in the children. Although they haven't found Social Services to be very proactive around contact, they say they do at least respond when information is needed: Lily had a number of health problems, and the agency asked the adoptive parents of other half-siblings for any information that would help a diagnosis. Through these contacts, which continue only sporadically, Kay found that two of Lily and Andy's siblings are functioning intellectually well below their chronological ages. She was distressed by this, concerned about what it might mean in terms of Lily and Andy's development and is wondering about the impact on them if they meet these other half-siblings. She felt at one stage that this information was more than she needed, but realises the benefits of being able to sympathetically prepare her children for a meeting that, without preparation, might confuse and upset them. Kay and Tim feel very strongly that children who are adopted have the right to know who their relatives are, even if direct or frequent contact is not appropriate. They are comfortable with the amount of control they have over contact arrangements, and visits to and from the children's half-brother are very much in line with visits to their own relatives and close friends.

Adoptive parents taking the initiative

It seems that adoptive parents are often braver than social workers give them credit for. I've talked to several who have initiated approaches to members of their children's birth families, sometimes against the advice of social workers (although where agencies have been reluctant to help, some individual social workers have been supportive, often actively so in locating birth family members). Where children are placed in the same general locality as their birth families live, adoptive families, through local knowledge, chance remarks and coincidental encounters, often have very much more than the "official" information given to them.

Joe and **Martin** met their birth mother when they were seven and five-and-a-half years old, having been in their adoptive family since infancy, with only occasional letterbox contact between their adoptive parents and their birth mother. It was Joe's yearning for more than occasional bits of information and his sadness at not knowing his birth mother that led Stuart and Beth to approach the Social Services whose letterbox facility they were using. After discussion, the choice of face-to-face meetings was offered to the boys' birth mother. Marialena had by then returned to her native European country, but her positive response to the chance of seeing her children again led to Beth flying out to meet up with Marialena and then to the family travelling out to spend an emotionally-fraught but happy few days with her, also meeting her new daughter, her parents, and other relatives. There was a similar visit the following summer, and then again two years later, when it was obvious that Marialena's mental health problems were returning; the little half-sister and another born the previous year were both in foster care. Stuart says that, although it was a difficult and disappointing time, seeing Marialena's vulnerability helped the boys to understand why they had been removed from her care as tiny babies. Through Marialena, the boys also later met their birth fathers, both African-Caribbean and both living in London, although contact has continued with only one of them. The boys, now in their late teens, manage the contact themselves. Joe continues to see his birth mother, in her native country, every now and then – staying usually with relatives of hers: he has learned to speak her language. His contact with his birth father in London continues – 'occasional, casual, friendly'. Martin makes plans to see his mother but these have not yet materialised. Both are busy with the normal concerns and preoccupations of adolescence, and Stuart does not feel that contact is currently very high on their agenda. When Marialena phones the family's home now, the boys are often out, and it is Stuart and Beth to whom she talks.

Jackie took the initiative in enabling her youngest son, **Tony**, to meet his birth mother, Ellen. The decision to do this came after all assistance for Tony had failed to help his severe attachment problems. Although Jackie had been writing regularly to Ellen through a letterbox, and had met her twice prior to Tony's adoption, it took two years, and a refusal from the agency, before Jackie managed to find Tony's original social worker, who agreed to visit Ellen. Tony was then 12 years old and had not seen his mother since he was two. Jackie says that Ellen was 'fantastic'. She dealt sympathetically and sensitively with Tony, explaining why her own mental illness had meant she had been unable to raise him herself. Tony's behaviour improved tremendously after this meeting: he seemed able to look forward and Jackie felt he had stopped blaming himself for his mother's illness. He spent more time with Ellen and met other members of his birth family, becoming more certain of his identity. Jackie says that Ellen has become 'very much part of our family' and they talk frequently on the phone. Sadly, at this moment, Tony has dropped out of touch with both his families. Both mothers are anxious about him.

When **Yvonne's** daughter **Kathryn** expressed sadness at not being with her birth mother, and fear that her birth mother would forget what she looked like, Yvonne took the initiative in sending photographs of Kathryn and her brother to the placing agency and asking for these to be forwarded to the birth mother. The children had been placed with no contact at all and the agency still felt this was in the children's best interests, although they did agree to forward the photographs. Yvonne felt that Kathryn would appreciate having more than this, and has asked the agency to request a reciprocal photograph from the children's birth mother. If her response to this is positive, then Yvonne may suggest setting up letterbox contact. Since then, however, Kathryn has been a lot more settled, and less rejecting of her adoptive family. Her mother feels that sending the photographs, talking and listening to Kathryn's concerns, and reassuring her that they would help her find her birth family when she is older has laid many of her anxieties to rest.

The role of foster carers

Several adopters spoke positively of the role that foster carers had played, both in providing valuable information about their children's early lives, taking photographs of the children and of their birth parents, beginning life story books for them and being willing to remain in contact for as long as this was needed.

One foster carer said that she regards herself as a bridge between the birth and adoptive families. She is godmother to several of the babies she fostered pre-adoption, is in contact with about half of the others and aims to 'send every child on its way with as much information as possible'. Recently, she was dismayed when an adoptive family accepted the life story book but said, 'We won't be needing this. Our daughter's life starts from the moment she's placed with us.'

An adoptive family, whose children's foster mother had wanted to adopt them herself, found the contact with her very difficult. There was no contact for several months after placement, and it was resumed only after the foster carer had let the social worker know she was "ready" to see the children again. The adopters did not feel the visits were helpful to the children, because of the still very evident emotional distress displayed by the foster carer. The adoptive mother commented, 'It's good for the children to know that the person who looked after them loved them, but it was really unsettling for them to have someone crying all over them.'

The role of the social worker

In all contact arrangements, at least two different, and possibly incompat-ible, family systems have to meet. It is a situation that some adoptive parents have likened to 'meeting up with the in-laws'. For some, it is a pleasurable experience, for others a tolerable one and, for a few, a stressful one to be endured rather than enjoyed. When families need help in managing contact, most will turn to their social workers for support and advice. Below are some of the comments received from adoptive parents:

- The role and the authority of the social worker become contentious when there is a conflict between what the social worker and the adoptive parent feels the child needs.
- Social workers don't have to deal with the repercussions of contact visits, which can sometimes spark off some very challenging behaviour in children.
- The agency's attitude to contact was good, but the individual social worker failed to make proper arrangements at the time of placement. We had to do most of it ourselves.
- Social workers should be aware of how much life and circumstances change – both in the adoptive and birth families.
- Contact was a fait accompli. We were told what the arrangements were, and we just went along with it.
- We wanted to set up a separate letterbox with some other birth relatives, but the agency wouldn't do this.
- Bits of anecdotal information are often the most interesting and useful.
- Social workers change so often that there's no one left now who knows the history of our adoption.
- Just as my daughter was ready for more contact, our social worker went off sick!
- Social workers once forwarded me a letter from the birth mother with her address on a post-it note. They said this was a mistake, and apologised, but I was really worried that they might do this the other way round and send the birth mother our address.
- We got good advice from the social worker to think in advance about what questions we wanted to ask before our meeting [with the birth parents]. She also warned us not to lose sight of why the children had to be adopted.
- One area that often gets forgotten by the professionals is the feelings of other children in the family who may not have contact with their birth families. This can cause major problems and social workers need to take this on board.
- When our children were placed, social workers were adamant that contact was not in the children's best interests. I never really found out why.

From a foster carer:

- Some social workers don't do their bit about taking photos of birth mothers at early access visits, don't collect information. Once a child is placed, birth mothers may drift away and the chance is lost.

And finally, from an adult adopted person:

- When I was going to meet my birth mother, the social worker talked to me about how it would be meeting a total stranger, even though she had given birth to me. This was very helpful.

If it were possible to briefly sum up the above, it would be to say that the service received is patchy. Contact is an important part of post-adoption work, and it frequently does not appear to be given the resources needed to run it efficiently and flexibly. There seems to be little indication that it is regarded as specialist work, or that there are systems in place to deal with the variety of requests that come in. Often the outcome appears to depend on the goodwill, or the expertise, of an individual social worker, who may even have to work outside the agency's official policy. When adoptive parents speak most positively and gratefully of the service they have received from social workers, it is usually when they have been treated with respect, their concerns about their children listened to, and their knowledge of their children's needs recognised.

Conclusion

One of the most striking things emerging from these conversations has been the uniqueness and individuality of adopted children and their families. There have been almost as many viewpoints and as many experiences as there have been individuals. It is hard to see how one model of contact could fit all. Arrangements need to be tailor-made, and flexible enough to take account of the changing needs and changing circumstances of the people involved, and regular reviews of contact arrangements should be built into post-adoption services.

Social workers cannot help going on sick leave, or changing jobs, or retiring, but their specific knowledge should not be allowed to disappear with them, leaving no one else able to take up a child or family's concerns.

To facilitate this, there need to be efficient systems for collecting, recording and accessing information. Workers with mediation and counselling skills also can offer useful advice and support if there are conflicts or difficulties between the birth and adoptive families, or if the children need help in dealing with any of the issues that contact may raise for them.

Several parents have spoken of the difficulties that one child's contact may have for other children in the family, even when all the children are biologically related, and this is something that should always be anticipated and prepared for, with support available for all the children. Birth children (and other members) of adoptive families also sometimes need help to understand that the contact a new family member has with their birth relatives does not make them any less a "real" brother, sister, nephew, niece or grandchild. Managing contact for your adopted child can mean managing a whole range of emotions in other family members.

Sometimes birth parents have allowed their own needs to take priority over their children's. One birth father was reported as frequently asking to borrow money from the adopters; three other families found that birth parents regularly talked about their own personal concerns to the adoptive parents, often to the detriment of their involvement with the children. Perhaps these parents were not able to get the emotional support they needed from anywhere else. In letterbox contact, letters were occasionally received from birth parents that contained information inappropriate to share with young children, or were so gloomy, angry or full of pain that the adopters were reluctant to let their children see them. Some were written in ways that indicated literacy problems (more prevalent in this country than many people may suppose). This suggests that more support, advice and practical strategies (perhaps audio tapes instead of letters?) may be needed to help birth parents manage contact arrangements.

Workshops on contact might also be a useful part of pre- or post-adoption training for adoptive parents. Letter-writing is not necessarily a modern-day skill. A number of adopters experienced difficulty in knowing, for instance, how to make letters meaningful without giving away too much information. One was told to 'keep it simple' because of the birth mother's learning difficulties, but would have liked advice on how to do this without sounding patronising. Moreover, writing to and meeting your child's "other parents" may unleash some unexpectedly disturbing and powerful emotions, or bring up some unanticipated practical problems. Workshops could help anticipate and prepare for some of these.

Children are quite often placed with contact arrangements already agreed. It is hard for prospective adopters with newly placed children to know whether these arrangements are going to be either appropriate or practicable since they do not, at that stage, even know their children very well. Perhaps it should be common practice, as part of the preparation for court, say, for agencies to invite prospective adopters to re-negotiate the original contact arrangements. By this time, they will have got to know their children's needs, thought about how they can best fulfil them and identified any potential difficulties. They will then be in a position to make an informed and positive contribution to managing contact.

Contact is a minefield of emotions and, in our 12 years' experience, changes and shifts all the time. What you have to remember is that you are not doing it for yourselves or for the birth family, but for your children – for their future, for their needs, and to make their passage to adulthood easier. (Jo, adoptive mother)

8 Contact in placements which match children's "race", religion and culture

Pauline Hoggan, Aminah Husain Sumpton
and *Wendy Ellis*

The Independent Adoption Service (IAS) was founded in 1965 as the Agnostics Society, a non-religious based agency, and has since placed around 1,400 children, mostly from local authority care.

In its early years, the agency placed babies from black and mixed heritage backgrounds with white adopters, a practice perceived at the time as being forward-looking. IAS critically reviewed its approach in the late 1970s, influenced by seeing the strengths of the London multiracial community in which we are geographically based and by taking heed of the views of social workers concerned about the overall needs of black children. From the early 1980s, a policy of achieving "same-race" placements has been followed. For many years the staff group, adoption panel and management committee have been multiracial.

Now, in 2002, we find that a considerable proportion of our adopters (approximately 50 per cent each year) can meet the needs of mixed heritage children in particular.

> ## Ethnic origins of the families approved 1999/2000
>
> 5 couples (White)
> 5 couples (African-Caribbean/White)
> 2 couples (Asian/White)
> 1 couple (Asian)
> 1 couple (Chinese/White)
> 1 single adopter (White)

"Race" is placed within inverted commas to stress that categorisation of people into different "races" is a social definition and one which has been used to determine hierarchies which have disadvantaged black people. It is not a biological definition as there is only one race – the human race.

Ethnic origins of the families approved 2000/01

6 couples (White/African-Caribbean)
4 couples (White)
2 couples (White/Maltese)
2 single applicants (White)
1 couple (White/Asian)
1 couple (Asian)

We recruit a high proportion of couples in mixed ethnicity partnerships and single adopters. As the demographic profile of London continues to change, we are finding that our applicants are coming from an ever-widening range of ethnic and cultural backgrounds including, more recently, from mainland European and African countries.

Since the policy of "same-race" placements has been introduced, another major shift in practice has been the degree of initial and continuing contact between birth relatives and the adoptive family, whether through letterbox exchanges or face-to-face meetings. We thought it would be useful to assess whether the adopters' ethnicity, culture or religion appear to be significant factors in their capacity to accept or manage contact arrangements well.

When more open adoptions began to be introduced in the UK during the 1980s, there was a perception that 'black and Asian, Hispanic and Native American families are far more familiar than white communities with the idea of contact' (Dutt and Sanyal, 1991, referred to in Triseliotis, Shireman and Hundleby, 1997).

Some years on, by observing situations in which we are involved, we can see no evidence that ethnicity itself leads to a significant difference in ability to sustain contact or in atittude towards contact. However, the fact that children are placed in adoptive families from their own "race", religion and culture is significant in reducing potential tensions and in clarifying the focus of the contact.

It is invaluable, for the identity and self-esteem of a child of mixed heritage, to be raised by parents who are confident and positive about their own mixed heritage partnership. It can also be reassuring for black and white birth parents of mixed heritage children to know that their child is being raised in this context.

McRoy (1991) comments [in the USA context] on the value of contact in transracial adoptions as a method of encouraging a child to acknowledge and learn about their ethnic background; in IAS placements which reflect the child's background, these aspects are promoted and reinforced by the adoptive family. When it comes to facilitating ongoing contact for the benefit of the child, it seems from our experience that both black and white adopters are equally able to do so if this is an expectation from the start of their preparation to adopt and where guidance and support are available.

Practical issues identified by IAS staff for adopters in managing contact include:

- coping with anxieties about initial and subsequent meetings with birth relatives and skills in managing these;
- understanding and appreciating the benefits for the child's welfare of keeping in touch;
- addressing practical and emotional difficulties in sustaining contact arrangements;
- dealing with inappropriate content in written information and lack of feedback from birth parents.

Meetings with birth relatives

The IAS preparation workshops for prospective adopters contain material on the benefits of ongoing contact for an adopted child; there is a role play exercise on meeting birth relatives.

Most prospective adopters are willing to have at least one meeting with significant birth family members, but understandably feel very anxious about it. Such meetings are usually held in an office or family centre and attended by a local authority worker who comes with the birth family, and by the adoption agency worker, whose role is to guide and support the adopters. Both the birth relatives and the adopters are prepared in advance for the kind of topics they can usefully discuss. Adopters are encouraged to make a note of questions about the child's early life they would like to ask the birth parents.

The adopters' reactions are positive following these meetings. As well as obtaining useful information and becoming aware that they can describe the birth relatives and their discussion directly to the child in the years to come, most also say that it is important in helping them to perceive the birth relatives as people, rather than just as subjects of a report, often negatively described.

For one adoptive couple in a black and white partnership, this was an especially moving aspect, as the young black birth father they met was experiencing many difficulties in his life. He was particularly concerned that the family who would bring up his child should understand that many of his problems had been caused by him being rejected as a teenager, and he expressed strong feelings that this family should not do the same to his child if he became troublesome. The adopters appreciated his honesty.

Understanding the benefits of contact for the child's welfare

A recent IAS workshop for adopters – "Explaining Adoption to your Child" – was attended by adopters with children in placement from six different families, and was a multiracial group. When asked to identify some of the positive aspects of contact, four of the families talked about the emotional advantages for the children, who have the opportunity to develop, or maintain, relationships with siblings living separately from them. The adopter of the child of a young birth mother commented on the positive aspects of meeting the birth mother and feeling privileged that she had entrusted her daughter's upbringing to them after having heard about them and met them. The plan now is to have ongoing letterbox contact.

One of the sibling contact arrangements referred to included five brothers and sisters, placed in three separate families in different parts of the country, but with all the carers feeling a genuine motivation to keep the children in direct contact. At present, we are aware of at least four other similar arrangements involving large numbers of siblings and sometimes other relatives such as grandmothers. There are considerable implications for supporting adopters in managing arrangements which are very complicated. For instance, will contact take place during school holidays or at times of religious festivals which are of significance? What kind of venues will suit all the children? It is helpful if one of the key social workers can arrange and facilitate an initial meeting of the adults involved and assist them in setting the ground rules about how they will communicate with each other from then on.

These arrangements involve black and white families, and one includes one white half-sibling placed with white adopters meeting up with his mixed heritage half-brother and adopters. There is no evidence of any group being more or less committed than another. They all have to address similar emotional and practical difficulties in sustaining contact arrangements.

Written information

Often in the past, adopters have been left without sufficient monitoring or guidance in dealing with ongoing issues in letterbox arrangements. This situation has improved, with most local authorities now having a designated point of service for these arrangements either provided directly in the Social Services Department or delegated to agencies like IAS. Almost all new adopters want help in setting up the arrangement, both with having some ground rules established and in being given practical help with the content and tone of the first few letters. We also always advise that there be an intermediary who looks at the correspondence, from both adopters and birth relatives, before it is sent on. This is not to censor communication, except where some kind of deliberate harm may be intended, but more commonly so that inappropriate material can be discussed with the party concerned and suggestions for a different approach made. In cases where one of the parties is regularly contributing without receiving a response, a professional can also assist in obtaining feedback.

One IAS family, who is sending regular updates to a birth mother, found that it meant a great deal to them to hear that she valued receiving these reports. The adoptive parents, who are an Asian/White couple and who reflect their adopted son's heritage, write:

At the time of D's adoption we agreed to have indirect contact in the form of a yearly letter and photographs.

An annual letter is clearly the minimum amount of contact; nevertheless, it still felt like quite a commitment at the time, especially as D was such a small baby when placed with us. However, as we have written each year we have actually found the process something very special and meaningful in our growing lives as an adoptive family.

Each year we write a newsy type account of major events that have happened to D such as holidays, starting nursery, learning to swim and ride a bike. We also try to describe his developing personality, likes and dislikes. We save significant photographs during the year to send with the letter. We have kept a copy of all the letters for D to have when he is older.

The contact creates a link to D's birth mother (J), that helps to fill in the blank space between her giving him up for adoption and the time in the future when he may or may not wish to meet her. As he becomes more aware of his background and what adoption means, he will understand that we did not sever the links with his past, but hopefully helped to maintain them for his birth family so that he is not a "stranger" to them should he want contact. We have the same wish to provide this for our new daughter [our second adopted child] and we are setting up a similar system for her.

We heard recently that J had said how pleased she is to receive the yearly letter and photographs. Up until this point I was always of the impression that, although important, the letters could only upset J and cause regret and suffering, and of course I am sure that to a certain extent they do. But it was revealing to hear that J also values them greatly and that she feels very proud when she reads about D and how well he is doing. She said she loves to hear about his holidays and all the activities that he gets up to. We also heard that she likes to see the photographs and even has some up on her wall. The most heartening comment was that, when she reads the letters, J feels that they confirm for her that she did make the best decision both for herself and her son. Of course J's reactions and feelings are unique to her and we are already aware that our second child's situation may be somewhat different. However, in D's particular case it was very important and moving for us to know how the letters are received.

I must admit that before this we felt as if we were writing into a vacuum and certainly couldn't tell if we were getting it right or not. We have also said all along that it would be good to have some information coming our way as well, so that we can answer questions D will inevitably ask as he gets older. However, we realise that such an exchange of information is a very emotional issue and whether it can be established depends on individual circumstances. For now, we can be secure in the knowledge that the feedback we did receive shows that the contact is very valuable both for J and for us; it will prove valuable in the long term for D himself.

We are increasingly placing children whose birth and adoptive families may have relatives who are based not only in different countries but in different continents and it is essential to maintain or set up links with family members outside the UK. Nowadays, it is often straightforward for these connections to be maintained through modern systems of communication, and it is important not to minimise the significance of people who live far away.

We recently placed two young mixed heritage children with adopters who reflect their heritage. The children have had difficulty in accepting their black identity because their birth family members encouraged them to value their white heritage only. There can no longer be contact with birth parents, but in addressing the children's cultural needs, the adopters are finding it invaluable that they have extensive life story material, including photographs of black and white members of the extended family and material such as maps and historical information on their country of birth. Another positive development is that the children have a young adult birth relative who lives in another continent and wishes to build an ongoing relationship with them via the adoptive parents; this will be conducted mainly by e-mail, letters, photos and telephone contact.

The IAS summer party

For many years now, IAS has held an annual Summer Party for adopters and their children in a local park. Originally, this was intended to provide an informal point of contact and support for the adopters to keep in touch with the agency and each other. However, the purpose has widened to also offer a significant opportunity for contact with birth relatives.

As there are organised activities, such as train rides, rounders and face painting, it means that the adults and children can spend time together and apart, while in a safe setting, with professional support available. Food from different countries and music are provided. This event is now attended by over 150 people and the impact of the families grouped together conveys a strong positive message about modern open adoption. As one young person, aged 12, commented, 'They are just like everyday families'.

Conclusion

The conclusion we draw from our experience is that it is indeed essential to treat the child's individual needs and welfare as paramount. In planning for adoption, there must be detailed knowledge and understanding of the child's ethnicity and religion to plan their future effectively. If these matters are the true focus of assessment and placement policy, then issues such as the need for ongoing contact in adoptions which reflect and promote a child's heritage, are most likely to be met with openness and understanding in a natural way.

References

McRoy, R G (1991) 'American experience and research on openness', *Adoption & Fostering*, 15:4.

Triseliotis, J, Shireman, J F and Hundleby, M (1997) *Adoption: Theory, policy and practice*, London: Cassell.

9 Managing contact arrangements for children with learning difficulties

Catherine Macaskill

This chapter considers a number of important issues in relation to managing contact arrangements for children with severe learning difficulties. It focuses principally on the issue of face-to-face contact. The information is based on the views of 15 experienced adopters and foster carers who have provided permanence for 18 children with very special needs. All the families whose views are represented in this chapter have had firsthand experience of face-to-face contact with one or both birth parents. The perceptions of such families are therefore uniquely credible because they are able to comment on the reality rather than the abstract concept of contact.

All the children were three years and upwards at the time of placement and a number of disabilities are represented. One boy and one girl have Down's syndrome. Other conditions include hydrocephalus, microcephalus, cerebral palsy and haemoplaegia. A few children are described as brain damaged but do not have a specific label attached to their condition. With two exceptions all the children are wheelchair bound, unable to use recognisable language and totally dependent on their foster carers or adopters. One child who was healthy when born suffered non-accidental injury at eight weeks and is now blind, epileptic and unable to walk or speak. Another suffered a cerebral haemorrhage after an angry parent lost control. At four years this child has very limited sight, poor co-ordination of his limbs, no recognisable language, and needs to be fed intravenously. He has already surpassed the medical prognosis about his life expectancy but his dedicated foster carers live daily with concerns about his fragility.

The danger of underestimating the importance of contact for children with severe learning difficulties

It is easy to ignore the idea of arranging contact for a child with severe learning difficulties especially when children are unable to use language to express their views and feelings. The following quotation from an experienced adopter is enormously relevant for children who are unable to articulate their wishes and feelings:

Listening carefully to behaviour. It may be the only language that the child can ever use.

Julian is now in his early 20s and is wheelchair bound. His language is limited to a few repetitive words. He transferred from residential care to his adopters when he was 11, at a time when professionals were less likely to consider contact as a viable option for adopted children. Although he had been seeing his birth mother and grandmother twice-weekly when he was in residential care, professionals considered that Julian would not notice if his birth family quietly disappeared from his life when he joined his adoptive family. Julian's tears and words tell a different story as his adopters relate their real experience:

He missed his birth relatives and wanted to see them. That was clear despite his disability. He was asking for them all the time in the only way he could. He was crying every day. 'Car-go-see nanny.' He remembers people's cars. We had a car so he could not understand why we could not take him to see his granny. He cried for over a year. He went through a real bereavement.

It took Julian's adopters a long time to persuade professionals that contact was relevant. At his first contact meeting with his birth mother and grandmother, his facial expression lit up the room. He conveyed clearly that he recognised them and that this was a significant moment for him.

Kathyrn was three years when she joined her adoptive family in 1997. Her adopter complains that social workers did not think that contact was worth discussing for a child with Kathyrn's special needs. Her disability has no label but her difficulties are enormous. She is now eight and totally dependent. She always seems to listen carefully from her wheelchair when others are speaking but it is virtually impossible to know what is happening in her world because she has no words. Her birth parents now visit her about three times annually. Kathyrn's adopter has no doubt that these visits are highly significant. She witnesses Kathyrn going through different stages of grief following each visit from her birth parents.

Kathyrn adores seeing her birth parents. Afterwards she gets very upset. It's very painful for her. When the birth parents come she cuts me out completely. She won't look at me. She refuses to eat. For days after it she's very withdrawn and upset.

It was often very upsetting for this adopter to witness Kathryn exhibiting such distress after each contact meeting. Like other carers of disabled children, her intuitive reaction was to want to protect her vulnerable child from anything painful. She admitted that it would have been very easy for her to block out any consideration of Kathryn's evident need for contact and to argue that she should be sheltered from additional stress because she was already carrying an excessive burden due to her disability.

Although all children with special needs may not be able to respond to their birth relatives in such a poignant manner as Julian and Kathryn, they are a reminder to professionals of how vital it is to "listen" to the deep needs of disabled children. They also demonstrate how important it is for children with special needs to be allowed to express grief in their own unique way for the loss of significant birth family members.

Dilemmas in relation to planning and preparation of children with special needs

Preparation of the child for contact is vital. **Suzy** is 15 and has Down's syndrome. A quotation from her adoptive mother illustrates one dilemma that has immediate implications for preparation.

She's a timeless creature so you can't prepare her in advance.

It is unlikely that any type of preparation for a child with learning difficulties can be undertaken over a prolonged period or far in advance of the event. Julian's adopters told him a few hours before his birth grandmother arrived. Kathyrn's adoptive mother told her what was happening as her birth parents were walking up the drive towards the front door. She explained:

Because we know Kathyrn so well we don't tell her anything in advance about contact. She doesn't sleep or eat if we do. We have a news black out in this family. Everyone is sworn to secrecy. Otherwise everyone would hear her ear piercing shrieks.

Karl (4) had only been one month in placement when his birth parents came to visit him. His adopters knew that he had difficulty distinguishing terms used for different family members like "mum", "dad", "granny", "grandpa".

He thought everyone was his cousin.

They therefore felt that it would be a meaningless exercise to prepare him for his birth parents' visit. When his birth parents saw him they were overwhelmed with emotion. Tears flowed. Karl stared quizzically at them as they wept. Later that night after they had left, Karl screamed and screamed for several hours. Nothing could console him. With his limited repertoire of language he was eventually able to demonstrate to his adopters that he was terrified that his birth parents were planning to steal him. His adopter role-played the scenario with him:

Mummy Rosemary comes to say 'Hi', to stay a little while, and then say 'Bye, bye Karl'.

Acting out the real situation over and over again helped Karl to grasp what was happening. Karl's level of sensitivity towards his birth parent's visit had been grossly underestimated by everyone who had been close to him.

Anne's adoptive mother described another dilemma associated with explaining adoption to her. She feared that introducing the concept of "two mums" would be bewildering and perhaps distressing for her:

Mummy is a very special word to Anne [15] but she'd be very confused if she found that she had a second mummy.

David is now 17 and has Down's syndrome. He has never seen his birth parents. His adopters have had many years' experience of adoption but they are unsure how they should address issues associated with David's birth family with him. His adoptive family has adopted other children who are not disabled. They have been sensitive to their adopted children's individual needs and have always believed that they should wait for each child to ask questions. David has been much slower than their other children to grasp what adoption means. Now they wonder if they should break their own resolve and initiate a conversation with David about tracing rather than waiting for him to raise the topic.

It was only two years ago that it dawned on David that he was adopted. He went around telling everyone. Everybody in the local supermarket knew. He's not got any contact with his birth parents. Should I initiate the thing or leave it to him? With a disabled child it has to be tangible before they can understand.

Whose needs are being met through contact?

In some contact situations children with special needs may be totally unable to identify their birth relatives. Is it appropriate for contact meetings to occur in such circumstances where it is obvious that only the adults can benefit? It is always important to remember that the central focus of any contact plan should be the child. Of course it may be possible for the child to benefit indirectly rather than directly. It could be argued that, if the adults are able to develop a harmonious relationship, the happiness of the adults will automatically have a positive impact on the child.

One adopter was able to develop such a positive partnership with a birth mother that they were able to research and plan together for her son's adulthood. An eight-year-old girl with cerebral palsy enjoyed being the centre of attention for a day at her birth mother's wedding when she took on the role of flower girl in her wheelchair. Another birth mother was able to undertake a fundraising venture for special physiotherapy equipment. In a very sad case the birth parents and adoptive parents shared their eight-year-old child's dying hours and were able to arrange his funeral together. In each of these situations, strong partnerships between both sets of parents had positive ramifications for disabled children even though their limited intellectual ability prevented them from recognising their birth parents.

Indirect contact through letters, telephone calls, e-mail, regular progress reports and updated photographs or videos can also be very meaningful for the adults even if the disabled child is unable to fully participate in these forms of communication.

Tensions and difficulties

- *The emotional element*

A contact relationship between any birth parent and adoptive parent has the potential to be difficult but there are some additional complexities underpinning adult relationships when contact concerns a disabled child. The trauma for any parent associated with giving birth to a disabled child is universally acknowledged. Stages of grief such as shock, denial, anger, guilt, and sadness need to be worked through. Unresolved feelings may remain for parents who have not only had to cope with a birth trauma but have also had to face the double tragedy of having to relinquish their child. Face-to-face contact with their disabled child may re-awaken some of these complex negative feelings. In contrast, adopters who do not carry any of the original feelings associated with the birth may embark on the task of caring for their "chosen" child with excitement, enthusiasm and even exuberance. One mother alluded to the birth of her disabled child as 'shattering' and causing her 'world to fall apart', while the adoptive mother described the arrival of the same child in her family as 'exhilarating' and 'one of the most special moments' of her life. When such contrasting feelings are evident to birth parents it is not surprising that they simply intensify their own feelings of woeful inadequacy. One adopter summed up the birth mother's feelings in the following way:

> It's like putting a dagger in an open wound for the birth mother and she's upset for days afterwards.

Sustaining an effective long-term partnership between the birth family and the adoptive family also presents a challenge. As the years elapse and the task of caring for a disabled child begins to take its toll on adopters, different feelings may emerge for them. As their bond with their disabled child deepens, it is possible for them to go through the same type of grief process as the birth parent faced at the time of the birth. Feelings of shock, denial, anger and disappointment may emerge as they observe their special child struggling to cope with life. These negative sentiments may be compounded by a sense of physical fatigue associated with the daily task of caring for a very dependent disabled child. One adopter, talking three years after placement, described the pain of watching her teenager cope with the pressure of being confined to a wheelchair.

At times I feel when I'm watching her as if the pain is going to devour me. I want to run away from it. I think she can't walk and she can't talk and she's going to be like this for the rest of her life. It just consumes me.

The fact that these phases of grief are occurring at different stages for both sets of parents creates the potential for unexpected stresses and conflicts to emerge between adults during contact meetings. Thorough preparation and sensitive management for all parties is essential if each person is going to understand what such a complex conglomeration of feelings means for themselves and for the other parties involved.

When there is a question mark surrounding the birth parent's responsibility for causing their child's disability, the carer's strength of feeling towards the birth parents can at times be quite overwhelming. **Colin** is now four years old. He has major medical problems following physical abuse by his parents. His dedicated foster carers take him three times every week to his local hospital. As they have watched him undergo painful medical procedures, they have felt his pain as acutely as if it was their own. This is how they describe meeting Colin's birth parents:

When we meet the parents it's hard to be polite. As you're trying to be civil to them your emotions are going full blast and you feel like exploding. We couldn't talk to them without thinking of Colin screaming and screaming and screaming in the hospital ward. It's hard to be forgiving when you see what they've done.

Another adoptive couple talked about how this issue affected them as they struggled to compose an annual letter that they had excitedly agreed to provide for the birth parents at the time their child was placed with them.

> *It takes us several months to put our annual newsletter together. We find it so difficult and each year it seems to get harder. I can't tell you how often we write it and then tear it up. We write general things but it just seems too bland. Then we add in some personal details and we feel uncomfortable because we're telling them too many private things. Then all the old angry feelings surface again and I start asking myself 'What right do they have to know anything anyway especially after the way they treated her?*

It is not just birth parents who are affected by contact. It is important to remember the impact on other children in the birth family who have to come to terms with the loss of a sibling. Some brothers and sisters who participated in the study, and who attended contact meetings, could become very distressed and unsettled through the experience of contact. Some struggled to understand why their special sibling could not return home. One older sister required specialist counselling because of her grief at the loss of her disabled brother.

Some adopters spoke with disappointment about the obvious lack of preparation available to birth families. Some felt that if social workers had been able to provide birth parents with adequate preparation about the unexpected feelings that might be engendered for them, then the entire experience of contact would have been more constructive for everyone.

- *Different stages of acceptance of the child's disability*

Contact brought birth parents face to face with the stark reality of their child's level of disability. There were times when it was difficult to believe that the adopters and birth parents were talking about the same child.

> *The birth parents came with us to the school to see **Mark** (15) in the school play. He was great in the play. For me it was so beautiful to see. From a disability point of view the birth parents just couldn't see it. His birth father seemed quite numbed by the experience. He just kept saying 'What made Mark turn out like that?'*

- *Birth parents' perceptions about the child's stage of development*

Some birth parents related to their children as if their child was still functioning at a much younger level. It seemed as if their view of the child had become "frozen" at the point in time when they had relinquished the child. This was sometimes evident in the gifts that they brought or in their manner of talking to the child. One adopter complained:

> *Although **Leanne** is seven years they see her as a three-month-old baby.*

Other birth parents had simply managed to block out the full extent of their child's disability. Distance from their child made it possible to do so. While adopters lived every moment with the stark reality of the child's impairment, it was easier for birth parents to cherish the fantasy that perhaps there was nothing significantly wrong with their child. Face-to-face contact changed the birth parents' fantasy into a sad and abrupt reality.

- *Physical management of the child during contact meetings*

Physical handling of the child was often awkward for birth parents. They were out of step with their child's current needs and felt clumsy, and embarrassed. They needed preparation to enable them to feel competent when managing the physical demands of the child.

Frequency of contact

Careful thought needs to be given to the issue of how often contact should occur. Obviously the degree of contact needs to be negotiated with all parties so that it is manageable for everyone. Annual contact is not likely to be very meaningful for a child with learning difficulties as one adopter of a seven-year-old girl explained:

> *When it's too spread out she isn't able to understand who they are. She can't remember things as far back as a year.*

On the other hand, excessive levels of contact can be overwhelming for everyone. The following factors need to be considered when determining the frequency of contact:

- the purpose of contact;
- the child's age, stage of development and memory retention span in relation to significant people;
- the child's emotional resilience;
- the adopter's emotional need to claim the child;
- the birth relative's capacity to understand and respond appropriately to the child's real needs; and
- the emotional impact on everyone involved.

In a recent study I conducted (Macaskill, 2002) about contact and permanent placement, it emerged that when face-to-face contact was established at more than four times annually in adoption placements it usually had to be reduced because it was unsustainable for all the parties involved.

Identifying a suitable venue

When identifying a suitable venue it is important to ensure that an appropriate degree of confidentiality is ensured for the child. Using the adopter's home may seem to provide an immediate and comfortable solution for all parties but it is always important to assess the long-term implications of using this venue. In situations where the child has suffered abuse, it is important to examine the current and potential connections between the birth relative who is in contact with the child and previous abusers. Although these relationships may appear to be somewhat tenuous or have even been terminated at the time when the contact plan is being made, it is possible that they may be rekindled in the longer term and consequently place the child at risk. These issues are especially important for disabled children who need extra protection because of their powerlessness to defend themselves combined with an absence of language to disclose abuse.

Suitable neutral contact venues that provide physical comfort, privacy, and appropriate activities are essential. They are often a scarce resource for any child but the special requirements of a disabled child, such as wheelchair access, make them even more difficult to locate. It is advisable to make maximum use of facilities that are already equipped for disabled children such as specialist play centres and clubs.

The value of a written contact agreement

In the Social Services Inspectorate study, *Moving Goalposts* (Department of Health, 1995), about post-adoption contact involving 37 local authority social services departments and 14 voluntary adoption agencies in the north of England, the authors state that written contact agreements are invaluable and should become standard practice.

The existence of a written agreement helps to prevent confusion not only between the various parties to adoption but within the agency itself.

They also state:

The negotiating process required to establish an agreement is a necessary and helpful one, and can play a major role in reducing and removing conflict.

Clear boundaries surrounding a contact plan are important in order to make certain that the safety of the child is ensured. It is vital that everyone involved is clear about the who? what? when? and how? of any contact plan. In situations where children have serious medical difficulties, decisions need to be made about how birth parents will be informed about significant developments in the child's medical condition so that they are not faced with a massive deterioration in a child's health at a contact meeting without any prior warning.

The process of negotiating a contact agreement is one way of ensuring that the views of all parties are heard and of anticipating difficulties before they arise. Of course a contact plan cannot be static. Children's and adults' needs change; disabled children may make remarkable progress or become increasingly impaired. There is a need for some type of review system to be set in place so that the contact plan does not stagnate but continues in a dynamic and creative manner.

The essential nature of long-term support in managing contact arrangements

Who should manage contact plans in the longer term? Should there continue to be any professional involvement after an adoption order has been granted?

Some carers may feel strongly that they want to manage contact with the birth family independently. **Kevin** was seven when he was placed for adoption. He has no speech and is totally dependent on his single adoptive mother. She is unsure about how much he understands. She suspects that he senses that his birth mother is a special visitor. After seven years of face-to-face contact with Kevin's birth mother, the adoptive mother has strong views about informality having been a key factor in the long-term success of their contact relationship.

> *I liked the fact that we had the freedom to arrange it ourselves. It was completely flexible. We all get something out of it. If there had been a lot of organisation I don't think that it would have worked for us.*

In contrast, other carers explained how contact had floundered for them because of the intensity of the relationship that had developed with the birth family. They had learned through hard experience that the availability of an intermediary was essential to prevent a contact plan reaching an impasse.

> *There's an urgent need for support. Social workers need to grasp the fact that you can't have an open adoption and imagine that it'll grow without fertilizer. Long-term support must be built in.*

Each situation is unique. The availability of an open system of support needs to exist so that families can choose to draw on this support as appropriate. The following should be key components of any post-adoption service:

- Emotional support and consultation for all parties to enable them to understand the complex feelings associated with disability that are liable to have an adverse impact on contact.
- The availability of an intermediary to negotiate in difficult situations so that the best interests of a disabled child remain paramount.

- Ongoing information for all parties about certain medical conditions underpinning disability and opportunities for birth parents to receive updated information about the progress of their disabled child rather than encountering unexpected adverse changes during contact meetings.
- Simple methods of helping disabled children learn about their origins and their birth family.
- Opportunities for briefing and de-briefing before and after contact meetings are essential for all parties.
- A system of review to ensure that the contact plan is adapted to meet changing needs and that children's best interests always remain paramount

The way forward

When disabled children are placed in a permanent family, it is easy for professionals to ignore any discussion about contact, especially as such children are unlikely to be able to articulate their depth of feeling. However, it is always important to assess carefully whether contact with significant family members should be retained or introduced. Abrupt changes or a complete severance of previous contact relationships with birth relatives are likely to be especially detrimental to disabled children who will view the sudden disappearance of key adults from their lives as incomprehensible. Preparation for contact for the disabled child needs to be simple and tangible and occur close to the time of the contact event. An acknowledgement by professionals of the sensitive feelings that are likely to be aroused by contact for all parties will have an empowering effect. Exactly what degree of confidentiality is required must be ascertained so that the long-term safety of the child is ensured. This is especially important for children who may have suffered abuse within their birth family in the past and who remain vulnerable because they are unable to articulate their fears. The availability of continuing professional support and access to an intermediary, when difficulties occur, are essential in order to ensure that contact plans can be sustained on a long-term basis and thereby provide the disabled child with continuity and stability.

When these safeguards underpin contact plans, the needs of disabled children will be appropriately promoted. They will begin to benefit in a practical way from having the same rights to continuity as other children in their peer group.

References and further reading

Argent, H (1999) *Whatever Happened to Adam? Stories of disabled people who were adopted or fostered*, London: BAAF.

Fratter, J (1996) *Adoption with Contact: Implications for policy and practice*, London: BAAF.

Macaskill, C (2002) *Safe Contact? Children in permanent placement and contact with their birth relatives*, Lyme Regis: Russell House Publishing.

Quinton, D, Rushton, A, Dance, C and Mayes, D (1997) 'Contact between children placed away from home and their birth parents: research issues and evidence', *Clinical Child Psychology and Psychiatry*, London: Sage Publications.

Russell, P (1996) 'The importance of contact for children with disabilities', in Argent, H (ed.) *See You Soon: Contact with children looked after by local authorities*, London: BAAF.

Department of Health, Social Services Inspectorate (1995) *Moving Goalposts: A study of post adoption contact in the north of England*, London: Department of Health.

10 Does the legal framework facilitate contact?: A view from Scotland

Paula Bell

Introduction

The questions facing social workers and carers managing contact for children in long-term care in Scotland are how to achieve this within the unique provisions in our legal system. The paramount duty is to promote the welfare of the children throughout their childhood (Children (Scotland) Act 1995) or throughout their lives (section 6 – Adoption (Scotland) Act 1978, as amended). The Human Rights Act has added a further dimension by confirming the right to "family life".

Do we seek long-term fostering or adoption with contact? Is there the evidence for a Freeing Order? What does the Children's Panel think? Have they imposed an order with conditions? The answers may not all be compatible but good practice has to function within this framework.

The case of Catriona, which is discussed below, had elements of most of these aspects and contact became the crucial issue. But first, I outline the legal system in Scotland, the placement, the management of contact, and planning for the child. I then end by looking at the knowledge, skills and values involved in this example of good management of contact and the main features for consideration. I will argue that the Scottish courts could improve the outcomes for children in long-term care by removing the adversarial nature of the process.

Legal framework[1]

Who is a "child"?

Definitions of "child" in Scotland vary:

- For child protection it is under 16.
- For initial accommodation by a council it is under 17.

---

[1] This is the situation at the time of going to press.

- If a child is the subject of a Supervision Order at the age of 16, they can remain so until the age of 18.
- For marriage, adulthood begins at 16; for voting it begins at 18.
- An adoption order can be made beyond the age of 18 if a petition has been lodged before the young person is 18.
- From age 12 a child will be asked to give consent to their own adoption: in other matters the child over 12 is 'assumed to have a view' and the child under 12 may have views taken into account.
- In Scotland, young people have access to birth and social work records at 16, and an absolute right to see court records at 16.

The legislation

The principal legislation is the Children (Scotland) Act of 1995 which, for the first time, laid out parental responsibilities and rights including the responsibility, even if not living with one's child, to maintain contact.

The Act also specified the duties of local authorities towards children in their care to include the duty to maintain contact and it amended the Adoption (Scotland) Act of 1978 to specify the duty to consider the welfare of the child *throughout his/her life* in adoption decisions.

The place of contact in Scotland's permanency options

Each option for permanency, whether long-term "accommodation" or an exit from the care system, offers a framework for considering contact.

- *Freeing for adoption* – the local authority petitions the court.
  A Freeing Order in Scotland cannot include a contact order and any arrangement is therefore at the discretion of the local authority initially and eventually of the adopter(s). Occasionally children freed are not adopted, perhaps due to their age at the end of the process, and full parental responsibilities remain with the local authority if the case is not reheard at court after a year has elapsed. A parent may seek revocation, if their child is not adopted or placed after a year, unless they have indicated that they do not wish to be notified. The local authority may similarly seek revocation but the Sheriff then has to make an alternative Parental Responsibilities Order. One council has made application to revoke a Freeing Order, with a simultaneous application for parental responsibilities, with parental consent, which was successful.

Good practice would suggest that another way of securing a child's future would be to award parental responsibility to the carers; it could be reassigned to the local authority if necessary in the future.

- *Adoption Order* – the adopters petition the court.
  This order can include conditions on contact but these can be inflexible over time if arrangements are specified too closely.
- *Parental Responsibilities Orders* can be awarded to local authorities in respect of children, usually those accommodated by them. As with the Freeing Order, contact decisions will lie with them and would be monitored through the Looking After Children (LAC) reviews.
- Carers or "any party demonstrating an interest" can apply to court for a *Residence Order*. Contact may not be affected by residence conditions because it is assumed to be maintained.
- *Children's Hearing Supervision Orders* can be used for some children whose sense of belonging to their birth family is strong, and for whom "belonging" to another family is not appropriate. It works particularly well where a carer or residential unit offers stability and acceptance. It is also the way that many troubled young people have decisions made for them over a long period; for them the Children's Hearing will be the place to resolve contact issues.
- *Parental agreement*: some children remain in the care of local authorities for many years with parental co-operation and no other legal order. These children may have been older at the time they were accommodated, or considered to be "too difficult to place" due to extreme behaviours. Contact is then agreed and monitored through the LAC review system.

Financial support

For children in long-term care, the method of financial support for contact arrangements depends on the permanency framework:

- Fostering allowances are available for children remaining in foster care.
- Residence Order payments are also available from the local authority.
- Adoption allowances can be paid by local authorities under certain conditions, and must now be means tested. These are often paid if

contact arrangements are anticipated, either with siblings, parents or other family members.

The Children (Scotland) Act 1995 has a general "welfare" clause which allows councils to make payments to relatives or friends who are caring for children who have no other order. Some councils do not use this as it specifies that payment can only be made "in exceptional circumstances".

Children's Hearing system

Scotland is justifiably proud of the Children's Hearing system which allows parents, children, relevant professionals (and legal representatives if they wish) literally to sit around the table with three lay, but trained, members of the public and the Children's Reporter in order to discuss the best way forward for their family. This must be reviewed at least annually.

However, the Panel of people who sit at each Hearing invariably changes, and this can pose difficulties for children who are in the care of the local authority or under their supervision for lengthy periods. Some Reporters attempt, especially in long-term care cases, to gain consistency by rostering at least one of the Panel members from a previous Hearing.

Parents, children and workers could be reporting on progress to three different volunteers every six months or year. Each of these Panel members may have quite new views on how best to help and whose position should be supported. Several local authorities report their experience of a long-term situation where a "permanency plan" comes up for annual review and is put back, and in some cases reversed, by a Hearing where a parent (often one who is failing to turn up for contact) attends the Hearing and asks for another chance.

Since a European judgement in 1995 (McMichael v United Kingdom), cases are reheard from scratch each time as no previous papers are given to panel members. Parents, including estranged partners, receive copies of reports. Following a Scottish judgement in 2001(S v Miller), children should also now receive copies of reports. This creates real difficulty for some children with divided loyalties who wish to see one estranged parent without telling the other. Both judgements are problematic for families with "secrets", especially secrets about a child's parentage.

Decisions

The options open to each Children's Hearing are:

- to make no order;
- to make a Supervision Order at home;
- to make an order requiring a child to reside away from home;
- to add conditions to either of these orders.

  Conditions can be added to specify contact arrangements or entrusted to social workers by using the phrase "at social work(er)'s discretion". This phrase allows flexibility when circumstances change, for example, parental illness or violence, or child co-operation. If the Supervision Order specifies the arrangements, changes will need to be brought back to a further Hearing. It is possible for children to be excused attendance at their Hearing, but it is not encouraged: it should happen only when considerable anxiety or distress is anticipated.

- In addition, and frequently in the case of permanency decisions, they can appoint a Safeguarder. A Safeguarder is an independent person, often a lawyer or former social worker, who looks at the case afresh and from the point of view of the child's best interests.

The status of the child in long-term care with annual Children's Hearing reviews can be unsatisfactory from the point of view of trying to offer security. One child described it at her LAC review as 'I know I can stay here but the Hearing brings it all back up each time and I'm not sure if there will be a change'.

Case illustration

Catriona – care history

Catriona was 28 months when accommodated, her mother having had two other children removed due to her alcohol abuse. All three children had different fathers who were variously committed to visiting or supporting their own child.

The eldest child had been living with relatives for long periods and the baby was placed with paternal grandparents following neglect. As middle child, Catriona had stayed many of her days and weekends with her maternal grandparents who were interested in continuing to see her but were not offering long-term care. It was not clear how much of a bond Catriona had with her mother or whether she could be returned to her care, which the Children's Panel wished to be explored.

Placement

Fostering at first provided good consistent care and a chance to assess Catriona's development, which was good. The carers were active in assisting Catriona to remain at the Council Family Centre group where she and her mother had been known.

Contact

The Children's Hearing Supervision Order specified weekly contact which Catriona's mother maintained initially and then was less consistent. Catriona also had contact with her siblings fortnightly with the support of the Family Centre and it was hoped that her mother would find this venue less threatening than the carers' home. But her mother began to bring other relatives with her "for moral support" which confused Catriona. The family would also bring bags of sweets and appeared to be more comfortable sitting Catriona on their knees and feeding her while talking to each other, than spending time playing or communicating with her.

The workers in the Family Centre encouraged play and the social workers spoke to the family about the importance of observing Catriona with her mother. The contact changed but only for a month or so before returning to the same pattern.

Catriona's mother's alcohol problems persisted and she missed some of the Family Centre sessions. When she attended for contact, she often smelled heavily of alcohol, although she was never drunk when there. Catriona was now making good progress with the carers and outgrowing the Family Centre for her own needs.

It was agreed at a planning meeting to stop bringing Catriona to the Family Centre except for contact; when her mother continued to miss her visits, it was agreed not to bring Catriona until the Family Centre called the foster carers to let them know that her mother had arrived. The social worker and Family Centre staff dealt with the additional family members who still turned up by occupying them on the first visits and then asking them to stop coming along.

The same workers assessed Catriona's attachments by watching her reactions to her family, her interactions and responses to separation. The assessment concluded that her bond with her grandmother was more positive than that with her mother.

Plans

With the lack of progress on the mother–child relationship, her mother's poor history of parenting, continued alcohol problems and the lengthy imprisonment of Catriona's father, it was agreed at a Children's Hearing that permanent substitute care was required. In view of Catriona's age, the Adoption Panel advised that she should be adopted and because of her mother's opposition to this, it went back to a Children's Hearing formally for their advice. They confirmed the plan and reduced contact to once a month to include the grandmother.

Members of both sides of Catriona's family were approached but none wished to care for the child. Her mother was seen as the "failure" of the family, a woman known to be aggressive towards others; her father's family felt no connection or responsibility for her.

Child's views

Although pre-verbal, Catriona's behaviour and emotional state were observed to gauge her comfort with her birth family and her carers. Her physical progress in care and her development testified to her security and her soiling and wetting after contact visits demonstrated her upset.

Going to court

Catriona's extended family initially agreed that permanent plans should be made for her and to the proposal for adoption. Because her mother did not agree, a Freeing for Adoption application was made to the local court. The case was heard some eight months after lodging the application: it was postponed three times due to the mother's failure to instruct a solicitor, her failure to see the lawyer she instructed, and then the withdrawal of the lawyer on her non-appearance. The Sheriff finally granted the application when, with advice from another lawyer, she withdrew her opposition. He heard Catriona's mother's views, her submission that the facts as presented were true and that Catriona required care.

Three months prior to the final decision, Catriona's maternal grand-mother decided to ask the court for leave to enter proceedings based on her wish to maintain contact with her granddaughter. The court agreed to hear her case six months after the Freeing decision, again delaying place-ment planning.

When a further court delay was suggested, the chair of the Adoption Panel proposed that the lawyer for the grandmother and the Council's lawyer discuss what she was seeking, on the basis that Catriona's relation-ship with her grandmother was agreed by all as important. Catriona was now four years old, obviously attached to her maternal grandmother who had continued to maintain regular and positive contact at weekends and was not opposing placement plans. She objected to Freeing because her contact could not be guaranteed in the future (as the Scottish Freeing Order does not allow contact orders to be made and so she had no other recourse in law than to object to Freeing).

The lawyers quickly established that the Council would be looking for a family who would offer contact to the grandmother and maintain that relationship. She did not wish to stand in the way of Catriona's security and accepted that her contact would not be based on legal rights. It has not been common Scottish practice to recommend a Contact Order in an adoption after a Freeing Order which cannot have a contact condition attached to it. Also, it may be thought that by setting up a "once and for all" arrangement, the needs of the developing child would not be met. Or it may be that changes to the Scottish adoption law, at the same time as local government boundaries altered, have meant a thinner spread of adoption expertise and confidence for some councils.

The case was settled out of court and an adoptive family was found for Catriona just before she started school. Contact with her mother and siblings was terminated but contact with her grandmother has been maintained; due to distance it is not always face-to-face, but Catriona's mother and siblings also get news of her indirectly through the grandmother.

The adopters now manage all the contact arrangements and they receive an adoption allowance to assist with costs. The arrangements were made by the social worker in the beginning, using neutral venues like a local park or museum but then left to the families to manage themselves.

Knowledge, skills and values

Knowledge

The main requirement for the good management of contact between children and their parents must be knowledge of attachment theory and its practical application, as described by Fahlberg (1994).

Assessing the parent–child relationship will also draw on knowledge of child development, in order to interpret the meaning, value and purpose of contact for the child. Social workers, managers and carers, including carer link workers, need to share their understanding of the relevant tasks for the child's stage of development to help plan the best conditions for contact arrangements.

Knowledge of identity (Fahlberg, 1994), direct work (Jewett, 1984; Oaklander, 1988) and resilience theory (Wassell *et al*, 1999) will promote the best practice in providing continuity for the child and taking their views into account.

A good working knowledge of the legal provision is essential, not necessarily for the social worker or senior social worker but for those empowered to make recommendations and/or decisions for including contact arrangements in the permanency plan viz. the agency legal adviser, Adoption Panel Chair, agency decision maker and reviewing officers.

Skills

Communicating with children is a key skill in this area and not to be underestimated, especially when presenting evidence to court. The court is seeking to know what the child's understanding and views are, and how these were ascertained. Often, social workers have not been regarded as credible witnesses on this issue and independent expert advice has been sought. If I could make one plea, it would be to move away from the adversarial approach to making contact arrangements in court, by any necessary experts being called by the court to advise the court impartially.

Perhaps more emphasis in social work training on face-to-face work with children and the use of play, and more experience in practice, would lead to more confidence and competence in the witness box. Triseliotis (Foreword, Fratter, 1996) and more recently Lowe and Murch *et al* (1999) concur with Fratter that a child-centred, rather than a rigid approach is required for good contact arrangements in adoption.

Values

The espousal of values relating to identity is perhaps the most important – it covers the issues of heritage, culture, ethnicity, religion, language, parental history and health, as well as recognising where parental contributions can be made to the child's positive view of him or herself. Research reminds us that even the most damaged and difficult parent can provide the child with a sense of their history and a real understanding of the circumstances of their separation (Lowe and Murch *et al*, 1999).

Comment on what worked in this case

Working together

The co-operation of the adults offering and arranging care of the child: the Family Centre staff, foster carers, social worker, grandmother and mother, while not always agreeing with each other, were able to work together sufficiently well to ensure that contact was at the best pace, place, and time for Catriona.

Child's welfare paramount

Although Catriona's mother and grandmother were often in conflict with each other and in the beginning would only unite against "the system", they could set aside their hostility during contact.

Staff and extended family tried to maintain contact through the worst of Catriona's mother's circumstances, her aggression and failures to attend. Their shared belief that contact was useful to the child was perhaps never voiced but evident in all their work.

Working with the child

The social worker played with Catriona using a doll's house and figures for each member of the family; this was crucial in order to understand her views, levels of comfort or distress. It was complemented by the carers who logged in their diaries the child's behaviour on a daily basis with close attention given to periods before and after contact sessions (whether they took place or not).

Constructive use of time

The imaginative contribution by the carers and Family Centre workers in setting tasks for family members gave focus to contact and helped the contact sessions with the grandmother develop from the initially passive experience they were for Catriona.

Flexibility

The flexibility shown by the foster carers in being prepared to take on weekend arrangements greatly enhanced continuity for Catriona: not all carers can take on tasks of transporting and supervising but these carers did, to the great benefit of final contact plans.

Shared values

The recognition by all parties of the value of contact for Catriona meant that they could work together to resolve very real conflicts of interest and manage an otherwise unpredictable situation.

Conclusion

Managing contact in Scotland has a unique legal framework, and requires knowledge and skills from all involved. Perhaps more than anything, though, it requires carers, social workers and family centre (or other) staff to share their values and beliefs in what is in a child's best interest. Co-operation is essential for the good management of family situations which are almost always likely to involve unreliable or damaged parents, and children in distress.

The Children's Hearing system allows a less formal setting in which to consider a child's future but it is hard to see how annual (or more frequent) reviews and possible re-framing of care plans can promote a child's sense of security over the years. The court process, as it stands, offers a less than flexible response in regard to contact orders attached to adoption, and the adversarial nature of the court system does not encourage easy resolution of contact matters when compromise may be possible, as in the case of Catriona.

References

Fahlberg, V (1994) *A Child's Journey through Placement*, London: BAAF.

Fratter, J (1996) *Adoption with Contact: Implications for policy and practice*, London: BAAF.

Jewett (now Jarratt), C (1984) *Helping Children Cope with Separation and Loss*, London: Batsford/BAAF.

Lowe, N, Murch, M, Borkowski, M, Weaver, A, Thomas, J, Beckford, V, with Thomas, C (1999) *Supporting Adoption: Reframing the approach*, London: BAAF.

Oaklander, V (1988) *Windows to Our Children*, Center for Gestalt Development, Inc.

Wassell, S, Daniel, B and Gilligan, R (1999) 'Putting resilience into action', *Adoption & Fostering*, 23:3.

McMichael v United Kingdom (1995) 20 E.H.R.R.; *Fam.Law* 478:[1995] 2 *FCR*. 718.

S v Miller No. 1 2001 *SLT* 531; No. 2 2001 *SLT* 1304.

11 **Protection and supervision:**
Making problematic contact safe and beneficial

Alan Slade

Introduction

Children who have formed attachments to, and identify with birth family members, generally benefit from some contact unless their proposed visitors are wholly unsuitable. In some cases, unrestricted or carer-managed contact is not feasible but, nonetheless, the maintenance of a link with the birth family is in the best interests of the child. To manage contact in those circumstances is a difficult and sensitive matter. A specialist setting for direct contact between the child and birth family following a final care order or adoption order should be considered in cases where a significant risk to stability is finely balanced by an acknowledged value for the child of continuing contact.

What is needed in these circumstances is a forum for contact that is at a distance from, and independent of, either of the child's family 'homes', a neutral meeting place that affords the child and his/her families a high degree of support and safety in an impartial environment: a specialist setting.

What is a "specialist setting"?

Research conducted in the late 1990s by Hedy Cleaver (2000) explores the impact of the Children Act 1989 on contact between foster children and their relatives. For about a quarter of the children in that study, contact took place at the foster home. These meetings were more popular with children than with their parents, who frequently expressed dissatisfaction and resented carers usurping their role. Contact at the foster home restricted the type of activities children and families did together. In nearly four out of ten cases, social services venues like nurseries and family centres were used as meeting places. However, these were unpopular with both parents and children. They offered little privacy and restricted normal family interaction.

In their study of children in care, Millham *et al* (1986) emphasised the strangeness of the visiting relationship, and how difficult and complex it is to maintain links for parents of children in care:

Visiting those we know intimately in strange contexts and before unfamiliar audiences is a particularly fraught experience . . . it should be obvious that a lone parent whose child lingers in the care of strangers in unknown territory, to whom the care intervention is a violation, a parent who is bereft of a meaningful role and is unversed in the rules of this unfamiliar game, will find visiting difficult. These barriers to contact are compounded by the complex feelings of guilt, powerlessness, anger and mourning that most parents experience on the removal of their children to care.

Millham and his colleagues pointed out that contact was all too often arranged in apparently "public" places; in noisy, impersonal and adult-orientated surroundings, busy communal rooms in residential homes or multi-functional spaces in social service family centres.

Cleaver's study (2000) also highlights how problematic birth parents find contact away from their own homes, particularly "supervised contact". Generally, they felt unsupported by social workers and unclear about what they could expect from contact and others' expectations of them. Foster carers recognised that contact in their homes could be a positive experience, but felt that poorly managed contact could have a disproportionate impact on the lives of their own family members. They sometimes felt under pressure to "do contact", including supervised contact, because no alternatives were available or resources were not available. Most of those taking part in Cleaver's study wanted to see more child-centred, purpose-built contact centres, with specialist workers to facilitate and supervise contact. As a well respected, highly experienced foster carer once complained:

I had a one-month-old baby just detoxed from crack, a seven-year-old who was just lovely but she needed time . . . and they told me I had to "supervise" James and his mother . . . on my own. The gasman came to read the meter, the baby needed changing . . . I had to leave James and his Mum alone for a few minutes . . . it was then that she told him that his dad would be coming to get him, which wasn't true.

A specialist setting offers a sense of "home from home" to children and families: private and homely sitting rooms – one family per room – with many child-focused activities, kitchens to prepare and share family meals, and a garden. The environment in which contact takes place can be, and frequently is, a powerful determinant of how beneficial and sustainable the child's contact is.

The A family

The eight children of the A family were referred to the specialist service while subject to interim care orders. The siblings were accommodated in five foster placements following consecutive breakdowns of two residential placements, reportedly due to 'disastrous' family contact. In both residential homes the children had, it was claimed, at their parents instigation 'trashed the place and threatened and assaulted staff'. When referred to the specialist centre, the A children had temporarily closed down their second residential home by smashing windows and kicking in doors during a contact visit. The parents, echoed by the older children, complained at feeling 'on display' in the homes and of 'so many workers . . . as if they expected trouble'.

Children's and parents' lack of any prior experience or preparation for the 'strange situation' (Bowlby, 1979) of supervised contact, 'of meeting one another by appointment' (Millham *et al*, 1986) is exacerbated by an embarrassing lack of privacy in uncomfortably public and impersonal surroundings. All this will result, theory suggests, in behaviour between child and parent that may be as much to do with the unhelpful environment, as it is to do with the actual child–parent contact relationship. The environment in which problematic contact takes place is then a crucial factor in either securing consistently safe and beneficial contact or obtaining unambiguous evidence for the restriction or termination of unsafe and damaging contact.

Following full care orders, the A family attended supervised contact for seven years. There was never an incident when the children or their parents wilfully damaged or threatened property or staff. At one of the early visits, the third youngest child asked mummy if she and daddy 'live here now'. Several visits later, the middle boy painted a picture, explaining 'it's a hotel where we can all be happy . . . like this place'.

This privacy and impartiality – a 'home from home' – was equally welcome to these adoptive parents:

We knew that Tracy, the mother, didn't like it there. But for us, having to keep going back to the family centre where the assessments all happened . . . all that and all sorts of people around . . . it just began to feel as if we hadn't actually adopted James.

More important, from the point of view of the local authority or the adoptive parents, is the specialist setting's provision of skilled and qualified staff to supervise contact. Proper supervision of problematic situations, as the example given above by James' foster carer demonstrates, requires the resources to constantly monitor and manage the child's contact. The following definition of supervised contact is used by the Coram Child Contact Service. It has been adapted from a court report* and describes both its purpose and goals and the means needed to achieve these.

Supervised contact aims to ensure safety from physical harm and emotional abuse and requires a high level of constant supervision from supervisors experienced and confident enough to intervene immediately and firmly if anything of concern arises. If safe contact is achieved supervision becomes therapeutic in the widest sense. The contact is managed so that the child is supported in resolving issues with the parent which he or she needs to understand; or to provide opportunities for a parent to apologise or in other ways make amends; or to effect a planned and humane ending to contact. In supervised contact, the supervisor plays a role in guiding parents to improve the quality of interactions and parenting; this may include "mediating" to improve the quality of interactions between a child's parents or between parents and substitute carers.

---

* *The Experts Court Report* in re: L (Contact: domestic violence [2000] 2 FLR 334).

Why use or request to use a specialist setting

The prime functions of the specialist contact setting for children in permanent substitute families are to protect the placement or adoption from stress and pressure – and the worst-case scenario – potential breakdown, and to afford the child planned and consistently good contact over many years. If the adoption was contested or the parent, older sibling or other relative has never fully accepted the care order and has limited understanding of the impact, on the child, of critical or derogatory comments about the placement, then effective, skilled supervision is definitely necessary. The birth parent may be suffering a serious mental illness or have learning difficulties that affect their ability always to speak or act appropriately in respect of the permanence of the placement and the contact arrangements. If contact, problematic as it may be, is to be an ongoing part of childhood, then it needs a secure base, a "home" in which the child's experiences and memories of birth family can be rooted and traced back, a place that becomes rich with associations and therefore meaningful.

> *Zahide was pregnant with Rashid when she fled East Africa for the UK following torture and rape during a civil war. Rashid's father had disappeared and Zahide had no family in the UK. When Rashid was three, Zahide suffered a chronic schizophrenic episode and had to be sectioned. The local authority twice attempted supported rehabilitation but Zahide's condition was worsening and eventually a full care order for Rashid was obtained in 1993. The care plan was for long-term fostering or adoption. Rashid was four when he began having frequent supervised contact with his mother in a specialist setting prior to the full care order being made. Rashid would arrive for contact 'running with a beaming smile' into his mother's arms. Zahide, however, often behaved in a florid, hallucinatory, and paranoid way. Supervision protected Rashid from the effects of this, while allowing him, over time, to begin distinguishing safely between his mother's behaviour and that of other, less troubled adults; 'What was she talking about?' he would ask.*

> *Zahide would bring cheap but lovely clothes and small toys for Rashid and take photographs; the supervisor also took photographs as the*

service kept an instamatic camera for such "moments". Three years after placement Rashid's first foster placement broke down; he was immensely fond of his foster mother, "Auntie Rose", but her husband had used corporal punishment on other children in their care. At this time, Rashid "lost" all his photographs and infant toys. The local authority actively began seeking adoptive parents for Rashid, but he settled well with his new foster mother, Janet. Contact was reduced to three times per year. Zahide was by now learning how to manage her chronic illness, adoptive parents were not forthcoming and Zahide managed to maintain this sparse, infrequent "identity contact" with her son for three-and-a-half years, until "Auntie Janet" retired to the Caribbean.

Rashid's third foster mother, Pamela, is committed to keeping him until he is 18. Together with the Contact Service and with the agreement of the local authority, she has promoted gradually increased contact. Rashid is now 14 and sees his mother frequently at the "setting" they have used for ten years. They pore over Zahide's store of contact photographs: 'I remember that teenage ninja turtle suit . . . I think I lost it', 'you remember, we played this game a lot?' Over time, the supervisor and mother have explained to Rashid about schizophrenia and that, 'you don't catch it, like you do a cold, but you can't stop it like you can't stop a cold'. Rashid now has photos of uncles, aunts, and cousins in Africa. Equally importantly, he has frequent contact with his second carer's family and he sees Janet when she travels to the UK once or twice every year.

"Contact" or the maintenance and development of important and beneficial social and relational links – despite trials and tribulations – have formed part of Rashid's personality. Specialist contact settings, few and far between as they are, have been used to supervise many other similar cases, where children in permanent alternative placements have maintained rewarding contact over many years with very few and often no placement changes; they have benefited immensely from learning the importance of "staying in touch" while understanding the reality of their birth families' problems.

When to use a specialist setting

This question is partly answered by Rashid's story above. Contact, despite its traditional "orphan" status in social work, is a specialism and one that, in circumstances of problematic contact following permanent placement, requires that social work activity does not 'drop off' after final decisions are made. Agencies must remain involved with the outcomes of their decisions about placed children long after those decisions are made and finally enacted. If the child's needs were for long-term contact despite the presence of risk, then ongoing professional involvement must ensure that contact plans are responsive to the child's changing and developing needs, while both birth and substitute families continue to receive the support, guidance and recognition they deserve in managing this difficult and sensitive matter. For a local authority, the benefit of purchasing a specialist service is that someone else is professionally managing and assessing the long-term contact, thus freeing the authorities' staff for other work.

There are three dimensions to consider in determining when to use a specialist setting. The first task is to identify the particular child's contact needs. The following list is adapted from Finkelstein (1980) who defined six categories of children "in care", each category highlighting a different set of needs. Given that this was produced in the context of permanency planning, it adapts very well to categorise the need for supervised, specialist contact.

Children requiring supervised contact in a specialist setting

1. Children with no attachment to the birth family – those who have never met or never lived with the contact parent and who require careful, gentle introduction and nurturance.
2. The child from emotionally committed birth parents and extended family, where supervised contact is short-term and unsupervised "family" managed contact the most likely outcome, once the birth family has been helped to work through issues of separation and parenting.
3. Children with attachments and roots who cannot be cared for at home or through unsupervised, staying contact, but who need continued contact with their birth family or non-resident/parent (attachments needing

nurturance rather than replacement), perhaps as a prelude to less restricted contact or family placement but not necessarily.

4. Children of parents who are intellectually committed to contact, but do not follow through on commitment – the child thus becomes increasingly confused, and often needs considerable time to work through his/her feelings of rejection before being able either to accept infrequent, long-term supervised contact or to say goodbye.

5. If parents/family members have been judged unfit in cases where interim contact work has failed, then long-term therapeutic contact is needed to help the child develop a real picture of his/her parent's strengths and weaknesses and the reason for intervention by the state.

6. Adolescents who can be helped to form independent views on future contact in the privacy of a specialist service away from the intimacy of family life.

Categories 1 and 2, where permanent alternative placements have been made, will rarely present situations which require specialist supervision. The remainder though all apply to situations of permanency and clearly, a child's developing needs mean movement between categories. Rashid's case illustrates how a child's contact aimed originally at meeting the need to sustain attachments and roots where rehabilitation was not an option, gradually changed to meeting his need to develop a realistic picture of his mother and the reasons for his situation. In time, the goal for contact moved to helping him, as an adolescent, to form independent views on future contact, as he did by requesting an increase in contact at his LAC review.

The second dimension in determining whether or not to use a specialist service will be the behaviour and attitude of the visiting parent or family member, as assessed during and following the care and adoption proceedings. If it is acknowledged that the child has an attachment to the birth family, of one form or another, then the need for properly supervised contact will be due to certain particular characteristics of the birth parent/family member.

The characteristics of birth parents suggesting a risk to the placement if contact is not in a specialist setting are shown below (adapted from Wolfe, 1987).

Birth parent's/family members' characteristics	Impact on placement
Inappropriate expectations of child	Inability to accept expressions of warmth and affection about new family and assigning inappropriate responsibilities like 'tell them you want to see me more', leading to likelihood that potential for making amends and apologising for past harm is low.
Ineffective (escalating) control methods	Inappropriate disciplinary and dispute resolution methods leading to likelihood that potential for helping develop healthy peer and sibling relationships is poor, expressed through open conflict with permanent carers and local authority.
Disproportionate rate of negative as opposed to positive interaction with others	Insufficient expressions of warmth, interest and affection in child and child's "new life" leading to likelihood of quality of contact relationship being poor.
Low frustration tolerance and high impulsivity levels with aggressive and violent behaviour patterns	Inability to provide safety and comfort through very poor capacity to contain and manage conflict leading to instability and disruption of placement.
Socially isolated and disadvantaged with no supportive networks	Inadequate emotional and social resources to provide for a consistently "good" and reliable experience of contact without supervision and support, leading to uncertainty and confusion for the child.

Having established the child's need and wish for ongoing contact and the likely problematic nature of it, given the characteristics of the contact parent/relative, the third dimension to consider is whether a specialist setting is necessary to ensure that the aims and goals of child contact are met. Again, the following list is general to all supervised child contact.

Aims and goals of specialist supervised contact

- To support children in maintaining and developing important emotional and psychological bonds with relatives and friends.
- To provide stability for children in care, and a source of support in young adulthood.
- To enable the child to develop a sense of identity and belonging.
- To promote the child's sense of self-worth and self-esteem.
- To foster the likelihood of a child successfully returning home.
- To help the child to develop a sound understanding of the reasons for separation from family and the adult's responsibility for this.

- To contribute to keeping children safe and in the public eye when they are away from home.

How a specialist contact setting works

If contact is to go ahead despite being problematic, and if it must be properly supervised, then the specialist setting ensures that there are sufficient persons present to avoid any "lapses" in supervision. Consistently safe and therapeutic contact cannot be provided by one person in isolation, as James' carer, cited above, would testify. The specialist setting provides a "cover worker", always available to contact supervisors and stationed close enough to be able to overhear and respond to problems. This cover worker is also crucial to therapeutic work. For example, if there is a need for the supervisor to speak briefly with the contact parent alone, midway through a visit, because the parent is verging on abusiveness, then the cover worker can step in and spend time with the child. This is an opportunity to learn how the child has been affected by the altercation, to provide reassurance and to assess whether the child wants to, or should, continue with the visit.

The attitudes of carers and adopters play a vital part in harmonious contact arrangements. Carers and adopters are more likely to play an active and positive role in promoting contact where supervising or "cover" social workers are available to work in partnership with them, to share feedback about the progress and purpose of contact and to listen to their concerns and anxieties. Birth parents also value time that contact social workers spend with them, feeling it helps them keep "in touch" with their children. Meetings between supervisors and parents enable them to talk about and share information about the child. Such meetings also serve to support contact between parents and their children because supervising social workers can instigate appropriate communication, as opposed to parents having difficulties contacting social workers. The specialist service has the time, focus and resources to provide this "family support". As contact post-placement is aimed at improving and sustaining relationships between children and their birth parents/families, it is important to provide therapeutic counselling for parents and/or children before and after visits and working with them to help change existing patterns of interaction.

Similarly as for children caught up in loyalty conflicts between estranged parents, research shows that it is rare for permanently placed children to share contact experiences with their carers or to make their true wishes known to them (Cleaver, 2000). An important function of the independent, specialist setting is to enable children to talk about and to understand their contact arrangements, for example, when they wish to change the frequency or duration of contact with parents or if they want to see other relatives or friends, or just be able to go on supervised outings to a favourite spot.

Carly, living with her mother and younger sister, was four when she, her mother and younger sister started coming for supervised contact to visit her older sister and brother who were looked after and fostered. When she was seven, her 15-year-old brother absconded from care and returned to live with their birth mother. Her older sister remained looked after.

At age eight, during a supervised outing to the local shops, Carly stationed herself beside the supervisor and challenged: 'Why do you have to be here? You don't have to be here . . . it's because they think mummy will take Gemma away but she won't, so why are you here anyway?'

'Well, look . . . sometimes things get said or done in these kinds of visits and the social workers get a mixed up message about what happened and what was said. If there's no-one like me there, to say Mum did or did not say or do that, Mum might get blamed for something she didn't do or didn't say. I'm here to look after you and Mum as well as Gemma.

'They could take us away from Mum because they think she did wrong and you saw she didn't so they wouldn't?'

'Eh well, maybe, but it's much more that Gemma's visits could be stopped, yes.'

'Okay, but you don't need to be here you know!'

'Well I'm glad to hear it . . . but we'll see, yes. Anyway I like being here with you all.'

'Okay . . .'

Carly's mother and Gemma's foster carer were able to meet and talk amicably about Gemma and her progress. For many children this is not the case and a specialist setting provides a safe space where parents and carers or adopters need never meet. A service that can contain conflict and acrimony between birth family and substitute family, while facilitating "good" contact, is a major advantage of an independent, specialist setting.

Paul was seven when he began supervised contact in the specialist setting. He had been received into care due to neglect at age five. His white mother, Eileen, had a borderline personality disorder and he never knew his African-Caribbean father. Eileen's older partner, Stanley, who had been her support and Paul's main carer for much of his early childhood, was angered by her apparent acceptance of the care proceedings and the care order. When Paul's carers applied to adopt him, Stanley made serious allegations against them in respect of their care of Paul and a major investigation was launched, culminating in their being exonerated of any misconduct.

However, from that point on, they stipulated that they never meet or see Stanley and Eileen. Paul, being almost eight at the time, made plain his wish to see Mum and Stanley every month and so supervised contact was resumed. Paul and his birth family maintained this level of contact for eight years, at the contact agency, without his adoptive parents and birth family ever meeting in all that time.

It was clear that Paul had in his own mind compartmentalised these two "split" families and the neutral, specialist setting enabled him to move comfortably and effortlessly between the two. When Paul, nearly 16, voiced his agreement with the Contact Service's proposal that the "two sides" finally meet again – he having decided he wanted unsupervised contact – his adoptive parents agreed but his birth mother refused and Stanley went along with her, albeit with misgivings. Paul then elected to have contact only on his own terms and when he wanted it, confronting the reality and taking charge of his circumstances.

Problems and pitfalls of contact in a specialist setting

As Paul's case illustrates, long use of supervised contact in a specialist setting can result in institutionalisation, with one or other of the families involved feeling unable to move forward from the once satisfactory and appropriate service, despite the child having "outgrown" the system. All too often courts, lawyers, and social workers struggle only to set up contact in the short term. Long-term planning for contact to match the child's changing developmental needs seems to be rarely considered. This can, and sometimes does, lead to a situation where children begin to refuse contact, not because the contact relationship is necessarily troubling them but simply because its context has become jaded and lacking in stimulation.

It follows that, if contact is to be long term in a supervised setting, then the more frequent it is from the outset the more likely are the child and parent to tire of it. The frequency of specialist, supervised contact must be proportional to the envisaged long-term placement outcome. If it is unlikely that contact will be able to become unsupervised and family-managed for many years, then the frequency must reflect this expectation. All the research into child contact, while often disagreeing, agrees on one fact: that it is the quality and not the quantity of contact that is important.

All long-term contact arrangements should be regularly reviewed. If the arrangement is supervised in a specialist setting, the supervisor will be in the best position to make recommendations. The danger of allowing contact to continue without review, simply because it is working well enough, must be avoided every time.

Conclusion

Being visited by one's parents or visiting one's children, by appointment, is a wholly artificial and unusual experience, a strange situation for which the participants are generally quite unprepared and largely unskilled. It is made even more unsatisfactory if the environment, in which such unrehearsed, sensitive, and necessarily private moments are to be shared, is "public" or in territory that belongs emphatically to one "side" or the other. Foster carers acknowledge that contact in their home can be positive; but problematic or unintentionally mismanaged contact frequently places them in invidious positions that impact severely on them and their own families, let alone on the fostered child.

If a child's best interests require that problematic contact should continue for many years, a specialist service providing a safe, homely and child-focused environment and staffed by skilled and confident workers, is best placed to effectively protect and support the child and the family. "Contact" has for too long been an "orphan child" and it is up to those that confront it on a daily basis, to ensure that policy makers and resource managers understand its complexities and the impact of poorly managed and under-resourced contact on children, families and carers.

Endnote

The above chapter is adapted from the Coram Family's *Guide to Best Practice in Supervised Contact* which, with the support of the Lord Chancellor's Department, is shortly to be published.

References

Bowlby, J (1979) *The Making and Breaking of Affectional Bonds*, London: Tavistock Publications.

Cleaver, H (2000) *Fostering Family Contact: Studies in evaluating the Children Act*, London: The Stationery Office.

Finkelstein, N E (1980) 'Children in limbo', *Social Work*, 61, pp. 100–105.

Millham, S, Bullock, R, Hosie, K and Haak, M (1986) *Lost in Care: The problems of maintaining links between children in care and their families*, London: Gower.

Wolfe, D A (1987) *Child Abuse: Implications for child development and psychopathology*, London: Sage.

• • •

11a Supervised contact in private law: A problematic example

Children who are not in the care system may become subject to supervised contact by court order in matrimonial proceedings. These contact arrangements would not become the responsibility of Social Services unless there were also child protection issues. However, contact supervision may be undertaken by one of the growing numbers of independent social workers. Even when contact supervision comes under private law, the needs of the children and their parents and the dilemmas facing the supervisor are the same as in all cases where children are separated from a parent on a long-term basis.

Although the exact details of the case have been changed, in the interests of confidentiality and possible identification, the contributor has chosen to remain anonymous.

Whose welfare and interests are being met?

In coming to its decision the court is required to make the child's welfare and interests paramount. Usually, this will be based on the recommendations of a Children's Guardian, child psychiatrist or other expert witness. An order for supervised contact in a matrimonial case can be made where one parent, and indeed the children themselves, are opposed to contact, but the experts consider knowledge and experience of the other parent will be important for the children's healthy, long-term psychological development. However, the court cannot legislate for good results. There is no formal provision for the appointment of a supervisor once the order has been made, so it is left to the parties and any professionals involved to find an acceptable solution. Frequently this will mean the use of a Contact Centre run by volunteers. In the situation described below, I agreed to take on the task because one of the professionals knew that, although retired, I had past experience as a Court Welfare Officer and as a social worker with families and children. In this particular case, rather than a satisfactory pattern of contact becoming established, the children remained opposed. In fact their feelings became more entrenched as time passed.

The three boys, aged five, seven and nine, lived with their father following their parents' divorce. Until the mother left, the whole family was an integral part of a strict religious community which had only limited contacts with the everyday world. The mother's rejection by her husband, her own family and the community was total. None of them believed in the value or principle of continuing contact for the children but reluctantly accepted the power of the court to make such an order. The mother, on the other hand, felt it vitally important that her children should know who she was and that she would always be there for them, while nevertheless accepting that the boys would continue to live with their father in the community where she was no longer accepted. In this context I took on supervision of three times a year, three-hourly contact, believing that it would be for a limited period, after which it would either have become an accepted pattern or would come up for review.

Before contact started, I was introduced to the father and a community member by one of the professionals. At this meeting, suggestions for possible venues were agreed, such as a museum or adventure playground. Meetings on home territory, whether the mother's, mine or anyone else's were totally forbidden, as was the giving of presents or sharing of food. After this, all transport and other specific arrangements and all communications were made through the community member I had met. Once the father's approval had been obtained by this person, I finalised arrangements with the mother. There was no direct exchange between the boys' father or member of the community and the mother. Indeed, when the children were brought to the chosen venue by the person I had met, they would only be handed over to me, never to the mother, even should she have arrived before me.

On each contact visit, the children's reluctance was clearly demonstrated by their behaviour. They made no eye contact with their mother, stopped taking part in our ad hoc games of football if she touched the ball and, where opportunity offered, they hid or ran off. There were frequent questions about how long it would be before they were collected and we were likely to be found at the agreed meeting point well in advance of the appointed time. Despite my efforts, conversation with me always remained stilted and they refused to talk to their mother at all. While none of them cried or had a tantrum of any sort, a certain stubborn unwillingness to participate was very apparent.

What is the supervisor's role?

The case illustration demonstrates the need to ask this question but also suggests some of the answers. A supervisor may act:

- as a BUFFER between the children and the parent with whom they do not want contact;
- as a POLICE OFFICER to ensure nothing happens that the parent with whom they live would not wish, for example, mother holding the boys' hands or being alone with them at any time;
- as a GO-BETWEEN conveying messages to and fro between the parties, setting up contact arrangements and discussing them afterwards.

In my experience there were serious constraints on my role. Even the frequency and duration were set by the court, while locations and activities were severely restricted by the parent and the community within which the children lived. Many venues and events were considered unacceptable, including such mundane matters as the mother and supervisor going into a café with the children. More serious for me than these practical limitations, was the very restricted scope for the exercise of any social work or therapeutic skills. This was not apparent at the outset, but over time as the boys' attitudes and behaviour became more entrenched rather than relaxed, and as I learned more of the community's values and disciplines, I felt gagged and shackled by the context within which I was functioning.

To whom is the supervisor accountable?

Where probation or social services are still involved, there may be an agency to whom the supervisor is accountable. Somewhere and someone to whom to feed back and from whom to seek necessary direction, support and supervision should be provided by that agency. In matrimonial cases, however, there may be no direct route back to the court which made the order.

In the case above, despite professional recommendations to the court for review after a set period of time and the making of a Family Assistance

Order, there was no provision for review and the Family Assistance Order, which could have provided some guidance and support, expired soon after the first contact. (Unfortunately in this case, I was not provided with a copy of the order before starting contact supervision and it took several months' persistence before I got one.)

How and when should supervised contact end?

In making an order in matrimonial cases the court may expect either that contact will come to a natural end or develop positively, increase in frequency and become self-supporting. But what if neither of these happens? How long should supervised contact continue? With school age children, their responses and behaviour will be a clear indicator of their feelings and wishes. As time passes, improvement or deterioration in their relationship to the other parent becomes more evident. For the three boys and their mother, there was no real contact – just going through the motions.

Conclusion

While it is important to acknowledge that the case illustrated is atypical – indeed probably unique – it nevertheless raises a number of more general questions about contact supervision in matrimonial private law cases. The Order is made at a certain point in time but can make no predictions or provision for changes in both children and adults and their home circumstances. A contact order made for a young child will need amendment as the child grows up and develops friendships, interests and activities which do not mesh in with specified contact arrangements. Older children may come to resent direction about how and with whom they spend their free time. This may result in the gradual diminution and eventual discontinuation of contact in general. Sometimes parents are forced to seek help when their child becomes disturbed or antagonistic as a consequence of being forced to continue contact against their wishes. Currently there is no opportunity for review or amendment of contact arrangements other than going back to court for a variation of the Order. Frequently financial constraints will preclude this action.

At present there is no routine avenue through which courts and judges learn about the outcomes of the orders they make, although it seems that a number express interest and curiosity. No doubt there are many disrupted families where the separated parents themselves negotiate continuing, satisfactory contact for their children, making changes and modifications when necessary. However, there remain a worrying number of children for whom issues about contact continue to be contentious and who are affected adversely even into adulthood. It would therefore seem advisable that there should be a mechanism for periodic report, review and amendment if necessary, without the formality and expense of seeking a variation in the order. Feedback about the supervised contact sessions even in the extreme case example above, might have led to more realistic and achievable expectations for and from all concerned.

12 **Contact and terminal illness:**
Adopting a flexible approach

Margaret G Bell

In 1995 a Sheriff in Scotland made a highly unusual decision: when granting an Adoption Order she attached a condition of direct contact between a five-year-old child, Jane, and both her birth parents Sue and Ted. The decision reflected a probably unique situation – both parents had Huntington's Disease. The birth mother contested the adoption application in favour of custody (an order available at that time in Scottish law), though she did envisage the child remaining in care of the Petitioners, Meg and Bob. The Sheriff concluded that the birth mother was withholding her agreement unreasonably. The birth father was agreeable to adoption provided that he had ongoing direct contact with the child. The Petitioners were in favour of ongoing direct contact between the child and both her birth parents. It was considered that continuing contact would allow the child to have firsthand knowledge of her birth parents' inability to care for her because of their illness. It would also allow her to have a clearer perception and understanding of the nature and effect of the illness.

The birth mother appealed against the adoption and the terms of the condition of direct contact. The Court of Session refused the appeal against the adoption decision but made a minor amendment to the condition of direct contact. Once an Adoption Order is granted in Scotland, the papers are sealed for one hundred years, open only to the adoptee when aged 16, but the Court directed that all parties should receive copies of the court process so that it would be possible to return to court to vary the order if required.

Jane first became looked after when she was under a year old. Both of her parents had been diagnosed with Huntington's Disease but were, at that stage, unable to care for Jane because of their excessive drinking. Jane was placed with Meg and Bob who were temporary foster carers.

Apart from one brief period early on, Jane continued to be looked after because attempts at rehabilitation were unsuccessful. When Jane was three-and-a-half years old, the Social Work Service made the decision that Jane's interests would best be served by placing her for adoption. In due course, after great deliberation, Meg and Bob sought to be considered to adopt Jane and were approved four months later.

Jane's parents separated soon after she became looked after. Arrangements were made for her to have contact individually with them and this has continued since the granting of the Adoption Order. The contact has been supervised by social work staff who participated in a training session to enhance their knowledge of Huntington's Disease.

After the granting of the Adoption Order the contact between Jane and her birth parents continued to be facilitated and supervised by the child care social worker who had taken over case responsibility six months after Jane became looked after, and the social work assistant who had been involved in the case from the outset. The social worker moved post when Jane was seven years old so Meg and Bob's link social worker from Family Placement Services, who had had direct knowledge of the situation from the beginning, and was known to all parties, took over the support and supervision of contact between Jane and Sue while the social work assistant continued to support the contact between Jane and Ted. To help distinguish who is who, the terms "Mummy Sue" and "Daddy Ted" have been used by everyone. This has no doubt also helped to reinforce for Jane the importance of Sue and Ted in her life.

Over time the contact between Jane and Ted has been less complex and has presented fewer dilemmas than that between Jane and Sue. Reasons for this can be easily identified. Firstly, Ted's positive attitude to Jane's placement with Meg and Bob is something he has been able to convey to Jane. This, in turn, has generally resulted in good quality contact. Additionally, the effects of the Huntington's Disease have not been as far advanced and have not affected Ted's day-to-day functioning as much as Sue's. Until recently, contact between Ted and Jane has taken place in public: Meg or Bob would take Jane to the town centre; the social work assistant, Jane and Ted would then go to a café and walk round the shops to buy a "goody bag" for Jane before Ted caught his bus home. However, recently Ted's condition has deteriorated. His involuntary, jerky movements have increased notably, drawing people's attention to him in public places and thereby causing Jane some embarrassment. Ted's intellectual functioning is also now noticeably affected so his conversation has become very fragmented. Following discussion between the social work staff and Meg and Bob, it was agreed to offer a more private venue for contact: a flat used by the Social Work Service for family meetings. The social worker is also becoming involved alongside the social work assistant to facilitate the practical arrangements and to support Jane and her adoptive parents. In future this will, no doubt, have to be reviewed again as Ted's condition becomes worse.

Contact with Sue has always been more stressful. In the year following the adoption, contact was offered generally once a month with both birth parents. Several times Sue herself cancelled because of illness or because she had been drinking. On other occasions it was cancelled or terminated early by the social work staff because Sue had been drinking. In order not to raise Jane's expectations or let her down, the decision was made not to inform her in advance of the exact timing of contact.

Sometimes during contact Sue could say something inappropriate to Jane and, even if contact is supervised, once something is said it cannot be retracted. Sue's inappropriate remarks reflected her inability to relinquish her daughter to Meg and Bob's care: she would tell Jane off when she used her new surname and make such comments as: 'I'm the only one who can tell you what to do', or 'You mean your other mum, I'm your real mum' or she would tell Jane that she was coming home to stay with her. It was important for the staff member supervising to intervene at the time or clarify for Jane immediately following contact. It was also essential to ensure that Meg and Bob knew what had been said so they could reinforce points and clarify misunderstandings for Jane.

In September 1996, Sue was admitted to hospital and was to remain in residential care permanently. Within a few months Sue wrote to the social worker stating she did not want to have further contact with Jane and she maintained this stance for two months. Sue's changing wishes highlight the lack of control in ensuring contact even takes place, let alone that it is handled well by participants. However, Jane (now six) made it clear, when contact was discussed with her, that she would see her birth parents if she wanted to. When Sue indicated she wanted to resume contact it was reinstated but it was made clear to Sue that she should not lead Jane on to think she was being returned to her care nor should she make any remarks which undermined Meg and Bob's position.

From this time on, contact generally took place on a monthly basis with Bob always accompanying Jane, at her request, as Sue's physical condition visibly began to deteriorate. It was important to be aware of Jane's sensitivity to her surroundings. The venue within the hospital had to be changed to provide a more congenial setting and privacy. During this period Sue was unable to sustain any conversation with Jane. All Sue tended to say repeatedly was 'Do you love your Mum?' and 'Give your Mum a kiss'. Jane was clearly uncomfortable at times with such repeated requests and needed help to appreciate Sue's limitations. Given that a dialogue was difficult to maintain, Bob and the supervising worker spent the time keeping Sue up to date with Jane's activities and progress at school, encouraging Jane to share her news.

At one point Sue said her two grown-up daughters, Jane's half-sisters, who had met her only when she was an infant, wanted to see Jane. This was then discussed privately with Sue who said her daughters wished to speak to the social worker. Meg and Bob were open to exploring this further connection for Jane. The sisters were interviewed together and it transpired it was Sue, and not they, who had suggested getting in touch. On hearing how well settled Jane was in her adoptive family, the two young women decided not to pursue contact. However, Jane's curiosity was aroused and eventually she did ask more about her older half-sisters. Meg and Bob considered the possibility of contact at some length. They thought it could benefit Jane to be in touch with birth family members of the younger generation. The social worker contacted the sisters again but only one expressed an interest. A meeting was arranged with Jane, Meg and Bob in their home and this seemed to go well. Meg and Bob and the sister agreed on a second visit but the sister did not turn up, leaving Jane upset and confused and no doubt feeling rejected.

In the summer of 2000, Sue moved to a nursing home further away than the hospital but still within a manageable distance. Her physical condition continued to deteriorate – she became wheelchair bound and lost weight. This really upset Jane. It became increasingly difficult to understand the little that Sue was saying. A signal was agreed between

Jane and the social worker so that an interpretation of what Sue was trying to say could be made: Jane would tug her ear or rub her nose to indicate to the social worker she had not understood what was said.

There were a number of times when Sue gave £10 or more to Jane, leading Meg and Bob to have some concerns that Jane might be tempted to visit for money. However, Jane herself was clearly bewildered and concerned about being given such large sums: 'Can my Mum Sue afford to give me such a lot of money?'

It became undesirable to sustain visits for the usual half hour – Sue would generally fall asleep. On one occasion she became distraught, crying and demanding a cigarette. It was important to check Sue's condition in advance so that Jane could be better prepared before each visit. On what turned out to be the last visit, Jane became visibly upset, quiet with tears pouring down her cheeks – Sue's condition had clearly deteriorated further – and the visit was ended after ten minutes.

Sue died four weeks later. Meg and Bob told Jane together that Sue had died and discussed the funeral arrangements with her. Jane wanted to attend the Church service and Crematorium; she went with Meg, Bob and the social worker. Bob sat with Jane at the front during the second service when Sue's close family asked her to join them. Sue's father, Jane's grandfather, hugged Jane, offered kind words and gave her some small mementoes from Sue. Following the service, Sue's family asked Jane, Meg and Bob to join them for refreshments, which they did because Jane wanted to. Jane's sisters indicated they would like to maintain contact with her. Meg and Bob made it clear this would be welcomed but that if it started there must be ongoing commitment; Jane should not be let down again. Only one sister is keeping in touch so far and she has introduced her own two children to Jane. Apart from this, Sue's father telephoned once following the funeral to ask how Jane was and an aunt sent a Christmas present and some family photos. Jane still sees Ted almost every month but his illness is progressing. Jane has asked for Bob to stay with her during visits and this is what happens.

Over the years, the social worker and Meg and Bob have endeavoured to tease out with Jane how she felt about direct contact, its frequency and duration and to plan contact accordingly. Jane has been able to make her views known and hopefully she has felt she has had a voice and been listened to. She has also shown a remarkable capacity to consider Sue and Ted's position, but at what cost to herself? Following the last contact with Sue she commented 'Wouldn't my Mum Sue be upset if I didn't come to see her?' She also made it clear, while Sue was alive, that she wished her birth parents to be treated equally – if she did not have contact with one how could contact with the other continue?

This case highlights many of the problems that can arise in managing contact arrangements. However, it has its own unique elements:

- Given the steady turnover of staff in social work teams it is no doubt unusual – and obviously beneficial – to have two members of staff continuously involved in a case over a ten-year period. What has been important for all parties has been a sound knowledge of the individuals, the history and the issues.

- For a worker, it has not been an easy situation – support and supervision have been essential in order to consider all aspects of the case, especially as being so closely connected over a lengthy period carries with it the possibility of becoming too emotionally involved and being unable to retain sufficient objectivity.

- Although since the adoption was granted, the primary social work task has been to supervise contact, this has also included discussions with Meg and Bob pre- and post-contact and offering ongoing support to them as they help Jane with the various issues that arise, and to the birth parents as their circumstances change.

- It is important that recognition is given to the social work time that is required. In this case compliance with a court order merges with the statutory role of providing post-adoption support. Although this case is unusual, the backgrounds and traumatic experiences of many children currently being placed for adoption will necessitate ongoing or intermittent social work input for years to come.

- The whole process of contact has been difficult for Jane – she has had to witness her parents' condition deteriorate in the course of a cruel illness. However, even if circumstances had been different and she had been brought up within her birth family, living with or having ongoing contact with her parents, she would have seen them deteriorate just the same.

If contact had stopped at the time of adoption, Jane would be left with sparse, fragmented memories of her parents. Although the memory she has now may be painful it will, hopefully, give her a real sense of her parents. To have been cut off, aged five, would have been denying her the opportunity to know her parents in later life because they would not be there for her to seek out, as an adult, if she so wished.

As Jane gets older, her capacity to understand about her parents' illness and the implications for herself, grows. For Meg and Bob this is the most difficult ongoing dilemma – ensuring they answer Jane's questions and provide an appropriate level of information at each stage of Jane's development. It is important for them to be able to tap into social work and the genetic service, which is part of the Health Service, when required, to seek support and guidance.

The granting of the Adoption Order vested parental responsibility for Jane in Meg and Bob so they have the decision making role if or when contact with the extended birth family comes into question. They have consistently demonstrated a capacity to be open and flexible to an extent that many couples might not be able to contemplate, as they endeavour to make decisions focused on Jane's very special needs and wishes in relation to her history and connections.

13 **The Paraguayan Connection**

We have made a commitment to Elena, a commitment to her family and a commitment to Paraguay. This was enshrined in the adoption decree. You can't make a commitment without having contact with the country and knowing who the family is. We would have found it difficult to adopt from a country which does not allow access to records; in Paraguay adopted people of 21 can see their records but Elena won't discover anything she does not already know. The Paraguayan connection has opened a whole new vista for all of us.

Elena lives with her adoptive parents, Anne and Brian, in a large house in West London. She is ten years old and has lived with them since she was six months. Her brother, Emlyn, who was born to the family, is at university doing Latin American Studies. Their house, which reflects a congenial English life style, has many examples of Paraguayan art and artefacts comfortably placed alongside Victorian prints and family photographs which include pictures of Elena and her birth family. Anne told me their story during the best part af a day, sitting at the kitchen table having coffee, lunch and yet more coffee. She spoke into a tape recorder and I took notes. Both the voice and the words are her own.

Hedi Argent, Editor

Making connections

We've always been an open family. We were able to answer all our son's questions; he knew everything about his family and his roots and connections, so when we thougth about adoption we knew how important it would be to be able to answer an adopted child's questions – even more important than for our son. My husband and I have lived and worked in South America, so we were not daunted by the idea of a child from Paraguay and we were determined to establish contact even before we were told about Elena. Our only concern was that the birth mother should agree to our taking her child to the UK as part of a legitimate legal process.

The adoption was arranged through an attorney according to the law in Paraguay. Unfortunately his views were reminiscent of British attitudes in the 1950s and 60s. He said: 'You've got the child, forget about her past. If you make contact they will only ask you for money.' The only photo he could come up with was a copy of the birth mother's identity card; it was very dark and you couldn't see the features. Although I wasn't happy about it, I had to settle for it. But there were nice girls in the office who didn't exactly say they knew anything but I noticed that their faces perked up whenever I asked all these questions.

We knew that, even if we couldn't have contact with the birth family straight away, we could keep in touch with Elena's foster carers who had been looking after her since she was a few days old. They would be her Paraguayan family for the time being and probably long into the future. They are a lovely family with a daughter, Sandra, almost the same age as Elena. When Sandra is older we hope she will come to us for a holiday or for a gap year before she goes to college.

I think one of the things that worked to my advantage is that I had to stay for four months in Paraguay before I could bring Elena home. I didn't stay of my own choosing but, on reflection, it was an advantage because I became familiar with the country and the particular area Elena comes from. I made initial contacts with the girls in the attorney's office and with one of our translators, which eventually led to the birth family. And I established a lasting relationship with the foster parents. I know inter-country adopters want to bring their baby home as soon as they can, but it does really pay off if you can stay longer that very first time and make the effort to contact as many people as possible who are part of the picture of the baby's life at that time.

Not long after we came home, we were asked whether another of our translators could stay with us because other arrangements she had made had fallen through. We said, 'of course', and a little later, Alicia from the attorney's office came to stay too. She had changed jobs and was now independent and free to make enquiries and to follow leads. She became our friend and our avenue to connections with Paraguay. She quickly traced Elena's birth family and she has managed our contact arrangements ever since. She was careful about her approach in case the birth family didn't want to know or some members were even unaware of the baby's existence, but they were all delighted. They had no photos of themselves, so Alicia took them to a studio to have some taken to send to us and we sent some of our family. After that, Alicia visited them and us regularly and we exchanged news through her; she was our go-between and our fairy godmother. You don't have to have a fairy godmother but it helps when you don't know the language well and the birth mother doesn't read or write. Alicia is tactful, efficient and low key.

We think it important for adopters always to give the child the security of knowing that they have "permission" to talk about their birth mother and family. Children should know that it will not hurt their adoptive family if they say they want to meet their birth family. I make this point bacause I don't feel it always happens: Families I know say, '*They show no interest in their birth mother, family, country*'. I'd go as far as to say it is up to the adults to inculcate this interest.

So Elena has always known her story and been proud of her heritage. Her birth mother, Elizabeth, became known in the family as her "Paraguayan Mum" and her photograph stands in Elena's bedroom so that she can see it when she goes to sleep and when she wakes. She is growing up with her life story book which is growing with her.

First meeting

By the time Elena was seven, she started to say she would like to meet her birth family and we began to make arrangements to go to Paraguay. It took time to get around to it; I think I was keener than my husband and we wanted to make sure that Elena was ready for this next step. I didn't want contact to be the only thing we were going to Paraguay for. Sometimes people say they want something and then they don't; the birth family might have got cold feet or anything, so you have to plan for every eventuality. We planned a holiday in Paraguay to include all the other people we knew: our translator and Alicia and their families; the foster family and their many relations, and we would stay in the little family hotel where I stayed for four months with Elena when she was a baby. We would also travel and get to know the country and perhaps venture into Brazil.

The first time we went, Elena imagined we'd go straight from the plane to see Elizabeth but I deliberately held back a few days because we needed her to see the real Paraguay first. No matter what she was told, she had this rosy picture of sunshine and people dancing in the street. We wanted her to see how different life is for people in the country she was born in. So we just spent time walking around the town and shopping in the markets. When Elena and Elizabeth met, they were both quiet and subdued and they both cried a little. By this time Elena had seen how poor people live and there was nothing shocking about her family. They knew what to expect of each other from the photos but it must have been very strange for her birth family to meet people who have a standard of life they cannot comprehend in a country they really know nothing about.

Before we went to Paraguay, we already had information about Elena's extended family. Elena has two nieces and loves the idea of being an aunty. Her three older sisters have never lived with Elizabeth either, but her only brother, Pablo, does live with her. Father figures are often absent and this is the case here. There is also "the granny", aged 86, and her wider family of cousins, uncles and aunts. She is not a blood relative but an important older person who brought up Elizabeth as her own and holds most of the family history. I'd got the branches of the family tree but the leaves weren't on it yet; "the granny" has filled in all the details now.

When we meet, Alicia interprets and we also manage with my little bit of Spanish and our will to communicate. But there isn't always a need to say much, it's enjoyable to just be together: we usually buy food for a barbecue or take everyone out for a meal or go visiting. There is a limit to what I can ask. For instance, I can't ask: why did you give this child up? When I know one reason was the worst kind of poverty.

Meeting again

It was definitely easier the second time we went – you know everyone, you've met them, you can laugh about certain things and Elena was more relaxed. I'm not a big ahead-planner myself, we just go and I take it from there. People in Paraguay may go away for a weekend but we have plenty of time to meet up and to fit in around them. Some days all Elena wants to do is stay in the hotel and play with the other kids round the pool or just read a book and that's fine. There isn't an expectation of having to fill every day with seeing the family. 'Go with the flow' is the expression I use. Out of a four week holiday this year, we saw the birth family five whole days and several half days. Then we visited the foster family once a week, met up with Alicia and her friend who also keeps in touch with the birth family and saw our translator, so we were pretty busy seeing people but it isn't all we do. We went to museums and galleries and met a well known Paraguayan painter who showed us all his work. I'm keen for Elena to have contact not only with her family but also with South American doers as well as artists; with her classical as well as contemporary heritage. She comes from Indian roots and we have introduced her to Guaraní culture.

Elena would like to find one of her sisters who lives in Argentina and her father, but it's not possible yet because we don't know where they are, and Elizabeth has a right to privacy just as we have. Each time we see them, things have come out and you don't have to find out everything all at once. The important thing is to keep connected. The more often you go, the more people you meet and the more Elena feels this is part of her.

We can't afford to keep going every year. We said last time, it will be two years before we come again and "the granny" said, 'Don't worry, I'll stay fit and well and we'll all be here when you come back'. Elena accepts we can't go every year but Alicia will turn up as usual and the connections remain firm. We are in touch with Alicia by telephone nearly every week.

Back home

Elena has become more stable since she has met her birth family. She still has moments of sadness about them but they are less frequent than before, and she talks about them easily. Her "Paraguayan Mum" has become Elizabeth. She feels better about not knowing her birth father because even Pablo doesn't get to see him. When she was asked to bring something she treasures to her interview for her new secondary school, she brought her up-to-date life story book with her *Memories of Paraguay*.

I don't think it's all plain sailing but perhaps that's my way of approaching things. Everybody has to find their own way; it's not impossible. You really can trace your child's family and you can afford to go there if you think it's important enough. I can't think of anything else that's more important. It's her birthright isn't it? It's not up to me to pick and choose whether she has contact with someone who gave birth to her. It isn't enough to know about your birth family. Elena has seen them – she actually knows them – she sees that she looks like her birth mother, that she has the same eyebrows as her sister, the same fingernails as her brother and that she shares some family mannerisms. She knows that there isn't anything we are hiding and that there is nothing we know that she doesn't. Not knowing is worse for a child than knowing – however hard it may be to have to face painful truths like poverty, brothers and sisters who stayed at home, cultural strangeness, language barriers, issues of ethnicity and even rejection.

Because Elena is not academic, the sixth form will probably be the end of her formal education. She may then want to live in Spain for a year or in Paraguay to learn the language. She already goes to Spanish classes and she's been learning Paraguayan dancing. If she becomes fluent in Spanish she might want to live part of her life in Paraguay; she may even come back with a Paraguayan husband! We have kept her dual nationality for her and because Brian and I also have Australian nationality she will have an Australian passport too. She thinks that's really cool!

After we came back from our first visit, Elena wrote an essay for school which says it all:

Last summer my Mum took me to Paraguay for three weeks so that I could meet my family, my foster parents and see where I lived when I was a baby. We stayed at El Lapacho which is the hotel I stayed at with my Mum. It was great to see Elizabeth, my real Mum, and Pablo my brother, and Lorena my big sister. Lorena has two baby girls so I am an aunty. We had a barbecue and Pablo and I got into trouble because we played with the puppies when "the granny" told us not to. I also got to see some of "the granny's" family who are the family who brought Elizabeth up. Elizabeth gave me a photo of my real granny but she lives in Buenos Aires. My big disappointment was that I didn't get to meet my real Dad, but maybe I will one day.

Names have been changed to shield Elena and to protect the people from Paraguay.

14 **Remaining connected:**
From an overseas adoption perspective

Introduction

I adopted my daughter Sofia when she was 10 months old, 12 years ago, from a Latin American country in which I had lived and worked. I had met Sofia's birth mother through a mutual friend, and the adoption was a direct arrangement. In keeping with the thinking of the day (with which I agreed wholeheartedly at the time), I maintained contact with the birth family, sent letters and photos, and paid fairly regular visits to them. When Sofia was four, they asked me to adopt her half-brother who was then 14 months old. Mario is now nearly nine years old. I have maintained the contact over the years – we have a number of close friends there who the children see as "family". They are both much more ambivalent about their actual birth family whom they have seen every 18 months or so, all their lives.

For various reasons, a couple of years ago, we went back to the children's country of origin and spent a year there. The children went to school, became very good at Spanish, made friends, but also learnt some very hard lessons. Whether or not this experience met their developmental needs is a question which will remain forever unresolved, but it certainly went a long way towards giving them a sense of themselves and who they are in the world. We made two visits to their birth family that year, and I think that it was the relative frequency of contact, and the information that emerged during the course of the first of the two visits, that began to make me seriously question what I had previously accepted to be the positive benefits of contact.

History

When I first adopted Sofia in the late 1980s, received wisdom and hence "advice" given to adoptive parents, was to ALWAYS re-frame everything positively and NEVER criticise the birth mother. Within an overseas adoption context, this meant, for example: 'Your mother left you in a latrine so that you would be found quickly' rather than 'she dumped you in a latrine like a piece of garbage which is probably how she felt about herself and you as well'. By the end of the 1990s this approach had shifted from one paradigm to another, and much of the work done by child psychotherapists working within the adoption field is now focused on a commitment to the "whole truth". It is generally accepted that children internalise pre-verbal trauma and need to know the truth as a way of validating their internal psychic experience.

I now think that truth always "outs" and it is always better to face it, although this does of course beg the question as to how many adoptive parents (both domestic and overseas) have enough information about their children's early histories to enable them to offer the "whole truth". Any negativity attached to the experience of tracing and contact has to be weighed against the effects on children of **no** contact, of no access to their birth families or their country of origin, because an empty void of un-knowingness can be worse than unpleasant reality. According to anecdotal evidence from the UK (and presumably the same applies to other countries), the overseas adoption world has a shockingly high number of unhappy children and teenagers (most of whom have had no access to their country of origin let alone their birth families) who are self-mutilating, delinquent, and/or generally dysfunctional. It would be doing a disservice to all adopted children, inter-country or otherwise, if any of the issues raised in this article were used by adoptive parents in denial, as a way to justify their unwillingness to address the issues of identity/ethnicity, and "belonging".

Issues of tracing and contact

Tracing and contact within an overseas perspective raise both similar and different issues to those of domestic adoption including language and how much or indeed whether to introduce the culture of the country of origin. I want to look at some of the questions that are rarely addressed and critically re-evaluate the "received wisdom" of current adoption practice and that of the recent past. In this paper I consider the issues raised by contact from the perspective of the children, as opposed to that of the birth family. In particular, I examine the changing models of best practice and subsequent repercussions on children, and focus on my own children's experience and that of some of their overseas-adopted friends. Although this is personal, any debate of this nature clearly has wider implications for future overseas adopters.

Tracing means, among other things, facing the pain and loss for all of us. The impact on the children's lives needs to be processed at each stage of every child's development. It is critical that all the players in the adoption field remain open to revising previously hard and fast opinions, and, above all, look at the individual needs of each child which may change over the years, sometimes radically. I think that I have now learnt that it is only possible to know you got it wrong after you did it wrong, and damage may already have been wrought.

I would not argue against tracing. I am all too aware, from detailed discussions with friends with overseas-adopted children who have "traced", from talking to their children directly, and from our own experience, that "knowing who you are" is of enormous benefit to a child's sense of self and emotional development. Feelings of finally being "whole" or "complete" are commonly articulated. Certainly, tracing successfully can and will bring with it a sense of connection, which clearly is facilitated if the adoptive parent/s have some access to the language spoken by the birth mother. An absent birth family can possibly be included in an overseas adoptive family much more easily without contact, by talking about them, but this position raises all sorts of questions around the child's fantasies and is clearly not the most developmentally healthy choice.

While the possibilities brought by contact are critically important, I also think that the limitations are enormous, principally because of unbreachable cultural rifts and economic inequality. A distant, but known, birth family also raises all sorts of issues such as 'suppose you don't actually **like** who they are and where you come from?' or 'you like the country but not your birth family,' or 'you like your birth family but not the country?'

In the year that we spent in their country of origin, my children, on a daily basis, witnessed that there were babies and children who were visibly loved and cherished living in families that were even poorer than their own birth family. I watched them internalise the harsh reality of the implications of this – that basically they were not wanted, or were an inconvenience. It was very painful for them (and me) to make sense of this, and to articulate it. They have done so more easily since we have been back in England. Of all the children I know who have been able to contact their birth families in their countries of origin or whose adoptive families knew something of their circumstances, none come into the category of really dire poverty (in the context of their particular country). These children, like many who are adopted domestically, have to face the painful truth that, rather than a fairy tale of poverty making their devastated birth family unable to keep them, they were not, in fact, "wanted". Most young women in my children's birth mother's situation have little control over their lives and would be unlikely to be able to access abortion for both cultural and financial reasons.

I know well three families whose children are adopted from overseas; all were committed to tracing and were successful, all have made two or more visits to the birth families, and all now say variations on 'Yes, well, we've done it, but now it's really hard because we have absolutely nothing in common and I wonder what we go back for'. The extent and depth of cultural alienation between the birth and adoptive families is likely to be exacerbated by class and inequality (also true of domestic adoption), particularly if the adoptive family is not familiar with the culture of the country of origin. How many times do children need to visit their country of origin (with usually very little or non-existent language in common) in order to feed their sense of self? Whence comes our sense of self? As far as my own children are concerned, their reactions to their own country of origin have been mostly positive. Ironically (or otherwise), the year they spent there resulted in them defining themselves much more clearly as "British" although my daughter also defines herself as "other".

The children's experience

Given that I adopted my daughter in the 80s, I followed the prevailing orthodoxy and endlessly positively reframed some of the children's difficult history. They have both always asked a lot of questions about their past, specifically about why they had been adopted. I excused their birth mother's careless neglect by explaining that 'she was so young she didn't understand how to look after babies' which, notwithstanding other reasons, is culturally incorrect given that girls of three years old in Latin American countries know how to look after babies. I maintained contact with the birth family and spent years covering up why their birth mother never sent them a birthday card. Clearly all this festered away for both the children, essentially because I had so successfully "reframed" and had never told them the "whole truth" as we know it.

From observation of my children over the past 12 years, and witnessing the pain that they clearly experience so keenly, I have become opposed to intercountry adoption while at the same time recognising the contradictions and privileges of my position. I have come to think that many overseas-adopted children live in a kind of emotional diaspora. They are never quite "there" – never quite connected to the world in which they live. Both my children, at different times, have told me that the reason they find it so hard to concentrate is that they are always thinking of their country of origin. My daughter first expressed this several years ago in a voice which said: 'How can you possibly not know what my head is always full of?'.

Whenever I write about adoption, I always solicit my children's opinions, as the in-house adoption experts who are very articulate on the subject. It needs to be added that these interviews were conducted while our family was engaged in a therapeutic process with the Attachment Project (AP) which is specifically designed to work with adopted children and their families. The AP has, as a basic tenet, a commitment to the "whole truth" in order to access the children's internalised experience.

I decided to talk to the children individually about how they felt about their own experience and contact with their birth family. Their responses were very different; they show the impact of changing practices, and illustrate that some may work better or worse for different children, a point adoption policy makers should address. I began the discussion by asking my daughter Sofia how she felt about her birth mother at the moment (given that I already know that her feelings are ambivalent and ever-changing). She replied, without hesitation, '*I'm not sure, happy in a way because I think that for people who are adopted it's better to know your parents and where you come from because your Mum* (meaning me) *looks nothing like you and I think it's better'*. My daughter knows some of the details surrounding her early infancy and her adoption, and I went on to ask her if, given what she knows about her birth mother, she would rather not have known her or despite everything, whether she was glad that she did? Sofia replied,

> *'I just feel bad knowing someone like that is my mum – it's kind of upsetting cause mothers aren't like that . . . but I'd much rather know her and know what she does because all the kids should know what their parents are like instead of just being puzzled about why she had you adopted, and feeling like an alien, like out of space, like you don't belong. If I hadn't have known her, I'd just be really confused because I just would have felt really upset like you were hiding one big thing about me – something in my life isn't right, something about me . . .'*

(This is from a child, to whom I thought I had effectively given a positive message for the past 12 years, but for whom clearly her psychic experience was very dominant.) I then went on to ask her about her Dad, who walked out on her birth mother when she was three months pregnant, and deliberately walked out of Sofia's life when she was four years old, never to be heard of again.

> *'How about your Dad?'*

> *'Really upsetting.'*

> *'Is it worse than Maria* (their birth mother)?'

> *'Yes, I just feel I'm not part of the world because my Dad isn't there for me and it makes me feel worse because Mario* (her brother) *has got a Dad and I feel absolutely jealous.'*

Sofia has enormous difficulty with the subject of Mario's Dad, although on the surface she copes very well.

In order to keep the discussion alive, and to benefit from the free-flow of feelings, I asked her what I have asked her many times in the past:

> *'If you had a choice, do you wish you weren't adopted?'*

> *'Yes, partly, a bit sometimes.'*

'Would it have felt better to have stayed where you came from?'

'I don't know. Why isn't Anielka (her best friend in her country of origin) *adopted?'*

'Why do you think?'

'That's what I don't understand.'

Sofia recently told the Attachment Project that basically the problem was that she had never really understood why she had been adopted. The Attachment Project encouraged, persuaded, and forced me to see that truth was the critical issue of the day. During a session with them, I told her the truth, which is basically that Maria didn't want her. She fell into my arms and cried although she "recovered" much more quickly than I had anticipated.

The main point of all this detail is to illustrate that for Sofia, who is now generally much more relaxed and less over-compliant than previously, current orthodoxy has worked really well, notwithstanding what damage I may have wreaked during the first 12 years by positively reframing the children's painful and difficult history and experiences in line with the late 80s thinking of the day.

It was different for my son. During the first visit of our year away, it became clear that the children's birth mother had told a web of appalling and monumental lies about the circumstances surrounding Mario's adoption, the upshot of which was that I decided that I was no longer going to present her in a positive light – I would not be actively negative, but "balder" with the truth. He was horrified, cried, and was very shocked (although what I told him was *very* mild). Mario has always been a somewhat difficult and challenging child and his behaviour deteriorated from around this time, although there were a lot of other factors which undoubtedly contributed to this.

I asked Mario a similar set of questions to those I had asked Sofia. On previous occasions, he has been furiously impassioned about the subject of having to come to terms with the fact that his birth mother obviously hadn't wanted to have children, but had gone on to have two, neither of whom she had bothered to look after. I began by asking:

'How do you feel about knowing her?'

He launched into an articulate and eloquent monologue:
'She didn't want us, you tell us about how she didn't feed me, and only gave me coke and coffee to drink (a common habit among the poor in globalised and coffee-producing countries because coca-cola and coffee are, ironically, only a different sort of health hazard than is milk) *and I feel so cross and angry and furious and fuming – having a Mum who's torturing you really, especially to a child, and she treated me like that all the time and she doesn't love me or Sofia and it makes me feel that no one loved me and no one talked to me and I had a really horrid life and I feel so let down by her and so unhappy and it's the worse thing that's happened in my life. Why?? Why was no one nice to me and talk to me and love me and I feel so unloved and just used by her. It's because I'm not loved, it's so hard to have life, to live when you've been treated like this. I wanted to be loved, someone to be nice to me and they all thought I was worthless. She doesn't treat me like I'm her son and I feel so unhappy. What's the use of having a child if this is how you treat them? I wish I didn't know her anyway cause she didn't treat me right – why should I remember her anyway?'*

I asked him if he felt that knowing Maria gave him more of a sense of self. Given that he is only eight years old, he was unable to conceptualise this, but gave a reflective and mature reply:
'Maybe she was treated like that when she was little, so I don't completely blame her cause that makes it not her fault. Being not loved is a really sad thing. I wondered if I was going to live in this misery forever – why does no one talk to me?'

I think that this last question points to his fixation that no one talked to him as a baby.
'I feel a bit cross with her and sorry for her at the same time. I'd rather not have known her, but if you hadn't told me I was adopted, I'd feel really unhappy because you hadn't told me the truth, and be angry with you for lying. I wish I knew her, but not the details, and because now I know she didn't love me I feel so lonely and unloved. Other

children in England have nice lives and have always been loved but it's no one talking to me that I can't bear. I just feel so let down from all that.'

I also asked Mario if he thought he would have preferred not to have been adopted? He laughed and said:

'Of course I'd rather live with you. I feel happier about my Dad but if only he wasn't at work, had spent time with me, then life would have been a bit easier. Maybe if it was just my Dad, but it's difficult to get on with life when you've got someone like Maria around.'

Since attending the Attachment Project, his behaviour, predictably, is a lot worse. I think that access to the reality of his birth family has had a negative effect and I would be tempted to go so far as to say a damaging effect. I am aware that his internal structures are **already** damaged, and seriously question to what extent these are reparable. Although there is a lot of emotional space in our family, talking with him in-depth on this occasion was very enlightening for me. Two weeks after this conversation, I asked him again if he thought he would be happier if he hadn't met Maria. He replied immediately and unhesitatingly that he wished he didn't know her, and he'd certainly be happier if he didn't know about all the things she'd done to him. So a "commitment to the whole truth" hasn't necessarily done him any favours in the short term.

In the long term, Mario will work it through, and is in the process of doing so, but I still question whether the pain this process produces is not in itself differently damaging. A friend who has met the children's birth family on two occasions, and observed the complexities of the inter-actions, commented that Mario would be acting out not being or feeling loved, whether or not I had told him any of the details. There is a level on which the details matter, and one where they don't. He *behaves* as if he feels unloved, and knowledge of the details of his early life has given him a handle for that.

Conclusion

Reeling from all this, and having written this paper, it is imperative to re-assert that contact and connection are good things, but I want to re-pose the questions that have to be borne in mind. My children have very contradictory feelings now which potentially challenge the management of our contact in the future. I have come to the conclusion that my children's stories raise significant issues that need to be addressed, such as what happens when you don't like the person you know to be your birth mother? When you observe her and experience her as behaving in a very negative way? What happens when you dislike the country you came from? If the happy scenarios work out, then great, but what about when they don't? Appropriate counselling about these possibilities needs to be part of a preparatory programme for overseas adopters. Anecdotal evidence suggests that contact with birth parents is overwhelmingly a positive experience, but without doubt there are exceptions to this both within a domestic and an overseas context. Adoptive parents and those working with them should be aware that orthodoxies change. We should be prepared to adapt current theory to the developmental needs, situation, and personality of individual children.

After much thought and discussion with her children, the author has decided to remain anonymous in order to protect their privacy.

15 **Orders or agreements?**

Mary Jones

This chapter is dedicated to the memory of Anne Van Meeuwen, Principal Officer, Policy and Practice, at Barnardo's. Anne died suddenly on 28 October 2001. She had worked in the field of adoption and fostering for many years and had intended to write this chapter. She would have brought to that task a wealth of experience gathered in a career that included work in Hampshire and the London Borough of Newham. Anne's work directly touched the lives of many children in adoption placements and indirectly benefited many more through her influence on legislation and guidance.

As a colleague and friend of Anne and a previous Barnardo's adoption project leader, Mary Jones was well placed to complete the task of writing this chapter, drawing on Barnardo's service experience in much the same way that Anne would have done.

It is impossible in any consideration of what works in post-adoption contact arrangements to isolate single factors that alone impact on the outcome. A whole range of events and circumstances throughout the entire adoption process inevitably have an influence on whether effective contact arrangements can not only be put in place but also be sustained. Influencing factors are likely to include the reasons why a child was placed for adoption in the first instance; whether or not the adoption was contested; the age of the child on placement; the way in which the foster carers managed any contact arrangements and consequently the expectations established prior to an adoptive placement; the level of support, training and preparation the adopters received, their attitude to contact, the way their attitude was managed by the assessing agency and, most significantly, the social worker's own attitude to contact; the level of support that the birth family received and their emotional distance from relinquishment.

This list is potentially endless and itself serves to emphasise the complexity in establishing satisfactory contact arrangements.

One crucial factor in determining the outcome of contact arrangements in England and Wales is the way in which those arrangements are established. Where contact is on the agenda (in my experience, it still is not automatically given any priority as a dynamic part of the agenda during linking), the arrangements can be set up in different ways. Some agencies still rely on a broad agreement made during the planning meeting, once a link between a child and adopters has been agreed. This agreement is often based on very basic details about who will be involved in contact, the frequency, and who has responsibility for managing the arrangements. While the adopters will be present at this meeting, the birth family is rarely involved and although contact proposals are likely to have been discussed with them, they are not necessarily party to any agreement made at a planning meeting. With the exception of new arrangements set up for contact with the current foster carers, the discussion will often focus on agreeing existing contact arrangements. They do not, as a matter of course, involve the consideration of potentially new contacts or the reconsideration of past arrangements.

At a recent planning meeting, when a question was asked about possible plans for contact for siblings who had been placed apart in foster care and were to be placed in separate adoptive placements, the agency response was that, as the children had not had any contact for the fairly lengthy duration of their foster placements, there was no need or indeed any point in raising the issue again. No thought was given to the possible advantages of renewing their contact or to their changing contact needs in the future. One interpretation of the underlying message here was the desire to "leave well alone". While informal agreements made at the planning meeting can be revisited as part of the agenda at review meetings, there is often no system for review post adoption and it is then usually left up to the adopters to negotiate or make changes.

Many agencies now give contact a better hearing than this and have developed a more formal and dynamic process for formulating, maintaining and reviewing contact arrangements. I would like to consider the pros and cons of contact arrangements agreed in this way – through a "Contact Agreement" – and compare them to arrangements which are imposed by a legal process, resulting in an order with contact conditions.

Contact arrangements made through the courts do not require the agreement of any or all of the parties potentially affected by them. A Contact Agreement or Contract, on the other hand, is negotiated and agreed between all parties involved in any contact arrangements, usually at the linking stage of a placement. While it is a formal process, it is not a legally binding contract and relies on the commitment of all parties to the agreement. What, if any, are the advantages of each of these more formal means of meeting contact needs in specific circumstances or situations?

Court orders

Contact conditions imposed by the courts potentially add "teeth" to any expectations around contact, by putting the weight of the law behind them. Whether or not, in reality, the law would actually "bare its teeth" if required is another matter. It seems unlikely that a judge would ever remove children, or indeed ever be justified in removing them, from a placement, which might in many other ways be seen as successful, purely on the grounds that the adopters did not stick to the terms of any contact conditions or order. In fact, the evidence suggests that courts are reluctant to make additional orders at all in adoption proceedings, particularly against the wishes of the adopters. There is a frequently quoted passage by Lord Ackner, from a case in the House of Lords, where he stated regarding contact that '*in normal circumstances there should be a complete break and that only in the most exceptional circumstances would the court impose terms or conditions as to access to which the adoptive parents did not agree*' (re: C (A minor) [Adoption – access]).

Often decisions that have been made about contact during care proceedings are not reviewed at adoption hearings, despite the fact that the issues and circumstances of all concerned may well be completely different. The factors which played a part in the initial decision-making process will have included consideration of contact in the context of the events leading up to the children being looked after, possibly including child protection issues. At the point of the adoption hearing this context may, if re-examined, present a very different picture. But even where such arrangements are revisited, it seems the courts are still unlikely to consider making an order without the agreement of the adopters.

Interestingly, while I have come across very few cases in Barnardo's service experience where contact arrangements have been imposed by the court, this was not because applications were not being made. I have found a number of examples of cases where applications for contact orders or conditions were made, which were ultimately either not granted or, for a variety of reasons, the application was withdrawn. We might consider, therefore, the motivation of those making such an application and the reasons why no order was made. In most of the examples I found, applications for contact were made not because the applicant wished to establish contact where none existed, or increase the level or nature of the existing contact, but because they had no trust in the commitment of adopters to maintain any agreement made. A birth mother applied to the court for contact despite the fact that an agreement was already in place and despite the fact that the adopters had a proven track record for maintaining contact in a previous adoptive placement; she just didn't "trust" the adopters to continue contact, post adoption. For parents who have perhaps lost their children and have little faith in the system in which they find themselves, it is hardly surprising that they cannot trust agreements which are largely reliant on the goodwill of others.

The experiences of the birth relatives leading up to an adoptive placement will also contribute to their expectations with regard to contact. In one case, a contact order was established during care proceedings, recommended by the Guardian on the basis that she didn't "trust" the foster carers to maintain contact between siblings, placed separately. The carers had intimated that they 'did not see the point of contact' as, in their view, 'the siblings did not have a meaningful relationship'. This not only begged the question as to the role that the local authority played in managing their foster carers, leaving the Guardian in a position where she felt that this somewhat heavy-handed approach was the only option, but also gave a message to the birth family that carers will not adhere to contact agreements, unless forced to do so. The contact arrangements set out in the contact order were reviewed at the adoption hearing; the level of contact was appropriately reduced, but the order remained in place, leaving the adopters to carry the legacy of mistrust.

I have not found examples, which is not to say that they do not exist, of court orders being intentionally used, or indeed applied for, in a positive way, to establish the parameters of contact and set up a framework. The intent was always to establish an "enforcer", against the wishes of at least one part of the triangle. Even where there was the potential for some agreement between parties about contact, an application to the courts for contact was generally an indicator of the level of mistrust and disbelief that any agreement would be kept. This in turn seemed to have a negative impact on the attitude of adopters towards the contact. Even those adopters who had an apparently positive approach to the notion of contact and who were expressing a willingness to "negotiate" an agreement felt threatened by the idea of it being imposed on them. Had conditions been made, it could well have meant that the contact arrangements would have been carried out in a spirit of resentment and with the potential therefore to become a negative experience for the child or children involved.

I know of one single case of a court order having, almost by default, a positive outcome (at least as perceived by the adopters), when an order for a limited amount of contact removed the possibility of further negotiation by the birth family for increased contact. This was not seen as a welcome outcome by the birth family. How it will be viewed by the children in this example is difficult to predict at this stage, but there will be cases where a clear framework for restricted contact, established in the courts, could have a reassuring impact for children, particularly where there has been a history of abuse.

There are a number of examples where an application for a contact order was made but the Judges preferred to encourage the option of an agreement, apparently seeing this as a more viable and positive alternative.

Contact agreements

A contact agreement "involves" everyone, or at least sets out to do so. To some degree, all parties have some sense of being involved in the negotiations. A contract agreement is a voluntary exercise. It has no "teeth" but could inspire a sense of ownership and therefore a commitment to making it work. But does a contact agreement always inspire the sense of ownership that enables contact to be managed in a more positive way?

Are the contact arrangements established by these means more sustainable? Such agreements seem to be gaining favour on the basis that they involve negotiation, they include all parties, they require, at least initially, the agreement of all parties, and so start from the premise that some sort of contact, is going to happen (see Appendix).

To begin the process of establishing a contact agreement presupposes that work has been done to get all parties to agree that there will be contact. From this point the process can move a stage further to consider exactly what will happen; what will be the nature and content of the contact; whom it will involve; how often it will take place and who will be responsible for managing and monitoring the arrangements. An agreement pays attention to the content and purpose of contact, not just its existence and frequency, and individualises it. Its very process enforces discussion and negotiation. Its success over the long term lies in the continued commitment of all parties through rewarding as well as difficult times and through change. One of the main advantages of the contact agreement over the court order is the scope to build in evaluation and review and therefore the potential to be flexible. The contact needs of children change as they settle, as they grow and develop, as they formulate questions and desire understanding, as their identity needs become more important. The contact agreement should, theoretically, be able to respond to these changes.

> *Paul was eight when he was placed and loved the idea that information was being sent to his birth mother about his progress a couple of times a year. He liked to be involved in the process of actually providing the information. It was a one-way letterbox arrangement but had been agreed by all parties, through intermediaries, including Paul. However, when Paul reached 13 he began to resent the fact that information was being sent one way only. He didn't want information about himself to be given, without question, to people from whom he heard nothing.*

In this instance the contact agreement enabled the level of flexibility that was required to meet Paul's needs at the time. It might have been tempting, and perfectly understandable, for the adopters simply to have stopped all contact, in response to Paul's changing attitude, instead of renegotiating it. The agreement drew them to the latter course.

The flexibility of the contact agreement and the potential, if it is managed appropriately, to respond to individual needs at different stages, can also allow for a move away from the Eurocentric view and its consequent expectations about how people will or should respond to various aspects of adoption. Agreements can accommodate culturally different approaches to issues such as separation, relinquishment and subsequent contact, if they are given priority by those involved.

A Korean birth mother, who'd had a concealed pregnancy and had her options explained to her through an interpreter, made it clear just prior to a linking meeting that her short-term and long-term understanding of the implications of adoption were different. In the short term she understood that she would have no contact with her child at all and this met her needs, at that time. In the long term, however, she had understood that her connection to the adopters would be akin to that of an extended family and that, if and when her circumstances ever allowed, she would be able to contact them and to re-establish a relationship with her child. The linking was postponed while the birth mother was given the opportunity to reconsider her options based on better information. One of the options was to negotiate a contact agreement to meet both her own and her child's needs. Only an agreement that offered flexibility and an opening for renegotiation would, and did, have any chance of meeting these needs.

Having a contact agreement in place does not preclude the application for an order, though it seems to have an influence on the outcome. In one case a contact agreement had been established, at the linking stage of the placement, between a child's maternal aunt and the adopters, setting out arrangements for direct contact. At the stage of the adoption hearing, despite little previous contact, the maternal grandmother applied for an order for direct contact. While the Judge expressed some sympathy for the grandmother's circumstances, he seemed satisfied that there was the potential for a further contact agreement rather than an order, especially as the adopters had already demonstrated their willingness to be engaged in this process. The hearing was adjourned for attempts to be made to reach agreement. Although the grandmother did not get the level of contact that she had requested, her involvement in the negotiations and a commitment from the adopters to some form of contact, led her to withdraw her application for an order and allowed for at least some resolution.

In another case, the birth mother was contesting the adoption because, as she made clear, she believed that an adoption order meant that she would lose all contact with her child. The birth mother and the adopters were brought together to try and negotiate an agreement. The birth mother was reassured directly by the adopters about their willingness to agree to and maintain some form of contact. The fact that the reassurance came directly from the adopters had a huge impact on the birth mother, much more so, I suspect, than if such promises had been expressed second hand by a social worker. Also, because the adopters had made their commitment to her face and not through an intermediary, it became a much more personal contract on their part and potentially a much harder one to break. The birth mother withdrew her opposition to the adoption on the basis of the formal agreement that was subsequently drawn up.

The main disadvantage of a contact agreement is the fact that it is not binding in any way and any party can renege on the agreement at any time. In most examples that have come my way, it was the adopters who most commonly made a request or sometimes a decision that the contact should be reduced or stopped, usually on the grounds that, in their view, it was not continuing to be in the best interests of the child. Common reasons given were the children's distress before, during and after contact; the unreliability of the birth family in keeping to arrangements; the inappropriateness of the behaviour of the birth family or of letters sent. Whilst in some of these instances there could well have been a good argument for reviewing the contact, there is also the possibility that the adopters were not fully prepared for the impact of contact in terms of a child and birth family's grief and how best this could be managed. The key to the success of contact arrangements seems to rest fairly squarely on the shoulders of the adopters. Therefore good preparation should be followed by continuing support and expert advice from the placing agency.

Conclusion

Given that there seems to be a reluctance by the courts to impose contact conditions and a greater reluctance to enforce them, the contact agreement has just as much likelihood of ensuring and preserving contact arrangements. Even though an order may be "perceived" to carry more weight and this could be reassuring in some circumstances, it does not guarantee either that contact will take place or that it will be a positive experience.

The element of negotiation and ownership in a contact agreement, plus the built-in review as situations change and relationships adapt, do seem to give the contact agreement a better chance of durability than conditions imposed by the court, possibly as a result of mistrust and not necessarily with the consent of those involved. However, such an agreement still relies heavily on the commitment of the adopters, a commitment that can be difficult to sustain, in the long term. One post-adoption worker commented, 'when the going gets tough, contact is the first thing that goes'. If disclosures about abuse are made post placement, adopters can find it very difficult to go on promoting contact. Apart from continuing to discuss it with them, there is little agencies can do if adopters pull out of contact agreements. Indeed, trying to re-engage adopters with aims to which they are no longer committed, is virtually impossible. If adopters are ready to pull out at an early opportunity, then they may not have fully bought into the notion of contact in the first instance. They may also not be getting the level of support required to ensure that they have the emotional energy to maintain contact even through the difficult times.

Whether or not contact arrangements are established by order or by agreement, two factors are prerequisites of good contact arrangements:

1. *Adopters who have been prepared well and have understood the concept of contact as a reality.* If contact is discussed with them as if it were a choice, then that is the frame of thinking they will maintain: 'It is a choice, my choice'. The question often asked during the assessment is 'can you consider contact?' This signifies choice and does not confront the child's right and need for continuity. Yet every child, even if there are no existing contact arrangements at the time of placement, may need to have their contact needs addressed at some stage in the

future. The question 'how will you manage contact?' sets a different tone. It confirms that contact is likely to be a part of adoption, in some form or another, and helps adopters start the process of thinking about the advantages as well as the difficulties involved in managing the arrangements.

2. *Long-term and well resourced post-adoption support.* Such support should provide practical and appropriate responses to the range of issues that adopters face. This in turn should enable them to maintain the emotional energy required to be flexible, to renegotiate and to be responsive to the changing needs of all those involved in contact, and to recognise their own changing needs.

Further reading

Triseliotis, J, Shireman, J and Hundleby, M (1997) *Adoption: Theory, policy and practice*, London: Cassell.

Tunnard, J (ed.) (1996) *Adoption and Birth Families*, London: Family Rights Group.

New Families Project (1993) *Making Contact Agreements*, Colchester: Barnardo's.

Ryburn, M (1994) *Open Adoption*, Aldershot: Avebury.

Casey, D and Gibberd, A (2001) 'Adoption and contact', *Family Law*, January, pp 39–43.

APPENDIX

This is a sample contact agreement relating to contact between a birth mother, Mary, and her son, John aged ten. It makes reference to the birth mother's live-in partner, Paul and her daughter, Karen, who remains with her. It gives an idea of the level of detail that is required and consequently the amount of negotiation that is necessary to create clear guidelines and set out expectations from the very beginning.

CONTACT AGREEMENT

FOR

JOHN

This Agreement is made in good faith by all those involved. The best interests of John will be considered at all times.

This Contact Agreement refers to the arrangements between Mary, John's birth mother, and Peter and Val before and after they adopt John.

What sort of contact is agreed?

Indirect:
- Peter and Val will send written information on John and a photograph in February of each year. This will be sent to Barnardo's Post Box and forwarded to Mary.
- Val and Peter will send a birthday card they have chosen with John, to Karen via the Barnardo's Post Box. This will be sent 3 weeks in advance so there is time for it to be redirected.
- Peter and Val will let Mary know of any significant events in John's life and any serious illnesses he might have.

- Mary can send Val and Peter information about herself and Karen in April of each year via the Barnardo's Post Box.
- Mary can send a birthday and Christmas card to John via the Barnardo's Post Box. This should be signed from Mummy Mary, Karen and Paul. Should Mary no longer live with Paul or Karen then she should sign the card from Mummy Mary.
- Mary will let Peter and Val know via the Post Box of any significant changes in her life.
- Mary will keep Barnardo's informed of any change of address.

Direct:
- Peter and Val will take John to Mary, once a year, to spend time at an activity based around Colchester. The meeting will last for approximately two hours and Peter or Val will be present throughout.
- Whilst Mary continues to live with Paul he will be welcome to attend along with Karen. There should be no other family members at this contact.
- Arrangements for the contact will be made via Barnardo's Post Adoption Worker. It is anticipated that contact will usually be in the summer holiday at a date to be agreed by all the parties.

What role will the agency's Post Adoption/Post Placement Service play?
- Negotiate the Agreement
- Circulate the Agreement to all the parties
- Be available for support and advise over any aspect of the contact
- Arrange the venue and date of direct contact on annual basis
- Re-negotiate Agreements
- Provide information and review the Agreement as specified

Agreement
- I/We agree to the contact described above.
- I/We agree that all actions and plans must be in the best interests of John and consistent with his wishes and feelings.
- I/We agree to inform the agency of any change of address.
- I/We agree to respect John's wishes should he want to change the terms of this Agreement at any time.

- This Agreement will be reviewed after 3 years.

  Signed .... Date .... John

  Signed .... Date .... Mary

  Signed .... Date .... Paul

  Signed .... Date .... Peter

  Signed .... Date .... Val

  Signed .... Date .... BNFP

  Signed .... Date .... LA

(Reproduced with thanks to Jackie Trent and Colchester New Families Project)

End-piece with Lauren

Hedi Argent

Lauren's mother, Shirlee, had learning difficulties and suffered from recurrent depression. Her parents were both dead and she was not in touch with her extended family. Shirlee met Lauren's father, Mickey, at a club when they were both 19. They briefly lived together but Mickey left before Lauren's birth. He made one re-appearance when Lauren was three months old, but the police had to be called because he smashed up the flat. He has not been heard of since.

Lauren was born by Caesarean section at a hospital where Shirlee had been previously treated for depression. She had her own hospital social worker who arranged a comprehensive support package for mother and child at home. In spite of daily help from Social Services, it was a struggle for Shirlee to keep the baby fed and clean. A few times she left Lauren with neighbours and didn't pick her up until the next day; at home, Lauren was strapped into her pushchair for most of the day. By the time she was nine months old, she could not sit up unaided and made no effort to crawl or to play. Shirlee complained that the baby kept her up all night so that she was too tired to look after her in the day. Lauren was regularly seen by the health visitor and paediatrician at the clinic; no physical reason for the developmental delay was found. Shirlee was not able to get herself and Lauren ready to attend the various groups for mothers and babies to which she was referred, even if her family support worker offered to go with her.

When Lauren was nearly a year old, Shirlee became seriously depressed and had to be hospitalised. Lauren was placed with a couple in their late forties who had three grown up children living close by and two grandchildren around Lauren's age. Tim and Liz took Lauren to visit her mother two or three times a week. Lauren showed no emotion at this time; she never cried or laughed; she ate her food without relish and showed little interest in her environment except for a fear of water. She seemed not to react to the move and separation from her mother or to the initial overtures made by the foster family.

After three months, Lauren was like a changed child. She sat up by herself, crawled at full speed ahead and made determined attempts to stand and walk. She cried when she was thwarted or if she hurt herself and developed an infectious giggle. She loved playing outdoors while her carers did the gardening, had favourite toys, developed likes and dislikes about food, and began to be able to give and take affection.

It was only then that she showed distress each time she had to leave her mother in the hospital. The wise, experienced foster carers understood that this was a sign of emotional health and progress. They now waited patiently for Lauren to develop enough confidence to call them when she woke in the morning or from her afternoon sleep, instead of lying quite still, staring into space until someone came.

Before Shirlee was discharged from hospital, her social worker called a case conference to decide about the future needs of mother and child. Shirlee had already said that she could not look after Lauren, as it would make her ill again. Tim and Liz were prepared to keep Lauren on whatever terms were thought to be in her best interests. The possibility of adoption in the future was mentioned, but it was agreed that Lauren should remain in their care until the birth mother had settled back into the community. In the meantime, there was to be fortnightly, supervised contact at a local family centre. Lauren continued to catch up developmentally. The supervised contact arrangements were not wholly satisfactory because Shirlee did not always remember to turn up and felt under scrutiny when she did. Even so, the Contact Supervisor said that there was ample evidence of a healthy attachment between Shirlee and Lauren although, by this time, Lauren clearly regarded Tim and Liz as her primary carers. Occasionally, Liz took Lauren to the contact meetings; there was never a problem but Shirlee needed help to occupy Lauren – it was not really a question of supervising contact but more of enabling Shirlee to make the most of it and to keep Lauren, who was now extremely mobile, out of harm's way. Shirlee related well to Liz, she appreciated what was being done for Lauren and also how she herself was being included in the arrangements.

A year after Lauren was first accommodated, a second Needs

Conference was held. This time the local authority was determined to place Lauren for adoption: she was still making progress and could be linked with one of several already approved adopters waiting for a healthy toddler. They rejected the current foster carers on grounds of age and proximity to the birth mother. It was feared that Lauren would be confused if she grew up with face-to-face contact and that there would always be a danger of accidental meetings or unwelcome approaches from the birth mother or indeed, from the birth father, if he found out where Lauren was. Shirlee said that she wanted Lauren to live with the foster carers; she didn't mind if her daughter was adopted as long as she could go on seeing her.

The local authority produced a Care Plan which included placing Lauren for adoption with a young couple who lived outside the borough. Indirect letterbox contact only was to be allowed. Shirlee did not agree with the plan to move Lauren, and was supported by her hospital social worker in her request for face-to-face contact. She said that she had never threatened the placement with the foster carers and that she would not be able to either write or read letters unaided.

The local authority applied for a Care Order on the grounds that Lauren's emotional health and security would be at risk in the future if she was not placed for adoption in another area. They produced anecdotal evidence to suggest that local adoption placements led to identity problems and to disruption in the middle childhood years. Shirlee contested the Application; the local authority opposed the carers' intention to adopt Lauren. The Court made an Interim Care Order and directed that an independent adoption worker should be appointed to assess the foster carers as potential adopters.

During the assessment it became clear that the carers liked Shirlee and felt great compassion for any mother faced with losing a child. They wanted Lauren to belong to their family but they did not feel the need to exclude Shirlee completely from their family circle – they saw it rather like including the non-resident father after divorce. They had experience of severed contact within their extended family and did not want Lauren to grow up disconnected from her past. They had been so anxious about having her removed from them that they had thought it best to go along with the local authority plan for termination of direct contact. But they had not felt happy about it. They had privately believed that it would be an advantage rather than a disadvantage for Lauren to stay not only where she had made secure attachments, but also within easy reach of her birth mother.

With the help of the independent adoption worker and Shirlee's own social worker, they formulated a contact plan, which would include Shirlee in a family outing once a month. As it was difficult for Shirlee to remember and stick to arrangements, they would remind her in good time before each meeting, collect her and return her home. They planned to go to local adventure playgrounds, for picnics, on the river, to theme parks, the zoo and anywhere else Shirlee might suggest, or Lauren, as she got older. Liz also proposed to invite Shirlee to school events and medical appointments. Tim and Liz definitely did not think that contact should be supervised and they were confident that they could support both Lauren and Shirlee.

The assessment recommended that Lauren should stay with her carers, that they should adopt her and that they should be encouraged to manage their own contact arrangements.

The local authority opposed the recommendations and pursued their application for a full Care Order. The judge made a further Interim Order and directed the local authority to consider an alternative Care Plan along the lines of the recommendations. Following advice from their legal department, the local authority agreed to present the carers to their Adoption Panel for approval as suitable parents for Lauren. Liz and Tim were duly approved and Lauren remained with them. More Interim Care Orders were made and the adoption was delayed while the local authority tried to negotiate a post-adoption contact plan, which would reduce direct contact with Shirlee to twice a year and avoid potentially emotional events like birthdays or Christmas. Agreement could not be reached and this was reflected in the local authority's Schedule 2 Report to the Court when the Adoption Application was finally heard, a year after the carers had been approved to adopt Lauren. The Application was granted and Liz and Tim were told that the local authority had done their best to protect Lauren's future interests but that they, the adopters, were now on their own. There would be no support for Shirlee, or for them, in managing the proposed monthly contact arrangements.

The arrangements limped along for a few months. The adopters began to wonder if they were really doing the right thing; Shirlee often seemed unresponsive and Lauren did not particularly enjoy the days out together. Tim and Liz were quite relieved when Shirlee disappeared without leaving an address; they informed Social Services and were advised to leave well alone. They were also asked not to speak to other foster carers or adopters about their *discredited attempts at an open adoption*. Altogether, the experience of trying to open up, rather than to close in their family, has left Liz and Tim feeling discouraged and apprehensive about how they will deal with Lauren's need for continuity as she grows up.

• • •

There is another ending to this story: neither ending is true, and neither is false. Both are possible and even probable. Each belongs to a real case. Which one is played out depends on our understanding of the concepts of openness, continuity, connections, changing needs, sense of self and, above all, on our acceptance that adopted children have two families and will always be the children of two sets of parents.

• • •

The assessment recommended that Lauren should stay with her carers, that they should adopt her and that they should be encouraged to manage their own contact arrangements. The local authority accepted the recommendations, the birth mother agreed the plan, the judge invited the foster carers to make their application to adopt Lauren and no further Interim Care Orders were made. The adoption was finalised six months later. By this time, monthly contact along the lines planned had been well established and it continued after Lauren was adopted. Sometimes there are hiccups: Lauren has a bad cold or Shirlee feels too low to make the effort, or the adopters have to change arrangements to fit in with other commitments. But, on the whole, contact works as well as most family connections and if there is a problem it can be discussed. Tim and Liz keep a record of contact outings so that Lauren will be able to remind herself of them when she is older:

August 2001
Collected Shirlee from home at 11 am. The weather was fairly good, so
we decided to go to a nearby animal sanctuary, as there would be lots
of "hands on" activities to enable Shirlee to do things with Lauren. We
handled the kittens and rabbits and fed the goats – with our encourage-
ment Shirlee helped Lauren with all of it. She also took Lauren on a
donkey ride, for approximately five minutes, on her own.

During the contact, Shirlee is able to do things with Lauren without
being totally responsible, which I think she likes, and when things get
difficult, like Lauren running off, she can leave it to Tim and me. We
both feel comfortable with the situation and think that Shirlee does too.
She enjoys seeing Lauren and Lauren enjoys the outings. The meetings
always feel informal and relaxed and at the end of the day, we are
doing what is best for Lauren. These outings will continue on a monthly
basis as long as it works for all concerned.

The local authority post-adoption worker has overcome his original doubts
and has asked the family to speak to a group of prospective adopters
about contact with birth relatives. He supports the arrangements by
keeping in touch with the birth mother and by being available for the
adopters.

Tim and Liz are sensitive, committed adopters but they are not unique.
Encouraging families to open up rather than to close in when they adopt,
and inviting them to make contact arrangements which will meet a child's
needs, without prescription or pre-conception, can lead to creative and
satisfying ways of keeping in touch. It can even make happy endings
come true.

Appendix
Open Adoption Research Synopsis

Sally Sales

This book did not aim to debate the value of open adoption, but to explore ways of better managing contact arrangements for children post placement and post adoption. However, contemporary social work culture is increasingly dominated by the need for "evidence-based" practice and nowhere is this more apparent than in the field of open adoption. There is a general belief within social work that the practice of openness in adoption is not based on firm research foundations. There are two commonly expressed complaints about the existing research studies. Firstly, there are no longitudinal studies on open adoption, so social workers claim they have no "evidence" of its long-term effects on adopted children to guide their practice. Secondly, there is a prevalent view that the research is not sufficiently large scale in its design, so no generalisations about contact can be drawn from the findings.

I intend this research synopsis to go some way to address these two concerns, as clearly there is now a growing body of research that is both longitudinal in design and large scale in sample size. However, it is my belief that the continuing controversy surrounding open adoption will not be easily assuaged by more "research evidence". Open adoption poses a challenge to the culturally dominant understandings that operate about both the nature of parenthood and childhood. It is far easier to contest the concept of contact, than to open up for exploration the forms of family life that it unsettles and destabilises.

This synopsis summarises a selection of the most relevant research here and in the USA. I have divided the studies chronologically and according to country, as so many of the American studies focus on the voluntarily arranged adoption of babies – a very different constituency when compared to Britain. I always indicate what kind of adoptions make up the research sample – relinquished babies; older children from care – as this difference is critical in terms of thinking about open adoption practice in Britain. I also indicate whether the sample is adoption only or whether it includes long-term fostering – a form of permanency that has a very different practice around contact. Where possible I distinguish which forms of contact the studies are researching – letterbox, face-to-face – but some studies do not always differentiate.

Some of the studies are large-scale and ongoing; some are small-scale snapshots; some are small-scale and ongoing. These very different research approaches provide contrasting information about open adoption. I am by no means of the view that the larger, longitudinal studies are necessarily the best. Many of the larger research projects, in their desire to account for behaviour in general, do not include information about the particular individual's experience – this is where the smaller, qualitative studies excel.

I include together various accounts arising from one study; for example, under English Studies there are three papers by Ryburn, documenting different aspects of one research study. I have also included recent research funded by the Department of Health, which, whilst not having a dominant focus on open adoption, does include contact in its research findings.

USA studies

1) Barth, R and Berry, M (1988) *Adoption and Disruption: Rates, risks and responses,* New York: Aldine de Gruyter

This study of 927 adoptions in California of children over three years old compared disruption rates of placements with and without contact. The researchers found that disruption rates were not significantly different between closed and open adoptions. This finding has been debated and contested by English researchers (most recently Quinton *et al*, 1999; Ryburn, 1999), with Ryburn of the view that this study demonstrates that planned and arranged contact with birth parents *is* associated with placement stability.

2) Berry, M (1993) 'Adoptive parents' perceptions of, and comfort with open adoption', *Child Welfare* 72

Berry, M, Cavazos Dylla, D J, Barth R P and Needell B (1998) 'The role of open adoption in the adjustment of adopted children & their families', *Children & Youth Services review* 20 (1/2)

This is a longitudinal study of 1,396 adoptions made in California between 1988 to 1989. Less than 25% of the adoptions involved children from the care system. The research is based on the analysis of questionnaires completed by the adoptive families. The first findings (Berry, 1993) indicate that adopters were cautiously comfortable with a range of open arrangements, but concerned about the longer-term. In this study contact was less common for children who had histories of maltreatment, although this pattern was somewhat mitigated if the adopters had met with the birth parents prior to placement.

A follow-up of 764 placements occurred four years later and was reported in Berry *et al*, 1998. This follow-up sample is smaller than the original because the researchers excluded all placements where foster carers adopted. The findings showed that contact had decreased or ceased for 44% of the placements, often because of the decision of a birth parent. A reduction in the frequency of contact was most common amongst those adopters who had chosen openness at the agency's insistence. For all families in the fourth year of placement, satisfaction with adoption seemed to have little connection to the levels of contact that were taking place. As this study progresses, the researchers intend to test whether openness becomes a factor in adjustment in adolescence.

3) Etter, J (1993) 'Levels of co-operation and satisfaction in 56 open adoptions', *Child Welfare* 72

This study looked at the ability of adopters and birth family to co-operate in post-adoption contact using mediation. The research focused on 56 open adoptions of babies, followed up four years after the order had been made. The arrangements covered both letterbox and face-to face contact. High levels of compliance with agreements and satisfaction with arrangements were reported. It is important to note that these adoptions were made on the basis of agreement between the adopters and birth parents prior to placement, meaning that there was already a good foundation for using mediation to agree contact arrangements.

4) Gross, H (1993) 'Open adoption: A research based literature review and new data', *Child Welfare* 72

This paper begins with a review of six empirical studies of open adoption and then presents findings from two small-scale studies: one involving interviews with 32 adoptive parents and 16 birth parents of infant open adoption placements made between 1989 and 1991; the other involving analysis of questionnaires completed by 75 adoptive families who adopted infants between 1985 and 1990. The contact arrangements in the two samples cover the whole range from information exchange to frequent visits. The results of the interview and questionnaire studies indicate that most of the participants are satisfied with the levels of openness in their adoptions and that most feel confident that difficulties will ease with the passage of time.

5) Grotevant, H and McRoy, R (1998) *Openness in Adoption*, London: Sage

Miller Wrobel, G, Ayers-Lopez, S, Grotevant, H, McRoy, R and Friedrick, M (1996) 'Openness in adoption and the level of child participation', *Child Development* 67 (5)

This longitudinal study of 190 families aims to explore variations in openness in adoption (minimal information through to face-to-face contact) and the effects of these arrangements for all parties involved. All the children were placed as babies, with no special needs, and therefore caution is recommended in generalising the findings to older children adopted from care. However, the study does demonstrate that, in 'fully disclosed' adoptions, adopters feel more secure in the parenting role and more empathetic to the adopted child and to the birth parents. In terms of adopted children, the study shows that the provision of information about birth family will not confuse the child about the meaning of adoption or lower their self-esteem, but neither will it move them to levels of understanding beyond their cognitive abilities.

Scottish studies

1) **Borland, M, O'Hara, G and Triseliotis, J (1991) 'Adoption and fostering: The outcome of permanent family placements',** *Adoption & Fostering* **15:2**

   Borland, M (1991) 'Permanency planning in Lothian region: The placements', *Adoption & Fostering* **15:4**

This was a comparative study of disrupted and continuing adoption and permanent foster placements made between 1982 and 1985. The study reported a 20% disruption rate in the overall sample (194 placements) and studied in greater depth a sample of 60 to examine the factors associated with disruption. Age was the most significant factor, the highest disruption rate occurring in the 11–14 age category. Contact is a neutral factor in the study, appearing neither to stabilise nor undermine the placements. This research has been variously interpreted by English commentators (Quinton *et al*, 1997, 1998 & 1999; Ryburn, 1998 & 1999). Ryburn contends that the research does show that for older children contact is associated with placement stability, but Quinton *et al* dispute this interpretation.

2) **Stone, S (1994) 'Contact between adopters and birth parents: The Strathclyde experience',** *Adoption & Fostering* **18:2**

This study focused on the centralised Baby Adoption Service in Strathclyde and their policy of adopters meeting with birth parents prior to adoption (introduced in 1992). The service only places babies under two and has a conservative culture towards open adoption, rarely making placements with face-to-face contact. Thirty-five couples were approached to participate in the study that was exploring the effects of birth parent meetings on adoptive families. Out of the 35 couples, 15 had met with birth parents and 13 reported positively about the experience. These couples emphasised the importance of the meeting being facilitated by the local authority. The 16 couples that had ongoing letterbox contact were finding this a helpful arrangement.

English studies

1) Fratter, J, Rowe, J, Sapsford, D and Thoburn, J (1991) *Permanent Family Placement*, London: BAAF

This large-scale study looked at 1,165 adoption and permanent foster placements made by voluntary agencies between 1980 and 1984. All the children in the study had a constellation of special needs. The research was aiming to assess which factors were most strongly associated with placement breakdown. The study showed that the risk factor in placing siblings separately was mitigated if contact could be sustained. Contact with other birth relatives was also found to be a protective factor in this study.

2) Beek, M (1994) 'The reality of face-to-face contact', *Adoption & Fostering* 18:2

This small-scale study was undertaken in 1992 and involved seven families (12 children) from the same local authority, who all had face-to-face contact with birth mother and other family members. The children were aged between three and 15 and only three of the adoptions were with consent. The reported advantages of face-to-face contact were strikingly similar for all seven families. The adopters in this study did not believe that contact interfered with their parental responsibilities or with their attachment to the children.

3) Hughes, B (1995) 'Openness and contact in adoption: A child-centred perspective', *British Journal of Social Work* 25

This paper is part of an evaluation of services to birth parents at the voluntary post-adoption agency, After Adoption. The sample of 30 birth parents (28 birth mothers, two birth fathers) interviewed for this article had lost children to adoption between 10 and 20 years previously. Their adoptions were closed with no contact; only three birth parents had lost children through care proceedings. The researcher invited the birth parents to speculate on how they would imagine themselves experiencing both indirect and direct contact. The entire sample felt that mediated information exchange would be best and had serious reservations about face-to-face contact. The researcher uses this finding to cast doubt on what she sees as a growing contemporary trend towards more face-to-face arrangements in adoption. The paper concludes by arguing for a more child-centred approach to decision making about contact.

4) **Ryburn, M (1995) 'Adopted children's identity and information needs',** *Children & Society* **9:3**

Ryburn, M (1996) 'A study of post-adoption contact in compulsory adoption', *British Journal of Social Work* **26:5**

Ryburn, M (1997) 'The effects on adopters of adoption without parental consent', *Early Child Development & Care* **134**

This study was undertaken in 1993 and involved 67 families (74 children), recruited through PPIAS (now Adoption UK) all of whom had experienced a contested adoption. The study was exploring the effects of such proceedings on post-adoption contact arrangements. Out of the 74 cases, 40 had some form of contact, in spite of the trauma of contested proceedings. Ryburn identified three factors with the maintenance of contact: a meeting between the adopters and the birth parents before adoption; older age at placement; transracial or black placement. The adopters with the most contact were those who were best able to manage the difficulties arising from contact. The study also found that adopters with no contact or minimal contact reported low levels of interest on the part of their children in discussing adoption

5) **Fratter, J (1996)** *Adoption with Contact: Implications for policy and practice,* **London: BAAF**

This small-scale, two-stage study explores the experience of open adoption for 32 children placed in 22 adoptive families. The sample was drawn from the original larger study of 1,165 placements (see above Fratter *et al*, 1991). Fratter interviewed the families in 1987 and again in 1991, so her study provides some sense of how contact develops and is managed over time. In 1991 she also interviewed the birth parents of four of the families. None of the adoptive parents believed that the development of their attachment to their children had been delayed or impaired by contact. It was more often reported that contact had helped with attachment in the early stages of placement. The study also showed that adopters were more positive about contact when they felt in control of it. Variations in form and frequency of contact were not significant in terms of how contact was experienced by adoptive families.

6) Logan, J (1999) 'Exchanging information post-adoption', *Adoption & Fostering* 23:3

The focus of this study was to evaluate an information exchange scheme at a voluntary adoption agency. The sample group was 34 children under 12 months of age placed for adoption between 1992 and 1994. Despite the agency encouraging a two-way exchange system, this was not happening in the majority of cases. The most common pattern was a one-way communication from adopters to birth parents. The study found that letterbox contact is a complex and emotionally charged experience that needs supporting if it is going to work reciprocally. The researcher also suggests that in the longer-term some kind of review process would be important.

7) Logan, J and Smith, C (1999) 'Adoption and direct post-adoption contact', *Adoption & Fostering* 23:4

This study was exploring the advantages and disadvantages of face-to-face contact for older adopted children, who had mostly been adopted from care. The researchers interviewed 61 adoptive mothers, 52 adoptive fathers, 57 adopted children aged between 6 and 15 and 40 birth relatives (including siblings). The findings were mostly positive with reported benefits including adopters feeling more secure and confident as parents. Adopted children spoke positively about contact, whilst still sustaining an emotional investment in their adoptive families. Both adopters and birth families agreed that contact should be flexible. Contra-indications for direct contact included the birth family undermining or not accepting the child's adoptive placement.

8) Sykes, M (2000) 'Adoption with contact: A study of adoptive parents and the impact of continuing contact with families of origin', *Adoption & Fostering* 24:2

This study aimed to explore the effects of different forms of contact on adoptive family life. The study sample comprised 30 adoptive parents (17 families), 15 of whom were interviewed. The children were aged between 3 and 15 and had been in placement for an average of 5½ years. The study found that, the more control and influence adopters have over contact, the more parental confidence is promoted. Contact works best when adopters are supported in making their own decisions about arrangements. The researcher speculates that contact may provide the means whereby adopters can develop their own version of their child's past and that this process improves the quality of adoptive family life.

9) Neil, E (2000) *Contact with birth relatives after adoption:A study of young, recently placed children,* Norwich: University of East Anglia, unpublished PhD Thesis

Neil, E (2002) 'Contact after adoption: the role of agencies in making and supporting plans', *Adoption & Fostering* 26:1

This study focussed on 168 children aged up to four years and placed for adoption between 1996 and 1997. The aim of the research was to both find out what arrangements were being made for post-adoption contact (examined by postal questionnaire) and to look in more detail, through interviews, at the 36 children who had face-to-face contact with birth relatives. The majority of the children were adopted from the care system. This study found that the local authority culture was the most significant factor in decisions about contact for children. Agency-led arrangements were reported to be the least successful and the most successful were those where the agency was not involved. Face-to-face contact did not interfere with the development of close relations between adopters and their adopted child and adopted children could enjoy a relationship with birth relatives, even though they did not yet understand about adoption.

Other recent English studies that include a focus on contact

1) **Lowe, N, Murch, M, Borkowski, M, Weaver, A, Beckford, V and Thomas, C (1999)** *Supporting Adoption: Reframing the approach*, **London: BAAF**

This study examined the support services for older children (over five) who had been adopted from care, following their progress from the time of the decision to place until a year after the adoption order. The research comprised an agency study (both voluntary and statutory) and a family study that involved both questionnaire (226 families) and interviews (48 families). The study includes a chapter on contact.

The study found that, out of the 226 families who responded to the postal questionnaire, 89 had direct contact and 113 had indirect contact (letterbox, telephone calls). Direct contact was most commonly arranged for relatives other than birth parents (i.e.: grandparents; siblings; aunts and uncles). In the family study, families did not commonly have written agreements – only 39% had such an agreement in place. Most reported arrangements were informal and self-managed. 95 per cent of the agencies participating in the agency study had a letterbox system in place and most agencies (over 80%) encouraged a meeting between adopters and birth family. However, practice around contact differed vastly across voluntary and statutory agencies and across regions, with the authors identifying contact as 'one of the most contentious practice issues' they encountered. Notwithstanding this, the authors reported benefits for children in sustaining different forms of contact with birth family members, provided that birth parents are not undermining of the placement and adopters can accept the child's previous history.

Thomas, C, Beckford, V, Murch, M and Lowe, N (1999) *Adopted Children Speaking*, London: BAAF

The Thomas *et al* study focused on 41 older children from the original larger scale study (see above Lowe *et al*). The study aimed to gain a better understanding of the views and experiences of adopted children. The children were between 8 and 15 at the time of interview and had been with their adoptive families on average for over five years. Two-thirds of the children had some form of contact with their birth family, about which they had very clear views and understanding. Some of the children wanted immediate changes in the contact they were having, most commonly wishing to see more of their birth family members. The researchers reported that some children were mystified by the lack or absence of contact with important people from their past.

2) Quinton, D, Rushton, A, Dance, C and Mayes, D (1998) *Joining New Families: A study of adoption and fostering*, Chichester: Wiley

This study was conducted in the early 1990s to find out more about the permanent placement of older children. The study sample comprised 84 children, aged between five and nine, all of whom were placed permanently with a new and unrelated family. The sample was followed up at one, six and 12 months after placement; 75% of the children had settled into their new families within the first year, with only three disruptions. Contact is not a dominant focus of this study, but the authors reported no significant relationship between contact and the child's behaviour, or any association between contact and placement stability after one year. However, most parents reported that contact was either neutral or positive in its effects, with sibling contact regarded as more helpful than birth parents contact.

3) Thoburn, J, Norford, L and Rashid, S (2000) *Permanent Family Placement for Children of Ethnic Minority Backgrounds*, London: Jessica Kingsley

The 297 children of minority ethnic origin in this study were drawn mainly from the large-scale study of 1,165 children placed between 1980 and 1984 (see above Fratter *et al*, 1991). Seventy-one per cent of the children had been placed with white parents; the rest where at least one parent was of similar ethnicity to the child's own. Two-thirds of the sample had been adopted; one-third had been long-term fostered. Interviews were conducted with 38 parents and 24 of the young people between 12 and 15 years after placement. Again, contact was not a major focus of this study but was included in the findings. Over a third of the children had contact with birth parents and 22% had contact with siblings placed elsewhere. Whilst the disruption rate was 24%, contact was found to be a neutral factor with respect to placement breakdown.

References

Quinton, D, Rushton, A, Dance, C and Mayes D (1997) 'Contact between children placed away from home and their birth parents: Research issues and evidence', *Clinical Child Psychology & Psychiatry*, 2:3

Quinton, D and Selwyn, J (1998) 'Contact with birth parents after adoption: a response to Ryburn', *Child & Family Law Quarterly*, 10:4

Quinton, D, Selwyn, J, Rushton, A, and Dance, C (1999) 'Contact between children placed away from home and their birth parents: Ryburn's "reanalysis" analysed', *Clinical Child Psychology & Psychiatry*, 4:4

Ryburn, M (1998) 'In whose best interests? Post-adoption contact with the birth family', *Child & Family Law Quarterly*, 10:1

Ryburn, M (1999) 'Contact between children placed away from home and their birth parents: A reanalysis of the evidence in relation to permanent placements', *Clinical Child Psychology & Psychiatry*, 4:4

Contributors

Hedi Argent is an independent adoption consultant, trainer and freelance writer. She is the author of *Find me a Family* (Souvenir Press, 1984), *Whatever Happened to Adam?* (BAAF, 1998), the co-author of *Taking Extra Care* (BAAF, 1997) and the editor of *Keeping the Doors Open* (BAAF, 1988) and *See you Soon* (BAAF, 1995) .

Shelagh Beckett is an independent consultant specialising in fostering and adoption. She has undertaken service and case reviews both in the voluntary and statutory sectors and is regularly used as an expert witness on issues relating to siblings, adoption placements and contact. Shelagh has also advised ITV and the BBC on many television series covering fostering and adoption, including *Love is not enough – the journey to adoption* and *Love is not enough – the journey after adoption*.

Margaret G. Bell completed her social work training at Edinburgh University and has worked in Fife and Ayrshire. She has been a social worker with the Family Placement Service in Fife since 1991.

Paula Bell is a Service Development Officer with West Lothian Council. She started in social work in 1974 and has been a senior social worker and Practice Team Manager in Children and Families. She was a member of the West Lothian Adoption Panel for nine years and, latterly, its Chair. She also chairs BAAF's Scottish Practice Development Forum, and is their representative on BAAF's UK Social Work Practice Advisory Committee.

Maureen Crank is the Chief Executive and founder member of *After Adoption*, the largest independent provider of adoption support in the UK. She is a member of the *Adoption and Permanence Taskforce* and was on the Expert Working Party for the *Adoption Standards*. She is currently on the Department of Health working party which is developing a *Framework for Adoption Support*. Maureen is co-author of *Still Screaming* (After Adoption Manchester) but says she would rather 'do' than write.

Hilary Galloway and Fiona Wallace
Hilary is Team Manager and a member of the Adoption and Fostering Panel in Wandsworth Social Services. She is also a member of the *Kinship Care Development Group.*
Fiona is a Team Manager, and a member of the *Kinship Care Development Group.* She initiated Family Group Conferences in Wandsworth and is currently engaged in developing the *Family Support Strategy and Action Plan* for Wandsworth.

Pauline Hoggan, Aminah Husain Sumpton and Wendy Ellis
Pauline is from Scotland and has been Director of IAS since1999, having previously been manager of the Lothian Regional Adoption Team and Head of Service for Children and Families in Argyll and Bute Council.
Aminah was born in India and has lived in several different countries. She is Muslim and speaks Hindi, Urdu and English. She is a senior practitioner with IAS and a Children's Guardian. She has trained professionals and school children on topics such as adoption, religion and the individual needs of black children.
Wendy was born in England and is of African heritage. She qualified as a social worker in 1987 and then worked in the Children and Families team for Wandsworth Council. She joined IAS in 1992 and in 1999 she took up the post of Principal Post-adoption Social Worker.

Mary Jones has been a practising social worker for over 20 years and has worked at Barnardo's, in the field of adoption and fostering, for 14 of those years. Her most recent post was as Project Leader of a family placement project, based in Wales.

Catherine Macaskill is currently a freelance social worker, providing training and consultancy for statutory and voluntary agencies. She has extensive experience of working in adoption and fostering and also in the specialist area of disability. She is author of *Against the Odds* (BAAF, 1984); *Adopting or Fostering a Sexually Abused Child* (Free Association, Books, 1991); and *Safe Contact? Children in permanent placement and contact with their birth relatives* (Russell House Publishing, 2002).

Elsbeth Neil is Lecturer in Social Work at the University of East Anglia in Norwich. She has been carrying out research into contact after adoption since 1996 and she completed her PhD on this topic in 2000. She is currently undertaking a longitudinal comparative study of direct and indirect post-adoption contact arrangements for children aged under four.

David Pitcher is a senior social work practitioner in a childcare team in Plymouth. He set up and co-ordinates *Parents Again*, a support group for grandparents who care for their grandchildren. David also works as a family mediator. He has recently won the *Professional Social Work Award* (British Association of Social Work) for best practice and the Plymouth City Council Award for *Public Servant of the Year*.

Sally Sales worked at *The Post-Adoption Centre* from 1994 to 2001, developing the *Mediation & Contact Service*. She is now doing research for a PhD on open adoption, while working as a freelance trainer and psychotherapist in private practice.

Alan Slade was Head of *The Child Contact Service* at the Thomas Coram Foundation from 1991–96. He returned to the post in 1998 and has remained head of the service under the re-named Coram Family Organisation. He is a qualified social worker and has published articles on child contact in professional journals and spoken at national and international conferences. Alan is also an experienced social work practice teacher.

Patricia Swanton has been involved with adoption for over 30 years. She is currently the Editor of *Adoption Today*, the bi-monthly magazine of the UK adoptive parent support group, *Adoption UK*. She has had 12 years experience as an Adoption Panel member in both voluntary and statutory agencies and she is an approved volunteer for *After Adoption Yorkshire*. Patricia is the mother of seven children – three born to her, two adopted as babies and two adopted as older children.

Alison Vincent and Alyson Graham are both qualified social workers with a range of childcare experience. They work at the *Berkshire Adoption Advisory Service* which offers support, training and advice in adoption and permanence and facilitates adoption panels. The authors manage the *Information Exchange Service*.

Index